93
/13

THE RHETORIC OF SENSIBILITY IN EIGHTEENTH-CENTURY CULTURE

The Rhetoric of Sensibility in Eighteenth-Century Culture explores the burgeoning eighteenth-century fascination with the human body as an eloquent, expressive object. This wide-ranging study examines the role of the body within a number of cultural arenas – particularly oratory, the theatre, and the novel – and charts the efforts of projectors and reformers who sought to exploit the textual potential of the body for the public assertion of modern politeness. Paul Goring shows how diverse writers and performers including David Garrick, James Fordyce, Samuel Richardson, Sarah Fielding, and Laurence Sterne were involved in the construction of new ideals of physical eloquence – bourgeois, sentimental ideals which stood in contrast to more patrician, classical bodily modes. Through innovative readings of fiction and contemporary manuals on acting and public speaking, Goring reveals the ways in which the human body was treated as an instrument for the display of sensibility and polite values.

Paul Goring is Senior Lecturer in British Literature and Culture at the Norwegian University of Science and Technology. He has published in journals including *Representations*, *The Shandean*, *Literature and Theology*, and *Word & Image*, and has edited Laurence Sterne's *A Sentimental Journey* for Penguin Classics.

THE RHETORIC OF SENSIBILITY IN EIGHTEENTH-CENTURY CULTURE

PAUL GORING

CAMBRIDGE
UNIVERSITY PRESS

PUBLISHED BY THE PRESS SYNDICATE OF THE UNIVERSITY OF CAMBRIDGE
The Pitt Building, Trumpington Street, Cambridge CB2 1RP, United Kingdom

CAMBRIDGE UNIVERSITY PRESS
The Edinburgh Building, Cambridge, CB2 2RU, UK
40 West 20th Street, New York, NY 10011-4211, USA
477 Williamstown Road, Port Melbourne, VIC 3207, Australia
Ruiz de Alarcón 13, 28014 Madrid, Spain
Dock House, The Waterfront, Cape Town 8001, South Africa
http://www.cambridge.org

First published 2005

Printed in the United Kingdom at the University Press, Cambridge

Typeset in 11/12.5 pt Adobe Garamond [PND]

A catalogue record for this book is available from the British Library

ISBN 0 521 84509 2 hardback

For Jan and Mike Goring

Of bodies chang'd to various forms, I sing.

Ovid, *Metamorphoses*
trans. John Dryden (1693)

Contents

Preface   ix

Introduction   I

1 Spectacular passions: eighteenth-century oratory and the reform
  of eloquence   31

2 Bodies on the borders of politeness: 'Orator Henley', Methodist
  enthusiasm, and polite literature   60

3 Thomas Sheridan: forging the British body   91

4 The art of acting: mid-century stagecraft and the broadcast of
  feeling   114

5 Polite reading: sentimental fiction and the performance of
  response   142

Epilogue   182

Bibliography   202

Index   214

Preface

This is a book about bodies – about the eloquence of bodies and their capacity to express symbolically the values of a particular culture. The 'rhetoric of sensibility' under scrutiny here, then, is a bodily rhetoric. It is the passionate, emotional language of the body which came to be esteemed in British society in the mid eighteenth century, and which has since been regarded as one of the key markers of that period's culture (or often 'cult') of sensibility. I have aimed to illuminate the relations between this powerful bodily rhetoric and notions of politeness which were developing in Britain at the time. The body, I suggest, came to be invested with new representational functions as a medium for the emblematisation or performance of modern politeness.

The development of new protocols of bodily behaviour was a widespread and multifaceted eighteenth-century enterprise taking place within a range of different cultural arenas. To capture that breadth I have cast my net wide, and the book therefore presents a large number of characters – orators, elocutionists, rhetoricians, actors, acting theorists, novelists, and others – whose various contributions to eighteenth-century culture involved some form of shaping of, or commentary upon, bodily eloquence. These include the very familiar, such as David Garrick, Samuel Richardson, and Laurence Sterne, together with figures who are less well known today, such as Thomas Sheridan, Aaron Hill, and Richard Graves. I hope that by making the study wide-ranging I have not sacrificed too much in terms of depth.

I have published articles on the 'body projects' of several of these figures before, and some of that work appears in a revised form here. An early version of Chapter 3 appeared in *1700-tallet: artikler om språk, litteratur, musikk og estetikk* (Kristiansand: Høyskoleforlaget, 2000). Part of Chapter 4 began life as a paper for a National Early Music Association conference on 'Mime and Gesture in the Eighteenth-Century Theatre', and was subsequently published in the Association's journal, *Leading Notes* 13 (1997). An earlier form of much of Chapter 2 appeared in *Literature and Theology* 15:4 (2001) – I am grateful to Oxford University Press for allowing me to reproduce the material here.

Many other debts of gratitude have mounted up during the several years the book has been in the making, and I am pleased to be able to acknowledge the main ones here. Firstly, I must thank Linda Bree at Cambridge University Press for her initial interest in the project and for her guidance and enthusiasm throughout the writing process. Thanks are also due to the two anonymous readers assigned by the Press who have patiently endured drafts of the book and have given me invaluable advice on how to improve it. For making the production process agreeably smooth, I am grateful to the team at Cambridge University Press, as well as to Pauline Marsh, who copy-edited the typescript, and to Susan Forsyth, who produced the index.

Research for the book began at the University of Wales, Aberystwyth, where I benefited from help and support of various kinds from, amongst others, Ian Bell, David Shuttleton, Andrew Hadfield, Francesca Rhydderch, Chris McNab, Claudine Conway, and particularly Shaun Regan and Brean Hammond, both of whom have given useful advice on sections of the book and have been more helpful over the years than I suspect they realise. Base-camp for the writing has been the English department at the Norwegian University of Science and Technology in Trondheim. I am grateful to my colleagues Jeremy Hawthorn, Domhnall Mitchell, Ruth Sherry, and Eli Løfaldli for showing a keen interest in the project, for tolerating my less than avid interest in departmental matters during phases of writing, and to Jeremy, for his constant willingness to read drafts, explore problems, and lend friendly advice. I must also thank those who hold the purse strings at the Humanities Faculty at Trondheim – a body which has been remarkably generous in funding trips to research libraries in Britain and America. Thanks too to the many helpful staff at the British Library, the National Library of Wales, the university libraries in Cambridge, Aberystwyth, and Trondheim, and particularly the Huntington Library – in the balmy environment of the Huntington, the final stage of writing proved to be a great pleasure. Among other friends and scholars who have provided help of various kinds, I must thank Tom Keymer, Peter de Voogd, Aileen Douglas, Angela Rosenthal, Peter Miles, Juan Pellicer, David Noy, Andrew Biswell, Susan Deacy, Deanne Williams, Robert Hamm, Paulina Kewes, Bjørg Hawthorn, and Robert Jones.

My research trips to London have been helped and always made enjoyable by my many good friends there, particularly Claire, Hugh, Julia, Liz,

Luisa, Malcolm, Mary, Matthew, Penny, Tim and Tom. Tone Midtgård has been delightfully supportive and distracting throughout the writing, and the two dedicatees have been splendid parents since long before I started this project. I am grateful for their encouragement throughout, and am very pleased that 'Any news of the book?' is now, finally, a redundant question.

Introduction

On 29 October 1746, the printer and novelist Samuel Richardson (1689–1761) wrote a long letter to his friend Aaron Hill (1685–1750), a man of broad interests spanning commerce, trees, English wine, literature, and, of particular relevance here, the theatre and acting techniques. Richardson was in the midst of the composition of *Clarissa* (1747–8), the first volumes of which would be published the next year, and he responded to Hill's comments on a draft of part of the novel and discussed matters relating to *Clarissa*'s characters.[1] Towards the end of the letter he described his reactions to reading a work by Hill, a didactic verse essay entitled *The Art of Acting*, which he had agreed to print:

Last Sunday I attempted to read it not as a Printer; and was not aware, that I should be so mechanically, as I may truly say, affected by it: I endeavoured to follow you in your wonderful Description of the Force of Acting, in the Passion of Joy, Sorrow, Fear, Anger, &c. And my whole Frame, so nervously affected before, was shaken by it: I found, in short, such Tremors, such Startings, that I was unable to go thro' it; and must reserve the Attempting it again, till your *Oak Tincture* (but just enter'd upon) has fortify'd the too relaxed, unmuscled Muscles, and braced those unbraced Nerves, which I have so long complained of, and so shall hope to find a Cure, and the Proof of it, from the same beneficent Hand.[2]

It is not absolutely clear what Richardson intends when he writes that he 'endeavoured to follow' Hill in his account of how the 'passions' should be performed on stage. Does he mean that he tried to 'follow' Hill's argument and instructions in an intellectual sense? Or is he suggesting that he went some way towards actually acting out the signs of the emotions as described in the poem? Or is he referring to a type of reading practice that falls somewhere between these two senses of 'follow'? Whichever way we understand Richardson's approach to the poem, his letter to Hill provides a

---

[1] Publication dates in the main text are for first editions; dates of editions cited are given in the notes. Personal dates are given for figures to whom more than passing reference is made.
[2] *Selected Letters of Samuel Richardson*, ed. John Carroll (Oxford: Clarendon Press, 1964), pp. 74–5.

I

telling account of real emotional transport arising in response to a representation of the human body performing signs of emotional transport. Richardson's sabbatical reading of *The Art of Acting*, he claims, has provoked in him a state of nervousness of such intensity that any further dealings with the work must be postponed until he has prepared himself with some bracing tincture.[3] A work advancing a theory of acting has affected him to the extent that he feels physically weakened and ill – and he is by no means shy about reporting this to Hill. Indeed, Richardson seems almost to savour his nervousness, dwelling upon it in a lengthy self-diagnosis, which serves both as an assertion of his delicate condition and as a compliment to the captivating power of Hill's writing. Unexpectedly for Richardson, *The Art of Acting* inspires from him an eloquent performance of his own sensitivity, which in turn, through his epistolary telling, becomes a further image of bodily performance serving the benefit of both authors.

We are, of course, well used to the idea that representations – using literary or other media – can produce powerful emotional effects in their consumers. Since at least the time of Aristotle, who analysed the process in his *Poetics*, the arousal of emotion has been recognised as one of the fundamental functions that works of the imagination serve for their communities of readers, spectators, or auditors. So it may be that Richardson's response to *The Art of Acting* appears intense but ultimately unexceptional. However, what I believe *is* remarkable about Richardson's act of reading is the fact that he is not moved by the dramatisation or depiction of an affecting object or series of events – that would be the more traditional manner in which literary representations arouse emotion. Rather Richardson is moved in response to an account of the bodily characteristics of moved people, as constructed by Aaron Hill. The indices of emotion *precede* the emotion; the signifiers *produce* the internally felt signifieds. As when a car is pushed to make the engine turn, the attention to external movement here spurs the inner emotions into life. To understand the nature of Richardson's reading more fully – and this will be useful for seeing the implications of this *petite histoire* that I want to explore further – it will be helpful to look briefly at the material he had before him.

---

[3] Hill and Richardson shared a keen interest in each other's ailments, and the oak tincture is one of many nostrums discussed in their correspondence (see Christine Gerrard, *Aaron Hill: The Muses' Projector 1685–1750* (Oxford: Oxford University Press, 2003), p. 204, and Dorothy Brewster, *Aaron Hill: Poet, Dramatist, Projector* (New York: Columbia University Press, 1913; repr. New York: AMS Press, 1966), p. 243).

Richardson's copy of Hill's *The Art of Acting* was one in a succession of several different versions of the work. From a verse prologue of 1733 to an expansive prose 'Essay on the Art of Acting', posthumously published in 1753, Hill's literary treatment of acting techniques underwent considerable transformation and revision.[4] The 1746 version, read and printed by Richardson, approached the subject in something over four hundred lines of verse plus an explanatory dedication. Hill developed and refined his theory as he revised the work, but the various versions none the less have several key aspirations in common: to advertise affecting acting as a socially beneficial force, to provide a taxonomic analysis of 'the passions' and their bodily signs, and to describe ways in which the actor might summon up these signs in performance. In the 1746 version, Hill recommends that in order to be emotive an actor should:

> Print the *ideal Pathos*, on the *Brain*:
> Feel the Thought's Image on the *Eyeball* roll;
> Behind That *Window* sits th'attentive SOUL:
> *Wing'd*, at *her* Beck, th'obedient MUSCLES fly,
> *Bent*, or *relaxing*, to the varied *Eye*:
> Press'd, moderate, lenient, VOICE's organ'd Sound,
> To Each felt Impulse, tones the tunefull Round:
> Form'd to the *Nerves*, concurring MEIN partakes, –
> So, the *mov'd* Actor MOVES – and Passion SHAKES.[5]

Working through the curlicues of Hill's poetic style, we find the nub of the argument: bodily expression should be produced as a direct mechanical consequence of the actor's mental identification with a particular 'passion' – the eighteenth-century term for which the modern near-equivalent is 'emotion'. Hill advances an acting technique in which the performer should attempt to *feel* the emotions which the fictional character would feel in the various situations engineered by the playwright – a technique akin to that famously promoted much later by the Russian actor and producer Konstantin Stanislavsky and also by later 'method actors'. But while Hill promotes such an internalised technique, he is at the same time partly prescriptive when it comes to illustrating the bodily signs that feelings actually produce. In *The Art of Acting* he addresses various passions individually and anatomises their

---

[4] The essay appears in *The Works of the Late Aaron Hill*, 4 vols. (London, 1753), vol. IV, pp. 353–414. The original prologue (to the first performance of William Bond's *The Tuscan Treaty* at Covent Garden in 1733) also appears in Hill's *Works*, vol. III, pp. 119–22. The various versions are listed in Leo Hughes, 'The Actor's Epitome', *Notes and Queries* 20 (1944), 306–7.
[5] Aaron Hill, *The Art of Acting* (London, 1746), p. 22.

bodily symptoms in detail. Here, for example, is Hill's analysis of fear – one of the passions Richardson singles out for mention in his letter:

> FEAR is *elusive Sorrow*, shunning Pain;
> Active – yet, *stop'd* – it dims the doubtful Brain;
> Spirit snatch'd inward, *stagnating*, by Dread,
> Slow, through the Limbs, crawls cold, the living *Lead:*
> Form'd to the *Look* that moulds th'Assumer's Face,
> His Joints catch *Tremblings*, – Life's moist Strings *unbrace*;
> This Road, and That, – th'alarmful Passion tries,
> *Halts*, in the Motion – *flutters*, in the Eyes;
> Checks the clipt Accent's hesitative Way,
> And, on th'*evasive Muscles*, hangs *Delay*.[6]

So while Hill sees the proper way of 'acting the passions' as a 'natural' process requiring no imitation of conventional gestures, he also goes to considerable lengths in supplying descriptions of those gestures which should be within the capable actor's repertoire. Indeed, the bulk of the poem is devoted to detailed representations showing how particular passions should be rendered legible on a body's surface. There is, then, a certain methodological tension in *The Art of Acting*, as Hill invites his trainee actors to follow not only their imagined emotions but also his own illustrations of moved bodies moving.

Hill became influential as an acting theorist, but he was seldom admired as a writer. The author of *A Letter to David Garrick* (1769) indeed reflected upon how Voltaire's plays could please even 'in the pitiful translations of an Aaron Hill' – Hill is not merely deemed to be a bad writer here, but has become a typifier of bad writing.[7] So Richardson's praise of Hill's 'wonderful Description of the Force of Acting' may have gone against the grain of conventional opinion regarding Hill's literary capabilities, but if we credit Richardson's account of his distress, his admiration is clearly an apt secondary response to his own experience with *The Art of Acting*. Through encounter with Hill's words, Richardson apparently set off a transformation of his own body by fictional models of variously affected bodies;

---

[6] *Ibid.*, p. 14.

[7] H. W., *A Letter to David Garrick Esq; On Opening the Theatre* (London, 1769), p. 7. This letter appeared long after Hill's death, but during his lifetime there were frequent assaults upon his writing – including that on acting. An early expression of Hill's performance theory, 'The Actor's Epitome', in *The Prompter* 113 (9 December 1735), inspired a parodic 'Of the praise of Tobacco; or, The Smoaker's Epitome. Mr A. H—ll's Style imitated', in the *Gentleman's Magazine* 6 (September 1736), 547. The parodist targets both the style and content of Hill's work: 'On the *rais'd lip*, oft mov'd, obliquely strait/Let the glaz'd *tube* recline, with easy state – / *Pointedly* look: – *Fix* your attention high ...' and so on.

consciously or unconsciously, he was allowing himself to be moved in response to Hill's representations of abstract but emotionally shaken bodies, and this form of reading produced his own intense transport and weakness. As Richardson suggests, he was a long-term sufferer of nervous disorders – he had been a regular patient of Dr George Cheyne (1671–1743), the popular physician to the gentry and author of the medical classic *The English Malady* (1733) – so when he came to read *The Art of Acting*, he was bringing to the work an emotional condition that he and his doctor would have recognised as already acutely susceptible.[8] It is nevertheless a testimony to the effectiveness of Hill's poem – albeit written to its author, who would be flattered and encouraged by the report – that Richardson should describe such a degree of inner turmoil. It is, as I have suggested, a turmoil prompted not by descriptions of objects or events that might normally *induce* 'Joy, Sorrow, Fear, Anger, &c.', but rather by 'following' representations of the bodily states seen to be the natural, somatic consequences of these passions. *The Art of Acting* describes nothing *joyous* or *sorrowful*, but rather displays what Hill sees – and partially constructs through his writing – as the physical effects of joy and sorrow. Yet paradoxically, by encountering these effects through reading, Richardson is able to discover in himself the real passions that cause them.

What, then, is the significance of this intense record of a moved body? What is the relationship between this episode and cultural history – a relationship implied by the first subheading in this introduction? The implications of the episode for this study can be broken down into three interrelated points:

(1) Firstly, the episode exemplifies what I see as a preoccupation in British culture of this period with the human body as an eloquent object, whose eloquence arises from the performance of an inscribed system of gestures and expressions. This preoccupation is manifest in various eighteenth-century projects which, at some level, were engaged in training the body – in shaping and directing ways in which bodies, both male and female, should appear in public. Efforts to mould bodily eloquence are apparent, with varying degrees of explicitness, within an array of eighteenth-century social and cultural arenas, and this book explores particularly oratory, acting, and the reading of sentimental fiction as activities around

---

[8] On Richardson's nervous condition and his relationship with Cheyne see David E. Shuttleton, ' "Pamela's Library": Samuel Richardson and Dr. Cheyne's "Universal Cure" ', *Eighteenth-Century Life* 23:1 (1999), 59–79.

which vigorous discourse concerning the spectacle of the body in public was generated. These cultural sites are connected by their engagements in body matters, and I have found it useful in writing about their shared preoccupations to apply 'elocutionary discourse' as a short-hand tectorial label to denote the general enterprise of eighteenth-century thinking and writing about bodies as expressive, eloquent objects.

(2) The episode also has a more abstract significance in that it vividly displays a body performing on the boundaries of nature and culture. The letter provides a glimpse of the organic, pulsating mass of Richardson's flesh interacting with a cultural system – a historically specific style of acting – and indeed serving as a textual space upon which marks of that cultural system are represented. The eloquence of Richardson's body, and of the bodies implicated within 'elocutionary discourse' more generally, can thus be seen to extend beyond the display of individual emotional transport so as to become indirectly expressive of the cultural circumstances of the somatic utterance. In this way, Richardson's performance illustrates a basic premise of this study (and of much other recent writing on 'the body'): that human bodies have textual potential and malleability.

(3) The third significance of the episode is a synthesis of the two previous points: the episode is suggestive of the particular cultural work that was advanced by 'elocutionary discourse' through the textual medium of the body. The eighteenth century is typically seen as a period in which British society was radically transformed so as to witness a 'birth of polite society', and I shall argue in what follows that the body served as an important (and problematic) textual space for the symbolic inscription of politeness and for the 'working out' of what it meant to be 'polite'. The body image presented by Richardson is, in many ways, innovative – or at least it participates in a discourse which was developing in Britain at the time. Attesting to his weakness and nervous trembling, Richardson gladly advances – or even trumpets – a self-image which is notably unheroic (in traditional, classical terms). Such nervous, emotional bodies – or, to use the adjective emerging during the period, such 'sentimental' bodies – held, for a time, significant cultural authority as components within the developing signatory system of politeness, and an aim of this study is to demonstrate how 'elocutionary discourse' functioned as a crucible within which such body images were fashioned.[9]

---

[9] The first recorded use of 'sentimental' appears in a much-quoted letter of 1749 to Richardson from Lady Dorothy Bradshaigh (1705–85), an aristocratic admirer of Richardson's novels who became his

These three general points underlie each of the chapters which follow, and it is worth while exploring them in turn and in greater detail.

EIGHTEENTH-CENTURY 'ELOCUTIONARY DISCOURSE'

The manner in which a body should appear and behave in public was clearly a major concern in eighteenth-century Britain. Efforts to codify somatic protocols mark numerous enterprises of the period which, in different ways, attempted to shape public conduct, and which, in the process, generated a mass of printed materials addressing the topic. To remain briefly in the area in which I began, *The Art of Acting* must be seen as just one amongst many acting manuals and other similar works related to the development of stage practice. Indeed, the literature directed to the training of actors constitutes a significant sub-genre of Enlightenment publishing in itself. In numerous works such as Charles Gildon's *The Life of Mr. Thomas Betterton... Wherein The Action and Utterance of the Stage, Bar, and Pulpit, are distinctly consider'd* (1710), Samuel Foote's *A Treatise on the Passions, So far as they regard the Stage* (1747), John Hill's *The Actor; Or, A Treatise on the Art of Playing* (1750; revised 1755), and Roger Pickering's *Reflections upon Theatrical Expression in Tragedy* (1760), different systems of acting – revealing different systems of understanding the body's capacity for eloquence – were theorised, developed, refined, and recommended for application on the stage.

This literature on theatrical performance was far from confined to a specialist market of actors. Acting manuals often appeared under a highly marketable gloss, such as the verse form used by Aaron Hill or by the anonymous author of the Edinburgh-published *An Essay on the Stage, or the Art of Acting: A Poem* (1754). In Gildon's *Life of Mr. Thomas Betterton*, the appealing guise of a biography of an outstandingly popular actor was used in order to sell an acting manual. Shorter pieces on acting reached wide readerships through the popular and affordable outlet of periodical publication, and journals devoted particularly to theatrical matters, such as *The Prompter* (1734–6) or the *Theatrical Monitor* (1767–8), included acting styles among the topics they addressed. Acting, furthermore, attracted

---

long-term correspondent and friend. 'What, in your opinion', she asked, 'is the meaning of the word *sentimental*, so much in vogue amongst the polite, both in town and country? ... Every thing clever and agreeable is comprehended in that word' (*The Correspondence of Samuel Richardson*, ed. Anna Lætitia Barbauld, 6 vols. (London, 1804), vol. IV, pp. 282–3). On the emergence of the term and its meanings, see R. F. Brissenden's classic study of sentimentalism, *Virtue in Distress: Studies in the Novel of Sentiment from Richardson to Sade* (London and Basingstoke: Macmillan, 1974), pp. 11–55.

the interest of now-canonical writers of fiction such as Henry Fielding (1707–54) and Laurence Sterne (1713–68), who used their works as platforms for digressions on performance techniques.[10] For a non-acting readership, a discourse on performance theory could serve as an authoritative basis for judging actors; it could feed into the development of an individual's 'refined taste', a claim upon which constituted an important strand of eighteenth-century polite identity.[11] Hill's *The Art of Acting*, for example, is offered in part as a work which will '*quicken the Delight of Audiences*' by qualifying them to '*form a Judgement of the Actors, in their Good, or Bad, Performances*'.[12]

Eighteenth-century histories and memoirs of the theatre – a genre which became increasingly popular from mid century as the theatre grew in respectability – also addressed acting techniques in their accounts of the theatre's most successful performers. William Rufus Chetwood's *A General History of the Stage, from its Origin in Greece down to the present Time* (1749) included, as its subtitle promised, *Memoirs of most of the principal Performers that have appeared on the English and Irish Stage for these last Fifty Years.* Chetwood had worked as a prompter at the Drury Lane theatre and so had been well placed for making the close observations of acting styles that inform his expansive catalogue of performers. In *A General View of the Stage* (1759), Thomas Wilkes similarly offered detailed descriptions of the gestures and expressions employed by leading actors in particular roles.[13] The poet Charles Churchill made his reputation with a work on acting styles: his satirical, mock-heroic *The Rosciad* (1761) depicted a parade

---

[10] Fielding, for example, digresses on acting in *The History of Tom Jones*, ed. R. P. C. Mutter (London: Penguin, 1966), pp. 398–9. For an example of Sterne's many references to the stage and acting, see *The Life and Opinions of Tristram Shandy, Gentleman*, The Florida Edition of the Works of Laurence Sterne, vols. I–II, ed. Melvyn New and Joan New (Gainesville, FL: University Presses of Florida, 1978), vol. I, p. 213.

[11] John Brewer explores the role of taste within polite culture, arguing that politeness 'placed the arts and imaginative literature at the centre of its aim to produce people of taste and morality because they were considered the means of achieving a polite and virtuous character' (*The Pleasures of the Imagination: English Culture in the Eighteenth Century* (New York: Farrar, Straus and Giroux, 1997), p. III). In *Gender and the Formation of Taste in Eighteenth-Century Britain: The Analysis of Beauty* (Cambridge: Cambridge University Press, 1998), Robert Jones similarly argues that the ability to form and express opinions on matters of taste served as a qualification for participating in eighteenth-century cultural discourse.

[12] So claims the full title of the version printed by Richardson: *The Art of Acting. Part I. Deriving Rules from a New Principle For Touching the Passions in a Natural Manner. An Essay of General Use, To Those, who* hear, *or* speak *in Public, and to the Practices of many of the Elegant Arts; As Painters, Sculpters, and Designers:* But Adapted, in Particular, to the Stage: *With View To quicken the Delight of Audiences, And form a Judgement of the Actors, in their Good, or Bad, Performances.*

[13] 'Thomas Wilkes' is thought to be a pseudonym for the writer and critic Samuel Derrick.

of contemporary actors, dissecting their styles and treating most with witty scorn. The poem's immediate popular success is a compelling testimony to the widespread interest that the subject of actors and acting could attract.[14]

Eighteenth-century stage practice is, of course, by no means uncharted territory. Following early accounts like that of Chetwood, the history of the period's acting has rarely been neglected, and modern eighteenth-century studies have been well served by scholarship from Alan S. Downer's fine article of 1943 to more recent work such as the monumental *A Biographical Dictionary of Actors, Actresses, Musicians, Dancers, Managers, and Other Stage Personnel in London, 1660–1800* (1973–93).[15] What such scholarship has not fully addressed, however, is the *cultural work* invested in stage practice, and I hope here to cast new light upon eighteenth-century debates over performance styles by considering them in relation to the contemporary emergence of notions of 'politeness'. The bodies of actors, I shall argue, became invested with the potential to symbolise politeness and to propagate its modes of expression, and consequently they were enlisted as civilising tools in both the legitimisation of the theatres and the nurturing of polite culture more broadly.[16] And this potential in theatrical performance will be brought into relief through its examination alongside a more shaded area of eighteenth-century culture – namely, oratory.

Eighteenth-century oratory has received only minimal attention from modern scholars, and yet it was a craft of immense cultural and political significance in Britain, and it attracted a similar kind of scrutiny and textual production to acting. Indeed, several of the manuals on acting were based on works originally written for the field of oratory – Charles Gildon, for example, borrowed extensively from an influential *Essay Upon the Action of an Orator* (1702?) when writing his *Life of Mr. Thomas Betterton*. This may explain Gildon's emphasis upon male actors, for where oratory is concerned, elocutionary discourse is focused primarily upon the training of male bodies. Writers on oratory were engaged,

---

[14] Raymond Smith describes the poem's success – its attainment of 'immediate fame' – in *Charles Churchill* (Boston: Twayne, 1977), p. 24.

[15] Alan S. Downer, 'Nature to Advantage Dressed: Eighteenth-Century Acting', *PMLA* 58 (1943), 1002–37; Philip H. Highfill, Jr, Kalman A. Burnim, and Edward A. Langhans, *A Biographical Dictionary of Actors, Actresses, Musicians, Dancers, Managers, and Other Stage Personnel in London, 1660–1800*, 16 vols. (Carbondale: Southern Illinois University Press, 1973–93).

[16] A valuable study which, while not specifically focused upon British stagecraft of this period, *is* attentive to the potential of acting to perform this type of 'cultural work' is Erika Fisher-Lichte's 'Theatre and the Civilizing Process: An Approach to the History of Acting', in Thomas Postlewait and Bruce A. McConachie (eds.), *Interpreting the Theatrical Past: Essays in the Historiography of Performance* (Iowa City: University of Iowa Press, 1989), pp. 19–36.

sometimes self-consciously, in a reconstruction of the forms of public conduct that could be understood as appropriate to masculinity, and by encouraging the use of affective delivery, they were elevating emotionalism as a means of empowerment for men in their public roles.[17] The reach of affective oratory was intended to embrace both men and women as spectators, but the role allotted to women here was more passive than in the fields of stagecraft or the novel, where the signifying potential of female bodies could be explored, and where women occupied a greater creative role as actresses and authors. It is to 'gentlemen', though, that tracts on oratory are addressed, as they offer to show the way to 'speaking well in public' – in fact, by conveying that skill, they are teaching one of the means by which men could lay claim to a gentlemanly status.

The need or desire to 'speak well in public' was addressed in numerous publications. In the century and a half between John Bulwer's pre-Interregnum *Chirologia; or, The Naturall Language of the Hand* (1644) and Gilbert Austin's *Chironomia; or, a Treatise on Rhetorical delivery: comprehending many precepts, both ancient and modern, for the proper regulation of the voice, the countenance and gesture* (1806), there appeared a rash of works offering advice to public speakers at the bar, in the senate, and particularly, in the pulpit.[18] And importantly, this advice was directed not only to *what* public speakers should say – the matter to be included in a speech or sermon, compositional structure, and so forth – but also to *how* they should say it, often including instructions on the finer points of expression and bodily gesture.

As with the instructional works on acting, public-speaking guides appeared in many formats, from cheap pamphlets, like the anonymous *Some Rules for Speaking and Action* (1715), to luxury items like John Ward's weighty, two-volume *A System of Oratory* (1759). Occupying the middle ground of this market were many slim volumes – John Mason's sixpenny, thirty-nine-page *An Essay on Elocution; or, Pronunciation* (1748), for example – and numerous other single-volume works. Most elocutionary works were written in prose, but verse forms were sometimes employed, as in the

---

[17] In this respect, the reform of oratory can be located within a wider eighteenth-century reform of male manners, involving the 'softening' of traditional signs of masculinity. G. J. Barker-Benfield describes the types of social practice around which such a reformation took place in *The Culture of Sensibility: Sex and Society in Eighteenth-Century Britain* (Chicago and London, University of Chicago Press, 1992), pp. 37–103 and *passim.*

[18] For a useful catalogue of eighteenth-century works on oratory, see the bibliography in Rolf P. Lessinich, *Elements of Pulpit Oratory in Eighteenth-Century England (1660–1800)* (Cologne: Böhlau, 1972).

anonymous *Advice to a Parson; or, the true art of preaching* (1691) or later in
Richard Polwhele's lengthy *The Art of Eloquence. A Didactic Poem* (1785).
Again like acting, the subject of oratory found its way into the fiction of the
period and was addressed by many novelists, notably by Sterne and by
Richard Graves (1715–1804), a clergyman and author whose *The Spiritual
Quixote* (1773) contains lengthy meditations upon the propriety of particu-
lar preaching techniques.

Public speaking was analysed and taught not only through the medium
of print. Several dedicated reformers, seeking to improve or transform
British eloquence, presented instructive lectures on oratory, and attending
such events became, as will be seen, a popular and fashionable pursuit.
From 1726 until his death, the eccentric John 'Orator' Henley (1692–1756)
maintained a London preaching house – the 'Oratory' – from which he
would regularly give lectures on techniques for public speaking. In 1762 the
Revd Dr John Trusler, who had gained considerable renown as a preacher
in his Hertfordshire parish, set up a school in London devoted to the
teaching of elocution. His school endured less well than Henley's Oratory,
but it nevertheless attracted 'a great many pupils'.[19] John Ward's *A System
of Oratory* was based on a series of lectures he presented at London's
Gresham College, home of the Royal Society, where from 1720 he served
as Professor of Rhetoric. And Thomas Sheridan (1719–88), the best-known
elocutionist of the century, exploited the public lecture in similar ways.
Sheridan toured England and Scotland with his lectures – printed as
Lectures on Elocution (1762) – and he regularly attracted large, paying
crowds.

In short, from the beginning of the eighteenth century there was a major
movement to develop public speaking in Britain, in the course of which
project appeared some of the century's most explicit writing on the
eloquence or potential eloquence of the body. And yet, while 'the body'
remains hot academic property – at a recent annual conference of the
British Society for Eighteenth-Century Studies no fewer than three panels
of lectures were devoted to 'The body and literature' – oratory, in the sense
of the *delivery* of orations, remains an obscure issue within studies of the
period. The topic has not been totally overlooked. The 'elocutionary
movement', as it has been termed, has been examined in unpublished
theses by William Phillips Sandford (1929) and Frederick Haberman
(1947), and Rolf P. Lessinich includes a chapter on 'The Delivery of the

[19] John Trusler, *Memoirs of the Life of the Rev. Dr. Trusler* (London, 1806), p. 186.

Sermon' in his *Elements of Pulpit Oratory in Eighteenth-Century England (1660–1800)* (1972).[20] The movement has also been discussed in Wilbur Samuel Howell's studies of rhetoric and logic (1961; 1971), which still provide the most accessible and comprehensive survey of eighteenth-century elocutionary writing.[21] This book has benefited from Howell's work, but I aim to open up the ramifications of elocutionary writing more widely than Howell, who, as a champion of classical rhetoric (an oddly anachronistic position, it might be said), is fundamentally dismissive of the movement.[22] I believe, like Michael Shortland, one of the few more recent scholars to have addressed the subject, that the investigation of works on oratory can bring forth valuable insights into the workings of eighteenth-century British culture. 'Elocutionary perceptions of the body', Shortland suggests, 'possess an importance far beyond the rather narrow limits of the history of linguistics and rhetoric' – I have devoted the first three chapters of this book to fleshing out some of that importance.[23]

---

[20] William Phillips Sandford, 'English Theories of Public Address, 1530–1828', unpublished Ph.D. thesis, Ohio State University (1929); Frederick William Haberman, 'The Elocutionary Movement in England, 1750–1850', unpublished Ph.D. thesis, Cornell University (1947); Lessinich, *Elements of Pulpit Oratory*, pp. 128–50. Short introductions to the major figures and texts of the movement are provided by *Eighteenth-Century British and American Rhetorics and Rhetoricians: Critical Studies and Sources*, ed. Michael G. Moran (Westport, CT: Greenwood Press, 1994), and a sketch of the movement is given in G. P. Mohrmann, 'The Language of Nature and Elocutionary Theory', *Quarterly Journal of Speech* 52 (1966), 116–24.

[21] Wilbur Samuel Howell, 'Sources of the Elocutionary Movement in England: 1700–1748', in Raymond F. Howes (ed.), *Historical Studies of Rhetoric and Rhetoricians* (Ithaca, NY: Cornell University Press, 1961), pp. 139–58; and *Eighteenth-Century British Logic and Rhetoric* (Princeton: Princeton University Press, 1971).

[22] Howell dismisses elocutionary works because their concentration on delivery tends to exclude other elements of classical rhetoric relating to composition. In 'Sources of the Elocutionary Movement' he shows reservations about the work of the elocutionists but nevertheless argues that the figures who comprise the movement 'should not be allowed henceforth to suffer the neglect that has been their lot since their own generation perished' (p. 157). In *British Logic and Rhetoric* his attack upon elocutionists has become caustic as he envisages a situation where, if the elocutionists had restrained their work on delivery, 'the practices which they identified as the whole art of rhetoric would have subsided into an early and well-deserved oblivion, and the true art of rhetoric would perhaps have avoided the eclipse that the nineteenth-century elocutionists helped bring upon it' (p. 458).

[23] Michael Shortland, 'Moving Speeches: Language and Elocution in Eighteenth-Century Britain', *History of European Ideas* 8 (1987), 639. Shortland builds on Haberman's work and provides a sound, descriptive introduction to writing on elocution, but he does not develop a discussion of the wider importance he recognises. Shortland has addressed other areas of somatic eloquence in further articles which have been useful for this study: 'Unnatural Acts: Art and Passion on the Mid-Eighteenth-Century Stage', *Theatre Research International* 12 (1987), 93–110; 'Skin Deep: Barthes, Lavater and the Legible Body', *Economy and Society* 14 (1985), 273–312; 'The Power of a Thousand Eyes: Johann Caspar Lavater's Science of Physiognomic Perception', *Criticism* 28 (1986), 379–408.

Considering the different types of practice through which the eloquence of bodies was constructed, it is important to recognise 'elocutionary discourse' as something wider than the sum of printed traces that now provide the primary routes for historical research into eighteenth-century acting, oratory, and other body matters. Martin Jay sounds a healthy note of warning when he describes 'discourse' as 'one of the most loosely used terms of our time', and it is as well that I clarify the fundamentally but not rigidly Foucauldian sense in which I use the term here.[24] With 'elocutionary discourse' I aim to refer broadly to the wealth of utterances and practices – some literary, some oral, some graphic, some somatic – which in different ways contributed to the construction of eighteenth-century understandings of bodily eloquence. Particularly it should be recognised that the practices of oratory and acting themselves – ephemeral practices, which are now only knowable as mediated through the meta-texts produced around them – also participated in this discourse. In some cases this participation was doubtless of greater significance than many printed utterances. For example, the practice of a prominent actor – David Garrick (1717–79) would be a prime case – is likely to have had considerably more impact than a pamphlet on acting practices upon the production of a body image.

I should further specify the character of 'elocutionary discourse' by adding that it is typically dialogic, in the sense that it is characterised by debate between *competing* body images. I shall be arguing – in Raymond Williams's still potent terms for describing cultural transformation – that an *emergent* sentimental body image came to *dominate* over a *residual* classical body image.[25] But sentimentalism did not achieve a secure hegemony. It would be misleading, therefore, to speak of 'elocutionary discourse' in the singular unless it were understood *prima facie* as inherently dialogic and internally variegated. Moreover, the contestation *within* this discourse was not only between classicism and sentimentalism: I shall chart further oppositions between 'polite' bodies and other bodies which were widely perceived as unruly or transgressive – particularly, the 'enthusiastic' bodies associated with Methodism.

It is appropriate to have opened up what I mean by elocutionary discourse – and I hope that by now I might liberate the phrase from

---

[24] Martin Jay, *Downcast Eyes: The Denigration of Vision in Twentieth-Century French Thought* (Berkeley: University of California Press, 1993), p. 15.
[25] Williams introduced the dominant/emergent/residual distinction in *Marxism and Literature* (Oxford: Oxford University Press, 1977).

inverted commas – before introducing the other cultural site under investigation here, since compared with acting and oratory, wherein the training
of the body is very obviously a key activity, this site's relevance to bodily
eloquence may initially seem more oblique. The site I refer to is the
sentimental novel or, more specifically, the *reading* of sentimental novels.
It is now well established that the sentimental novel figured in the mid to
late eighteenth century as a key agent and disseminator of bourgeois
ideology, and several studies have persuasively argued for the centrality of
this popular genre in the emergence of polite culture.[26] It has also already
been demonstrated, most fully in John Mullan's outstanding *Sentiment
and Sociability: The Language of Feeling in the Eighteenth Century* (1988),
that 'the body' is deeply implicated in the genre. 'In the novels of the mid-
eighteenth century', Mullan argues, 'it is the body which acts out the
powers of sentiment.'[27] Mullan has shown how the fiction of novelists
such as Richardson, Sterne, Henry Brooke (1703–83), and Henry Mackenzie
(1745–1831) promoted a physical language of feeling with a view to forging
sociability along lines of sympathy. Setting this cultural work performed by
the novel in a broader intellectual and social context, Mullan demonstrates
that the socialising tendency of the fiction is analogous to the contempor-
aneous projects of moral philosophers such as David Hume and Adam Smith
(1723–90), and that the vocabulary of the adopted somatic language is
mirrored in, or derived from, contemporary medical constructions of the
body. Mullan emphasises the novelists' preoccupation with the *ailing* body,
and presents suggestive parallels between the writings of novelists and of
physicians, such as Richardson's doctor George Cheyne.

In addressing the reading of sentimental fiction, I aim to develop the
picture of the genre's embeddedness in eighteenth-century thinking about
the body by re-exploring the methods by which it teaches somatic practice –
particularly those strategies by which fiction promoted the *performance* of a
language of feeling, including the performance of weakness. Readers of
sentimental fiction were invited to inhabit roles much like that taken on
by Richardson when he was reading *The Art of Acting*: such fiction urged
readers to rehearse a language of gesture, and it thus presented both
opportunities for the assertion of polite identities and a language of polite

---

[26] Secondary criticism of sentimental fiction constitutes a huge field. 'Central' works which I have
found particularly useful are: Brissenden, *Virtue in Distress*; John Mullan, *Sentiment and
Sociability: The Language of Feeling in the Eighteenth Century* (Oxford: Clarendon Press, 1988; repr.
1997); Janet Todd, *Sensibility: An Introduction* (London and New York: Methuen, 1986); Barker-
Benfield, *Culture of Sensibility*.

[27] Mullan, *Sentiment and Sociability*, p. 201.

self-presentation. And this didacticism is not only evident *within* the fiction, but also marks and consolidates the 'interpretive community' – Stanley Fish's term for the groups which, through *collective* processes, arrive at settled interpretations of literary works – which grew up around sentimental fiction.[28] Such didacticism, although mediated through the often convoluted path of narrative fiction, is analogous to, and analysable through comparison with, the didacticism at work in other areas of elocutionary discourse.

There are other enterprises which clearly could be seen within the fold of elocutionary discourse, but which could not be examined within the scope of this book – for example, practices within and around the visual arts involving the graphic representation of bodies.[29] Eighteenth-century medicine and anatomy are also clearly pertinent to the issue of somatic eloquence under scrutiny here. Thanks to the concerted recent work by historians of medicine – notably Roy Porter, G. S. Rousseau, Barbara Maria Stafford, and John Mullan – there is now extensive scholarship which deals with how, in physiological terms, the body was known in the eighteenth century, and with how this knowledge, formulated by physicians, was dispersed through British society via the medium of print.[30] In common with this book, the history of medicine shows that 'the body' cannot be simply understood as some epistemologically stable and natural given, but rather must be recognised as always partly mediated through the

---

[28] Fish develops his concept of the 'interpretive community' in *Is There a Text in This Class?: The Authority of Interpretive Communities* (Cambridge, MA: Harvard University Press, 1980).

[29] There is already considerable scholarship on the body and physiognomy within eighteenth-century theories of art. Good starting points are: Shearer West, 'Polemic and the Passions: Dr James Parsons's *Human Physiognomy Explained* and Hogarth's Aspirations for British History Painting', *British Journal for Eighteenth-Century Studies* 13:1 (Spring 1990), 73–89; and Brewster Rogerson, 'The Art of Painting the Passions', *Journal of the History of Ideas* 14 (1953), 68–94.

[30] A seminal work in the field is G. S. Rousseau's 'Nerves, Spirits and Fibres: Towards Defining the Origins of Sensibility', in R. F. Brissenden and J. C. Eade (eds.), *Studies in the Eighteenth Century 3* (Canberra: Australian National University Press; Toronto: Toronto University Press, 1976), pp. 137–57. Rousseau persuasively demonstrates the fundamental epistemological 'paradigm shift' which led to the predominant 'nerve science' of eighteenth-century medical thought. Mullan develops Rousseau's work in the final chapter of *Sentiment and Sociability* (pp. 201–40) – a reworking of 'Hypochondria and Hysteria: Sensibility and the Physicians', *The Eighteenth Century: Theory and Interpretation* 25 (1984), 141–74. From the deluge of medical history emanating from Roy Porter, the following might be singled out as particularly informative: *The Greatest Benefit to Mankind: A Medical History of Humanity from Antiquity to the Present* (London: HarperCollins, 1997); co-authored with Dorothy Porter, *Patient's Progress: Doctors and Doctoring in Eighteenth-Century England* (Cambridge: Polity Press, 1989); 'Civilization and Disease: Medical Ideology in the Enlightenment', in J. Black and J. Gregory (eds.), *Culture, Politics and Society in Britain 1660–1800* (Manchester: Manchester University Press, 1991), 154–83. The visual side of eighteenth-century medical discourse is well represented in Barbara Maria Stafford's richly illustrated *Body Criticism: Imaging the Unseen in Enlightenment Art and Medicine* (Cambridge, MA: Massachusetts Institute of Technology Press, 1991).

frameworks of science and ideology that are available within a particular context. Richardson's understanding of himself as a delicate collection of nerves, for example, is dependent upon the 'nerve science' that came to dominate eighteenth-century medicine. Where appropriate, my account of eloquent bodies draws upon findings from medical history, but it is with an emphasis upon the *performing body* that my own discussion develops.

THE BODY IN CULTURAL HISTORY

But what is the value of focusing upon the body in this way? Aside from intrinsic points of interest, why choose the performing body as the lens through which to explore wider issues of eighteenth-century culture? As a way into addressing these questions it is worth turning briefly to some of the scholarship which, over the last twenty years or so, has created what might now be recognised as a 'field' of 'body studies'. For it is upon insights generated by this field – particularly by studies of a broadly 'New Historical' stamp – that the current work builds.

Modern 'body studies' probably owes its greatest debt to the stimulating works of Michel Foucault, who in his investigations of various themes – treatment of the mentally ill, institutions of punishment, the history of human sexuality – has plotted the involuntary subjectivity of individual bodies to systems of power as they are manipulated or marked by different kinds of discourse. I alluded earlier to the nexus of nature and culture which can be witnessed in Richardson's dealings with *The Art of Acting* – Foucault's analysis of this fundamental yet elusive boundary has stressed the overwhelming power of culture to transform and create the experience of being human. In his seminal *Discipline and Punish* (1975; trans. 1977), Foucault argues that the body is 'directly involved in a political field; power relations have an immediate hold upon it; they invest it, mark it, train it, torture it, force it to carry out tasks, to perform ceremonies, to emit signs'.[31] His work vigorously asserts the body's embeddedness in culture, and repeatedly stresses the constructedness of practices involving the body which may normally appear under a veil of naturalising rhetoric. In Foucauldian terms, Richardson's body would be a version of one on the brink of 'docility' – a puppet of disciplinary power, the institutions of which, Foucault argues, were developed in Europe during the eighteenth century (or, as he prefers it, the 'classical age'):

---

[31] Michel Foucault, *Discipline and Punish: The Birth of the Prison*, trans. Alan Sheridan (London: Allen Lane, 1977; repr. 1991), p. 25.

The historical moment of the disciplines was the moment when an art of the human body was born, which was directed not only at the growth of its skills, nor at the intensification of its subjection, but at the formulation of a relation that in the mechanism itself makes it more obedient as it becomes more useful, and conversely. What was then being formed was a policy of coercions that act upon the body, a calculated manipulation of its elements, its gestures, its behaviour. The human body was entering a machinery of power that explores it, breaks it down and rearranges it. A 'political anatomy', which was also a 'mechanics of power', was being born; it defined how one may have a hold over other's bodies, not only so that they may do what one wishes, but so that they may operate as one wishes, with the techniques, the speed and efficiency that one determines. Thus discipline produces subjected and practised bodies, 'docile' bodies.[32]

Such forceful depictions of the coercive cultural transformation of somatic materiality have brought about significant shifts in how bodies are perceived, and Foucault has been highly influential in spawning a widespread post-structuralist enterprise which, from the early 1980s, has radically challenged foundational commonplaces of traditional humanist thinking. The conception of the individual as a core of action and meaning, which transcends local specificity by virtue of its centre of being in 'man', has been widely undermined by an alternative recognition of the subject as an unfixed construction of language and discourse. Viewed thus, the body's materiality recedes and tends to shed its signifying potential beneath the layered coverings of culture – indeed, for more radical proponents of such thinking, such as Judith Butler, materiality in itself is ever unavailable for scrutiny. The body, for Butler, is 'always already' sedimented in discourse, and is knowable only as its effect.[33]

Amid the scattered fragments of the post-humanist and post-structuralist subject, however, the body has alternatively been seen to stand with an awkward and insistent stability. Indeed, current interests in 'the body' have been attributed by some, such as Valentine Cunningham, to a recognition in the body of some kind of final centre of meaning in the face of the destabilising uncertainties of post-structuralist theory.[34] The body's

[32] *Ibid.*, pp. 137–8.
[33] This is a premise of Butler's *Bodies that Matter: On the Discursive Limits of 'Sex'* (London and New York: Routledge, 1993). Such arguments, it should be said, are not uniquely the product of post-structuralism, and comparable positions have been voiced before – see, for example, the claims by the sociologist and anthropologist Marcel Mauss that there is no such thing as 'natural' behaviour, in 'Les Techniques du corps', *Journal de la psychologie normale et pathologique* 32:3–4 (1936), 271–93.
[34] Cunningham notes this characteristic in an article criticising the trend for studies to focus upon the body. Semi-parodically he writes: 'The body is the presence we can rely on, our metaphysics of presence' ('Vile Bodies', *Times Higher Education Supplement*, 8 March 1996, 15).

varieties – its differences of sex, gender, race, age, health, ability, and those differences generated by mutilation, surgery, and so on – have received increasing attention across a range of academic disciplines, but the fundamental fact of embodiment, despite constructions around it, has none the less often been seen as something reliably universal. Aileen Douglas, for example, cogently points out in a study of Tobias Smollett's writing and the body that 'If you prick a socially constructed body, it still bleeds.'[35] Douglas is one of several recent critics who work from the premise, summarised by the editors of a volume on *Body and Text in the Eighteenth Century* (1994), that 'the body is neither simply in discourse nor out of it'.[36] These editors describe the body's 'survival within . . . discursivity as a kinetic potential' which can disrupt and transgress instituted models of somatic conditions.[37] Other body critics have seen the body's resistance to discourse as precisely the set of limitations within which discourse can operate. 'Cultural variations', Drew Leder has written, 'are always played out upon the keyboard of possibilities presented by our corporeal structure', and it is within the restrictions of these possibilities that a bodily essence is sometimes identified.[38]

As the passages quoted illustrate, criticism centred on the body is regularly preoccupied at some level with the distinction between nature and culture, and it is not uncommon for studies to attempt some mapping of that distinction. Such an ambition may be profitable grist to an anthropologist's mill, but when one is studying a cultural process – such as the growth of 'politeness' – it can be useful to remain critically detached from the distinction and to treat shifts in the perceived boundaries between natural and cultivated behaviour as potential indicators of broader cultural upheavals. In *Practicing New Historicism* (2000), Catherine Gallagher and

---

[35] Aileen Douglas, *Uneasy Sensations: Smollett and the Body* (Chicago: University of Chicago Press, 1995), p. xxii.

[36] Veronica Kelly and Dorothea von Mücke (eds.), *Body and Text in the Eighteenth Century* (Stanford: Stanford University Press, 1994), p. 4.

[37] *Ibid.*, p. 4. Catherine Gallagher and Stephen Greenblatt argue along similar lines: 'The way bodies are understood to function, the difference between men and women, the nature of the passions, the experience of illness, the border line between life and death are all closely bound up with particular cultural representations, but they cannot simply be reduced to those representations. The body functions as a kind of "spoiler", always baffling or exceeding the ways in which it is represented' (*Practicing New Historicism* (Chicago and London: University of Chicago Press, 2000), p. 15).

[38] Drew Leder, *The Absent Body* (Chicago and London: University of Chicago Press, 1990), p. 3. In a similar vein, Susan Bordo argues that materiality signifies 'our finitude. It refers to our inescapable physical locatedness in time and space, in history and culture, both of which not only shape us (the social constructionist premise, which I share with other postmoderns) but also *limit* us (which some postmoderns appear to me to deny)' ('Bringing Body to Theory', in Donn Welton (ed.), *Body and Flesh: A Philosophical Reader* (Oxford: Blackwell, 1998), p. 90).

Stephen Greenblatt provide a useful summary of how such a focus can generate historical insights. Following the 'linguistic turn in the social and humanistic disciplines', they write, what becomes

interesting about the nature/culture distinction ... is the very fact that it cannot be fixed because the boundaries between the terms and the significance of those boundaries vary too widely in different contexts. Like other crucial distinctions, the nature/culture divide should be read, in the manner of structural linguistics, as a key binary opposition, loaded with information for deciphering the various social codes one encounters in historical studies.[39]

This, in fact, is essentially the manner in which Foucault approached the cultural work surrounding 'the body'. Foucault, as Daniel Punday observes, uses 'the spatialized body to accomplish the "task" of historical analysis. The imprinted body provides Foucault with a text that can be read to understand historical changes ... The body ... is a site in which historical transformations can be observed in the codes for social behaviour and perception.'[40] This book presents a more tempered portrait of 'discipline' than that emerging from Foucault's work, but it proceeds none the less according to a similar view of the body's usefulness within historiography.

There are, of course, many other 'sites' in which one can observe historical transformations at work, but the body, I believe, displays a particularly acute capacity for representation because it is perpetually available in social relations – indeed, it provides an *inescapable* textual surface – and also because of the very resilience of its claims to being natural. Cultural representations gain power by their association with the body precisely because the flesh can bestow authority through the persuasive rhetoric of 'nature'. This has been admirably demonstrated in the groundbreaking (and effectively pre-Foucauldian) work of Mary Douglas, particularly her *Natural Symbols* (1970). Douglas presents and analyses numerous applications of the body which *naturalise* social desiderata; she describes, in fact, 'two bodies' – one social, one physical – arguing that the social body 'constrains the way the physical body is perceived. The physical experience of the body, always modified by the social categories through which it is known, sustains a particular view of society ...

---

[39] Gallagher and Greenblatt, *Practicing New Historicism*, p. 8.

[40] Daniel Punday, 'Foucault's Body Tropes', *New Literary History* 31 (2000), 513–14. Punday also makes the valuable point – one that applies to much work on the body – that bodies themselves are rarely objects of analysis for Foucault: 'the body itself never provides an actual text that is interpreted. All of Foucault's work ultimately discusses books that describe bodies; at no point does it actually observe physical bodies ... The body site, then, is less an object of analysis and more a rhetorical gesture – a trope – that justifies the textual analysis that he conducts' (p. 514).

The forms [... the body] adopts in movement and repose express social pressures in manifold ways.'[41] I shall be arguing that an aim – often an unconscious one – of those involved in elocutionary discourse was precisely that of *sustaining a particular view of society*. Bodies or fictional bodies exhibiting notably refined signs of the passions – including those clichés of sentimentalism: single tears, delicate sighs, gentle swoons – functioned within eighteenth-century culture in part as 'natural symbols' of 'politeness'.

But what was politeness, in this sense? The term now, as John Brewer puts it, 'conjures up ideas of etiquette, of conventions that help to smooth social relations, even if they are not essential to them'; in the eighteenth century, however, 'it meant much more'.[42] It is worthwhile exploring some of those wider meanings.

POLITENESS IN EIGHTEENTH-CENTURY BRITAIN

Brean Hammond has asserted that polite discourse was 'arguably the most significant crucible of aesthetic and social change in the eighteenth century'.[43] Hammond is in the supportive company of historians of British culture, including Paul Langford, Lawrence Klein, and G. J. Barker-Benfield, who concur in a recognition that political and economic changes from the end of the seventeenth century produced a concomitant transformation of manners and a growth of 'politeness' – a narrative which has been developed alongside the solidification of the view that this period saw the emergence of a 'bourgeois public sphere'.[44] Initiated principally by the philosopher and social theorist Jürgen Habermas in the early 1960s (and energised in English-language studies in 1989 with the translation of Habermas's *Strukturwandel der Öffentlichkeit* (1962)), studies of eighteenth-century European culture have increasingly investigated the discursive configurations made possible through the growth of this 'bourgeois public sphere' – a realm of public opinion and transaction which became increasingly prominent on the political map despite existing without official

[41] Mary Douglas, *Natural Symbols: Explorations in Cosmology*, 2nd edn (London: Barrie and Jenkins, 1973), p. 93.

[42] Brewer, *Pleasures of the Imagination*, pp. 99–100.

[43] Brean Hammond, *Professional Imaginative Writing in England, 1670–1740: Hackney for Bread* (Oxford: Clarendon Press, 1997), p. 147.

[44] See Paul Langford, *A Polite and Commercial People: England 1727–1783* (Oxford: Oxford University Press, 1989), especially chapter 3, 'The Progress of Politeness', pp. 59–121; Lawrence E. Klein, *Shaftesbury and the Culture of Politeness: Moral Discourse and Cultural Politics in Early Eighteenth-Century England* (Cambridge: Cambridge University Press, 1994); Barker-Benfield, *Culture of Sensibility*.

political status.[45] That an expanding bourgeois class should have claimed a greater stake in political and public life at this time was, in Britain, importantly connected to the devolution of power, following the revolution of 1688, away from the court and landed aristocrats and towards the urban bourgeoisie and those classes with trade interests. The economic relations of early capitalism, Habermas argues, dispersed political and commercial interests in such a way that state policy had a greater relevance to an increasingly large and economically enfranchised middle-class community. Bourgeois traders and property owners became culturally significant both as privatised individuals and as members of the public, in which they now had a share and upon which they, as links in a chain of commerce, largely depended. Such common interests prompted a growth in public life which was enabled both by the proliferation of new meeting places – clubs, salons, coffee-houses, assemblies, gardens – in which individuals could congregate and discuss the important issues of the day, and by a massive expansion in the production of printed matter.[46] Supported by rising literacy and a significant freeing of the presses from state control, printed productions of many kinds – newspapers, periodicals, fiction, tracts, and treatises – functioned as textual spaces in which bourgeois interests and identities could be formulated, exerted, and endowed with cultural authority. The press, then, became a central component in the emergence and structure of the public sphere; it was, as Bob Harris has written, 'the vehicle by which the private reasonings of bourgeois individuals were rendered public'.[47] In short, from the end of the seventeenth century there occurred in Britain an elaboration of public life and bourgeois interaction which was manifested within a range of newly created institutions, some taking the form of physical or architectural spaces, and others the form of printed text.

For this book, the most important feature of this established picture of eighteenth-century cultural transformation is the partially unformed quality of bourgeois identity which accompanies political and economic change and the growth of new social spaces and new discursive situations. The object of study here might be said to be the language, or an aspect of the language, that was developed (though it never became settled as any monolithic construct) so as to mediate new discursive situations involving

[45] Jürgen Habermas, *The Structural Transformation of the Public Sphere: An Inquiry into a Category of Bourgeois Society*, trans. Thomas Burger (Cambridge: Polity Press, 1989).
[46] On the expansion of urban club culture, see Peter Clark, *Sociability and Urbanity: Clubs and Societies in the Eighteenth-Century City* (Leicester: Victorian Studies Centre, University of Leicester, 1986).
[47] Bob Harris, *Politics and the Rise of the Press: Britain and France, 1620–1800* (London and New York: Routledge, 1996), p. 3.

subjects anxious to assert legitimate public identities but unsure of the protocols by which to do so. This language of politeness – operating on many levels, including the somatic – emerged as a form of social currency to smooth the relations of a developing community of socially and publicly engaged individuals. Politeness, defined in the mid century by Smollett as 'the art of making one's self agreeable . . . an art that necessarily implies a sense of decorum, and a delicacy of sentiment', allowed members of the middling classes to present a public image of civilised gentility.[48] Politeness became an ideal of sociable conduct – a touchstone of civilised behaviour that could be invoked within many different situations or activities. It was the quality that validated an individual's engagement in 'polite company', 'polite learning', 'polite letters', 'the polite arts', and so on. And the terms and forms of that gentility were also available to be employed by upper-class individuals, who could claim gentility through birth but sought to display the powerful alternative signs of civic virtue that were developing within the bourgeois sphere. As Hammond writes, 'genuine aristocrats could be encouraged to covet possession of the polite codes as a more virtuous and ethical alternative to those, like duelling and hunting, into which they were born'.[49] Politeness, then, contributed a type of refined cultural cement that supported sociable relations by bringing people together within the framework of shared social practices. As described by Lawrence Klein, a particularly lucid commentator on the subject, politeness had 'social, psychological and formal dimensions', and Klein succinctly elaborates on these facets of the polite phenomenon:

First, 'politeness' was situated in 'company', in the realm of social interaction and exchange, where it governed relations of the self with others. While allowing for differences among selves, 'politeness' was concerned with coordinating, reconciling or integrating them. Second, it subjected this domain of social life to the norm of 'pleasing.' The gratification nurtured by 'politeness' was psychological, the amelioration of people's senses of themselves and of others. Thus, 'politeness' presupposed an intersubjective domain in which the cultivation and exchange of opinions and feelings were involved. Third, 'politeness' involved a grasp of form. It was an art or technique, governing the 'how' of social relations. 'Politeness' concerned sociability but was not identical with it: while human sociability was a primal and original stuff requiring work, 'politeness' was a refined sociability, bringing aesthetic concerns into close contiguity with ethical ones.[50]

---

[48] Tobias Smollett, *Travels through France and Italy*, ed. Frank Felsenstein (Oxford and New York: Oxford University Press, 1981; repr. 1992), p. 57.

[49] Hammond, *Professional Imaginative Writing*, p. 151.

[50] Klein, *Culture of Politeness*, p. 4.

It is in this last field – 'the "how" of social relations' – that the performing body plays its most crucial role. Politeness was in part a language that could be *performed*, and while my focus here is deliberately upon practices like oratory and acting where a sense of performance is very obvious, a further aim is to suggest that these practices provided models which could be appropriated, adapted and internalised by both men and women as a manner of self-presentation more generally.

A revealing account of everyday social interaction as performance appears in an essay of 1770 by James Boswell (1740–95). Writing on the profession of acting for the *London Magazine*, Boswell makes a direct connection between the practices of the professional performer and of the figure engaged in society, and his account is striking for its knowing exposure of typically unconscious processes. Boswell seems to have had half an eye on his unconscious as he discusses his experience of a 'double feeling' – a feeling which

is experienced by many men in the common intercourse of life. Were nothing but the real character to appear, society would not be half so safe and agreeable as we find it. Did we discover to our companions what we really think of them, frequent quarrels would ensue; and did we not express more regard for them than we really feel, the pleasure of social intercourse would be very contracted. It being necessary then in the intercourse of life to have such appearances, and dissimulation being to most people irksome and fatiguing, we insensibly, for our own ease, adopt feelings suitable to every occasion, and so, like players, are to a certain degree a different character from our own.[51]

Like Jacques in *As You Like It*, Boswell finds all the world to be a stage as he reveals social intercourse to be a business steeped in rhetoric. 'Players' in society *adopt* patterns of expression whereby character is not so much *revealed* as *formed* at the point of utterance, and these self-formations occur according to expectations of behaviour which are predetermined as 'suitable' for different discursive situations. The performance is distinct from conscious dissimulation, being adopted 'insensibly', and the experience appears to Boswell, from his own interactions in society, as a slight awareness of himself in public as different from his private sense of self-identity.

With his 'double feeling' Boswell appears as the close relation of what Stanley Fish has called 'rhetorical man' – a figure aware of his own social construction, who 'manipulates or fabricates himself, simultaneously

[51] *London Magazine; Or Gentleman's Monthly Intelligencer*, 52 vols. (London, 1732–83), vol. 39, p. 470.

conceiving of and occupying the roles that become first possible and then
mandatory given the social structure his rhetoric has put in place'.[52]
Boswell is clearly content to recognise that society is structured by rhetorical codes and, seeing their beneficial sociable effects, he consents to his
own 'interpellation' – Louis Althusser's term for an ideology's 'hailing' –
and he satisfies the expectations of social rhetoric through his own performed politeness. The stratum of society described by Boswell sustains
a peaceful and polite surface because its rhetoric suppresses threats to that
public order – it is 'safe and agreeable' because 'real' characters, which for
Boswell are naturally fractious, are only socialised after passing through a
rhetorical filter.

While Boswell is not explicitly describing his body as the theatrical tool,
he is clearly aware of the power of 'appearances'. He lays bare the sense that
politeness, as Brewer puts it, 'thrived on being watched and seen'.[53] Self-
evidently the body functions as one of the primary texts in such visual
exchange. With its easy organic potential for impoliteness and its insistent
ever-presence in public situations, the body was a key site for the business
of constructing politeness, serving as a visible locus for the inscription of
legible notions of civic virtue. In eighteenth-century elocutionary discourse
we witness a culture promoting patterns of somatic behaviour which would
visually symbolise a polite, civilised status. The polite body itself can be
said to *perform* an act of civilisation. We might return to Samuel
Richardson, who suggests his own politeness when he declares his physical
sensitivity, for, as will be seen, possession of an easily moved character
became from the early years of the century a powerful sign of individual
moral worth and, as such, a sign of civility. The association of nervous
delicacy with virtue endowed the demonstration of emotional susceptibility with the force of moral justification.[54] Richardson's delicate body
serves, therefore, as a vehicle for civility, and if, with his 'so long complained of' condition, he should seem merely like an irritable valetudinar-
ian, it is worth noting that his illness produces not self-absorption but an
epistolary moment of sociality with his 'beneficent' friend.[55]

---

[52] Stanley Fish, 'Rhetoric', in Frank Lentricchia and Thomas McLaughlin (eds.), *Critical Terms for Literary Study* (Chicago: Chicago University Press, 1990), p. 208.

[53] Brewer, *Pleasures of the Imagination*, p. 102.

[54] As Barker-Benfield puts it, 'While sensibility rested on essentially materialist assumptions, proponents of the cultivation of sensibility came to invest it with spiritual and moral values' (*Culture of Sensibility*, p. xvii).

[55] It is also pertinent to remain alert to the genre of Richardson's self-portrait. Richardson's body as an object in civil exchange is presented in a medium that was circumscribed by expectations of

My argument will suggest that the bodies of orators and actors were important to the growth of politeness because they occupied supremely public positions in eighteenth-century life, and thus were ripe for taking on the symbolic function of embodying civility and for dispersing this quality through a broader public. The bodily eloquence of the moved actor or orator was deployed so as to echo among the viewing public: through 'sympathy', as contemporaries theorised the process, these public bodies embraced viewers within a physical code of politeness – to use Althusser's term again, they 'interpellated' spectators. For a brief glimpse of this process in action we can turn to Joseph Pittard, a self-appointed arbiter of good taste, whose *Observations on Mr Garrick's Acting* were published in 1758. Of a passage from *King Lear*, Pittard wrote that 'as it was imagined by *Shakespear*, it is spoken by Mr. *Garrick:* My Tears have ever testified this Approbation'.[56] Pittard is concerned to state that it is his body that provides the ultimate litmus test of good acting: his tears function as a sign of worthy emotional susceptibility – they display his 'weakness' and by doing so assert his good taste. A moment of moving drama produces a triple compliment to writer, actor, and audience member, as Pittard displays his own sensitivity through the act of body-based criticism and asserts a refinement akin to that shown by Garrick on the stage. The following chapters will describe both the production of polite eloquence and ways in which it penetrated the public sphere to be performed and lauded by spectators such as Pittard.

Considering the perhaps 'genteel' status of the examples cited thus far, it is probably worth clarifying the nature of this study's Foucauldian leanings and introducing briefly a further component of the polite phenomenon – namely, *leisure.* As the earlier discussion showed, Foucault's emphasis is classically upon the *utility* of the disciplined body – upon how bodies can be rendered more productive, and upon how unruly or criminal bodies can be prevented from disturbing state ambitions. His focus is typically upon prisoners, soldiers, and industrial workers, and upon how such categories of people are subjected according to state-defined needs of production. The polite eloquence under investigation in this study is connected with such production, but it also stands at one remove from it, since, far from fulfilling the *direct* needs of production, the growth of politeness is in many

---

civility. For an account of the letter as a site of polite intercourse, see Bruce Redford, *The Converse of the Pen: Acts of Intimacy in the Eighteenth-Century Familiar Letter* (Chicago and London: University of Chicago Press, 1986).

[56] Joseph Pittard, *Observations on Mr. Garrick's Acting; in a Letter to the Right Hon. the Earl of Chesterfield* (London, 1758), p. 20.

ways driven by the growing availability in eighteenth-century Britain of leisure – a by-product of increasing bourgeois economic power. Indeed, polite discourse can be seen in part as a masking justification of leisurely pursuits such as reading fiction, attending the theatre, or consuming cultural commodities.[57]

It is also worth adding some chiaroscuro to the picture of polite culture by stressing at this point that the rise of politeness did not sweep all before it, engulfing and transforming all that it touched. Just as 'Age of Reason' dogma has now rightly been overturned to expose the period's most unreasonable underbelly, so too should politeness be viewed in a dialectical relationship with alternative cultural possibilities. Challenges to polite eloquence – such as those posed by John Henley and, from the 1740s, some of the more frenzied Methodist preachers – provide a valuable context for regarding politeness as a phenomenon that could never achieve any settled or secure hegemony. I shall investigate these loci of 'the impolite' to suggest the hedged status of polite bodies, but also to reveal one of the processes by which politeness gained definition: namely, an active process of locating difference from perceived cultural 'others'. Exploring the margins of polite culture and considering unruly, carnivalesque bodies reveals the diversity of somatic possibility, and it adds suggestive contrast to the image of those whose aspirations to polite public status were marked upon their flesh.

AN OUTLINE

Thus far I have been in generalising mode, but it is time to turn to the particular and to provide some leads into the series of studies that follows. Taking the view that scholarly works are often not read *in toto*, I have aimed that each chapter should be reasonably comprehensible in isolation, but there is none the less some development of the argument across the chapters.

---

[57] It is in this way that Stephen Copley considers polite discourse: 'Instruction in polite taste is, in large part, instruction in cultivating standards of discriminating consumption, and expressing those standards in appropriate social exchanges. In this respect, the vocabulary of politeness provides a justificatory rationale for consumption by mystifying its relation to economic exchange, and concealing the status of the polite as leisured consumers. It thus offers commentators a mode of indirect endorsement of consumption, as an alternative to the traditional condemnatory discourse of luxury' ('Commerce, Conversation and Politeness in the Early Eighteenth-Century Periodical', *British Journal for Eighteenth-Century Studies* 18:1 (1995), 67).

Chapter 1 begins with an introduction to the social and political role of public performance in a period of comparatively 'untechnologised' media, and it presents the broad aspiration of the elocutionary movement to regenerate oratory by promoting modes of eloquence that would appeal to the passions. Innovative body images do not emerge *ex nihilo* but rather through the dynamics of cultural contest, and the chapter goes on to examine debate surrounding 'classical bodies'. I focus particularly upon the treatment in Britain of a French work, Michel Le Faucheur's *Traitté de l'action de l'orateur* (1657), the influence and interpretation of which were influenced by the teaching of classical eloquence formulated principally by Cicero and Quintilian. But Le Faucheur's *Traitté* is also significant because of the manner in which its doctrine became reinflected. Examining this modification of its Faucheurian eloquence, as shown by James Fordyce in *An Essay on Elocution Proper for the Pulpit* of 1753, I set in motion a running argument that emerging notions of politeness generated innovative forms of facial expression.

My use of the term 'classical' here is a traditional one, simply suggesting 'derived from the texts of classical antiquity'. It should be distinguished from a Bakhtinian sense of the classical body, denoting the forms of official high culture in contradistinction to a low grotesque body which resists interpellation in official discourse. Bakhtin's construction is a useful one, but it invites a potential confusion here since I seek to trace the *transformation* of classical aspects of eloquence which involved important questioning of classical and latinate traditional styles. I suggest that the transformation of classical eloquence and the emergence of newly powerful forms of expression amounted to a process of 'sentimentalisation' involving a freeing of signs of emotional susceptibility from a framework of 'classical decorum'.

The second chapter considers the margins of polite culture, and examines examples of public performance that ruptured a polite image of the body. It is here that I discuss the symbolic challenges to politeness posed by John Henley and by the Methodist movement, and I aim to describe the complex and nuanced relationships that these examples suggest existed between the 'centre' and 'margins' of British culture. I also consider the manner in which two writers – Oliver Goldsmith (1728–74) and Richard

---

58 Bakhtin develops the classical/grotesque distinction in *Rabelais and his World*, trans. Helene Iswolsky (Cambridge, MA: Massachusetts Institute of Technology Press, 1968). On his use of this opposition, see Laurie Finke, 'Mystical Bodies and the Dialogics of Vision', *Philological Quarterly* 73 (1988), 439–49.

Graves – approached the subject of Methodist oratory. Working with genres that situated their output within polite reading culture – the periodical essay and the quixotic novel – Goldsmith and Graves did not wholly 'other' the Methodists but rather suggested the advantages that a *qualified* incorporation of the somatic techniques displayed by (regularly condemned) Methodist preachers might bring to the 'official' discourse of eloquence. The chapter advances the argument that the eloquence of the body was never a settled construct in the eighteenth century, but was rather ever caught up in the intricacies of dynamic cultural contest.

The phenomena under discussion in this and other chapters, then, fall broadly into two types: firstly, printed texts which are usually aspirational in their modelling of idealised bodily conduct and which therefore must be considered as presenting semi-fictions of the body; and secondly, actual bodies which existed and performed in eighteenth-century culture, but which are now knowable only through the texts they inspired. My argument suggests an interaction of these phenomena, presenting points at which the didactic literature of the body is informed by the performance of particular individuals, and also cases of where actual performance may have been responsive to an impulse from printed elocutionary discourse.

Chapter 3 returns to the theme of sentimentalised eloquence and explores the remarkable career of Thomas Sheridan. That Sheridan was able to base the latter half of his career on the business of promoting polite eloquence (through publication and through lecturing) testifies to the immense public interest that surrounded the subject by the mid century, and I plot Sheridan's work within the commercial context that provided his support. The chapter also develops a further key theme and ambition of Sheridan's work: the connection between eloquence and the construction of Britishness. John Barrell has persuasively argued already that the extensive eighteenth-century project of Sheridan and others to standardise the English language represents a significant strand in the cultural activity which gave superstructural support to the political unification of Britain.[59] I pursue this argument by suggesting that Sheridan's dealings with the body were similarly underpinned by an aspirational view towards nation building.

Sheridan began his career in the theatre, and he maintained firm views that the stage was a resonant platform from which a reform of eloquence might be achieved. In Chapter 4, I explore the manner in which theories

---

[59] John Barrell, *English Literature in History, 1730–80: An Equal, Wide Survey* (London: Hutchinson, 1983), pp. 110–75.

and practices of eighteenth-century acting served the propagation of politeness. Through an examination of acting manuals and the styles of popular performers I chart a transformation of dominant techniques which is comparable with the sentimentalisation of oratory. Like the figure of the orator, the acclaimed actor can be seen to stand as a 'natural symbol' of his or her culture, and I explore how theatrical reformers such as Aaron Hill strove to refine theatre audiences – and British society more generally – by steering the symbolic potential within the spectacle of an actor's body.

In the final chapter, I turn to a consideration of the sentimental novel and of the engagement of the body in novel consumption. As with the earlier chapters, I am interested in considering the *dispersal* of body images, and I argue that, where that is concerned, the didactic sentimental novel attained a cultural position akin to the models of eloquence on public platforms. There is a movement in this chapter from public to private, although I maintain that the business of reading – even within intimate domestic, familial settings – retained a type of publicness, and that there were strong public or social pressures upon readers to perform or advertise proper responses to novelistic literature. Indeed, the low moral status that clung to the genre demanded that, if such literature was to have a place within polite culture, its consumption had to be *seen to be* virtuous. A central tool in such display, I argue, was the performance of emotional turmoil through the medium of the body. Novel reading – like oratory and acting – propelled into the public domain images of bodies symbolising politeness, and it is fundamentally this process of spectacularisation that occupies each of the following chapters.

Like all 'cultural projects', the development of polite somatic rhetoric attracted contemporary scrutiny and interrogation, and I conclude by considering the work of one of elocutionary discourse's most complex scrutineers, Laurence Sterne, whose fiction is rich in representations of and commentary upon the eloquence of bodies. Sterne's knowing and often wry treatment of both polite and exuberantly impolite aspects of embodiment provides the grounds for a critical consideration of the rhetoric in which so much was invested by Sterne's contemporaries.

CHAPTER I

Spectacular passions:
eighteenth-century oratory and the reform of eloquence

> To shake the armes with a kinde of perpetuall motion, as if they would straightway flie out of the sight of their Auditours, or were about to leave the Earth: is a Prævarication in Rhetorique. Such Oratours have been compared to Ostriches.
>
> John Bulwer (1644)[1]

> *Grief, sudden* and *violent*, expresses itself by *beating* the *head; groveling* on the *ground; tearing* of *garments, hair,* and *flesh; screaming* aloud, *weeping, stamping* with the *feet, lifting* the *eyes,* from time to time, to heaven; *hurrying* to and fro, running *distracted,* or *fainting* away, sometimes *without recovery.*
>
> James Burgh (1761)[2]

PUBLIC SPEAKING AND THE 'ELOCUTIONARY MOVEMENT' IN
EIGHTEENTH-CENTURY BRITAIN

The bodily production and broadcast of words were serious issues in eighteenth-century Britain. Public address, in its various forms in churches, courtrooms, political assemblies, theatres, and schools, remained, despite a burgeoning print culture and increasing levels of literacy, a dominant medium for popular communication. 'It is by speech', Thomas Sheridan wrote in 1780, 'that all affairs relative to the nation at large, or particular societies, are carried on.' And he elaborated to convey the range of institutions whose everyday business depended upon effective public speech: 'In the conduct of all affairs ecclesiastical and civil, in church, in parliament, courts of justice, county courts, grand and

---

[1] John Bulwer, *Chirologia; or, The Naturall Language of the Hand* (London, 1644), pp. 113–14.
[2] James Burgh, *The Art of Speaking* (London, 1761), p. 16.

31

petty juries, vestries in parishes, are the powers of speech essentially requisite.'[3] Furthermore, the public speech of this period served numerous purposes which are now alternatively performed by newspaper, television, and radio reporting and, more recently, by the Internet. Church services, for example, fulfilled a public role the practical and secular functions of which were far greater than those of religious services in the modern developed world. Anglican services not only functioned to inculcate religious doctrine, but could also be occasions for disseminating essential practical information to the congregation. Several of Laurence Sterne's sermons, preached to his Yorkshire flock in the 1750s, are concerned with a serious cattle plague, and the churches were used to announce how diseased cattle during this epidemic should be destroyed.[4] It was obviously important that the communication of such information should be effective, and the techniques for public delivery were crucial to society at many further levels. Public address was a principal instrument for the political, religious, and moral commerce of the nation, and turned to dramatic ends in the theatres, it was furthermore a key medium of public entertainment.

The eighteenth century is, of course, typically viewed as the age which saw the rise of print culture in Britain, and certainly print was taking on some of the roles that had previously been fulfilled through public perform-ance. For example, the private reading of sermons – a cornerstone of the eighteenth-century print trade – to a small degree reduced the consump-tion of sermons in the churches, where attendance was beginning to decline.[5] And print was furthermore enabling new forms of discourse which had no real precursory counterparts in public performance – for example, the novel. But despite the expansion of the print trade, public address remained a central conduit of information for a population which,

---

[3] Thomas Sheridan, *A General Dictionary of the English Language*, 2 vols. (London, 1780), vol. i, preface (n. p.).

[4] See Melvyn New, 'Sterne as Preacher: A Visit to St. Michael's Church, Coxwold', *The Shandean* 5 (1993), 162–3. James Downey similarly notes how 'many former functions of the pulpit have been taken over by other agencies' (*The Eighteenth-Century Pulpit: A Study of the Sermons of Butler, Berkeley, Secker, Sterne, Whitefield and Wesley* (Oxford: Clarendon Press, 1969), p. 1). Downey's study usefully stresses the centrality of pulpit oratory to eighteenth-century cultural life, but it is primarily as a literary phenomenon that he regards the importance of the sermon: 'The tendency of modern scholarship to neglect the contribution of pulpit oratory to English *literary* history arises from a failure to appreciate the importance that sermons once had in secular as well as religious life' (p. 1; my italics). Downey does not, therefore, explore the significance of oratory as a live medium, as I seek to do here.

[5] See Roy Porter, *English Society in the Eighteenth Century*, revised edition (Harmondsworth: Penguin, 1990), p. 226.

in 1750, was still basically only half literate.[6] Occupying this key position within the structure of British society, oratory had an importance and prominence great enough to generate a lively and multifaceted discourse preoccupied with questions such as: how should oratory properly be practised? What are the most effective or persuasive oratorical modes or styles? How should weak orators improve their performances? To what other cultural projects might oratory be harnessed?

For Thomas Sheridan, it was the centrality of, particularly, the church service in British society that rendered oratory not only an instrument worth using well (and in need of reform), but also an effective channel of communication through which broader cultural reforms could be implemented throughout the nation. One strand of Sheridan's project was the standardisation of English pronunciation, and he argued that in ancient Rome an exactness of pronunciation was maintained through the frequent opportunities for the populace to see, hear, and emulate admirable public speakers. He saw even more such opportunities in modern Britain:

For besides those of the senate-house, bar, &c. which we have in common with them [the ancient Romans], our churches furnish one of more frequent, regular, and general use, than all the others. These are daily open to all ranks and orders, and it is part of the duty of every person in the nation to attend divine service at least one day in the week. If therefore the pronunciation of our language were fixed by certain rules, and were uniformly and invariably observed by all the clergy, if they had also an equal power with the orators of old of captivating attention, and charming the ear, is it to be doubted but that a general good taste, and exactness of speech, would be diffused thro' the whole people?[7]

Further examination of Sheridan's writing will reveal his frequent tendency towards hyperbole and exaggeration, but from his statements there never-theless emerges a useful commentary on the significance of oratory to eighteenth-century British culture. The orator was the immediate focus

---

[6] J. Paul Hunter summarises current thinking on eighteenth-century literacy rates and, emphasising their rapid rise, states that 'By 1750 at least 60 percent of the adult men in England (and perhaps more) could read and write ... at least 40 percent of adult women (and possibly as many as half) could read' ('The Novel and Social/Cultural History', in John Richetti (ed.), *The Cambridge Companion to the Eighteenth-Century Novel* (Cambridge: Cambridge University Press, 1996), p. 20). Remembering the half or so who are left out of Hunter's figures is not to gainsay the importance of rising literacy, or to suggest that the audiences of the fashionable lectures I discuss later were there because they were illiterate. But considering literacy from the point of view of who could *not* read usefully reminds us of the continuing orality of much eighteenth-century cultural life.

[7] Thomas Sheridan, *British Education; or, The Source of the Disorders of Great Britain* (London, 1756), pp. 246–7 (hereafter *BE*, with page references given within the text).

of Sheridan's proposed reforms, which in order to increase the speaker's persuasive power were directed towards both pronunciation and the management of the eloquent body as a whole. But Sheridan also stressed that the orator, from his influential position at the centre of attention at regular events in public life, could equally be the agent of more widely diffused cultural changes. The public speaker's example, Sheridan insisted, could set a standard of politeness for the conversational transactions of all Britons.

Sheridan articulates here a view of the public performer's importance and cultural authority which is embedded in much eighteenth-century thinking about oratory and acting. He assumes – although he does not elaborate upon here – a fundamental connection between the manner in which language is delivered and the dispersal of 'a general good taste'. In fact, from his perspective as a reformer, Sheridan expresses a version of my own argument that the performing body has the potential to symbolise and broadcast a particular society's notions of civility. A public speaker is clearly no mere fount of words – an invisible medium of verbal language – but is a far more complex signifying site where verbal language and the language(s) of the body inevitably mingle. Displayed before the public, the body of an eighteenth-century orator formed an important part of his or (much less commonly) her communicative capability, and the signs generated through that body not only modified the meanings of the orator's verbal utterances but also carried a wider symbolic potential. What is apparent in Sheridan's work and in other eighteenth-century writing about oratory and acting is an endeavour to harness the wider potential within the physical performances of public figures and to exploit those performances in the development of politeness.

Sheridan recognised that the eloquence of a public performer carried with it a symbolic significance distinct from the 'content' of a performance, and that performers could exert influence in terms both of *what* was said and of *how* it was said. Others too recognised that audiences were permeable – that public figures could function as models from which standards of eloquence could be diffused throughout an impressionable populace. In a published letter to David Garrick, John Hill (1716?–75), a prolific writer, medical man and acting theorist, observed with regard to delivered speech that 'as the Stage takes nothing now from Life, the Tables may be turned, and Life take every Thing from the Stage'.[8] Far from any idea of drama

---

[8] John Hill, *To David Garrick, Esq; The Petition of I. In Behalf of Herself and her Sisters* (London, 1759), pp. 11–12.

holding a mirror up to nature, Hill suggests that stage practice is a *source* of patterns of behaviour. Other commentators, as we shall see, similarly note how the theatre or the pulpit could function as a 'school of eloquence', the educational effects of which could be instilled merely by virtue of attendance, with the spectator assimilating certain codes as a side-effect of some other pursuit such as religious observation or entertainment. But it was not only through such 'education by osmosis' that the public performer could function as an exemplar for more widespread behaviour. A more structured didactic process is witnessed in the several cases of actors and public speakers who developed parallel careers as teachers of elocution. Most notable among such figures is Sheridan, who built up his long career as an elocutionist via his work in the theatre. Sheridan presents an exceptional case, but there were other actors, such as Charles Macklin (1697?–1797) and James Love (1721–74), who cultivated sidelines teaching elocution, and there were public speakers including the Methodist John Wesley (1703–91), who published treatises on oratory and elocution. Wesley's twelve-page *Directions concerning Pronunciation and Gesture* (1749), priced at one penny, made readily available within the public domain a practical science of oratory, which readers could associate with one of the century's most successful and widely known preachers. (Wesley largely escaped the censure of 'excessive preaching' which, as will be seen, attached to other Methodists.) Public performance, then, was a key channel of communication for eighteenth-century British society, but it was additionally implicated in a didactic enterprise concerning the shaping of delivered speech and, with it, the dispersal of 'a general good taste'.

The eighteenth-century 'elocutionary movement', as the enterprise to regenerate public speaking has been called, was energised, in part, by a recognition that the quality of oratory in Britain, particularly in the first half of the century, was frequently poor. British orators, it was complained, lacked the power to be interesting and were failing to put across the import of their addresses – be it religious, moral, political, or judicial. Some writers on eloquence found laudable models among British orators: the author of *Some Rules for Speaking and Action* presented a list of contemporary speakers 'in the *Senate*, on the *Bench*, at the *Bar* and in the *Pulpit*' who would be 'worthy Imitation'.[9] But this writer and many others were drawn to the subject by what they saw as failings in oratory as it was being practised generally. The complaint attached particularly to Anglican divines. From

---

[9] Anon., *Some Rules for Speaking and Action; To be observed at the Bar, in the Pulpit, and the Senate, and by every one that Speaks in Publick. In a Letter to a Friend*, 3rd edn (London, 1716), p. 32.

the early years of the century it was noted that the delivery of many
Anglican clergymen was uninspiring and that their oratorical techniques,
both for addresses which were read and for those preached extempore, were
inadequate for the purposes of popular persuasion. Poor oratory was
addressed several times in *The Tatler* (1709–11) and *The Spectator*
(1711–12) – periodicals which were central to the early development and
consolidation of polite culture.[10] A 1711 issue of *The Spectator* was devoted
to the subject of reading the liturgy, and it carried Richard Steele's
complaint that 'The well Reading of the Common Prayer is of so great
Importance, and so much neglected.' Steele blamed this upon the dominance of Latin teaching in schools, where boys were 'look'd upon as above
English, the Reading of which is wholly neglected, or at least read to very
little purpose, without any due Observations made to them of the proper
Accent, and manner of Reading'.[11] Related analyses of oratorical standards
continued to be put forward for much of the century.[12] When the second
edition of Sheridan's *British Education* was reviewed in the *Gentleman's
Magazine* in 1769, the writer found Sheridan's claims regarding the powers
of good delivery exaggerated, but none the less agreed that 'oratory, as well
with respect to composition as utterance, is certainly a desirable thing, and
is shamefully neglected among us'.[13] An elaborate and detailed critique
of contemporary oratory had earlier been put forward by Oliver
Goldsmith, who contributed essays on the subject to several periodicals
in 1759 and 1760. To the readers of the *Lady's Magazine*, Goldsmith
offered 'Some Remarks on the Modern Manner of Preaching', and he
complained that clergymen's 'discourses from the pulpit are generally
dry, methodical and unaffecting; delivered with the most insipid
calmness, in so much, that should the peaceful preacher lift his head
over the cushion, which alone he seems to address, he might discover
his audience ... actually sleeping over his methodical and laboured

---

[10] On the role of the early periodicals in the emergence of politeness, see Hammond, *Professional
   Imaginative Writing*, pp. 145–91.
[11] *The Spectator* 147 (18 August 1711), in *The Spectator*, ed. Donald F. Bond, 5 vols. (Oxford:
   Clarendon Press, 1965), vol. II, p. 78. Steele echoes John Locke's advocacy of teaching English in
   preference to classical languages – see *Some Thoughts Concerning Education* (1693), in *The
   Educational Writings of John Locke*, ed. James L. Axtell (Cambridge: Cambridge University Press,
   1968), p. 300.
[12] Commentary on poor public speaking is found, for example, in Jonathan Swift's *A Letter to a
   young gentleman lately enter'd into Holy Orders* (1721) and in his sermon 'Upon Sleeping in Church'.
   Dull speakers were a popular target for satirists, including Henry Fielding, Richard Graves, and
   William Hogarth, who depicted a soporific preacher in his 1736 engraving *The Sleeping
   Congregation*.
[13] *Gentleman's Magazine* 39 (June 1769), 306.

composition'.[14] Goldsmith addresses two issues here: the composition of the sermon, and the manner in which it is delivered. He levels his criticism at those Anglican preachers who direct their attention to the sophisticated composition of highbrow sermons, and in so doing neglect matters of performance. It is a complaint that can be traced back to at least the Interregnum and the early advancement of so-called latitudinarian preaching – the style which was promoted through the efforts of such prominent clerics as Bishop John Wilkins and Archbishop John Tillotson and which was characterised by a new emphasis upon verbal clarity and upon accessible appeals to reason and to feeling.[15] Latitudinarians reacted against obscure or arcane verbal formulations in sermons: Wilkins censured verbal elaboration in his *Ecclesiastes, Or, A Discourse concerning the Gift of Preaching* (1646), where he argued that the most effective sermon was one not 'darkened with the affectation of *Scholastical* harshnesse, or *Rhetorical* flourishes'.[16] Wilkins also gave attention to the manner of the sermon's delivery, and here again he argued that the ideal to strive for was clarity and accessibility, so long as the preacher retained his performance within bounds of 'modesty and gravity'.[17]

Efforts to reform oratory – and to arouse congregations as a consequence – were directed, then, both to composition and to delivery, but it can be said that the campaign for improved delivery also developed a degree of autonomy distinct from debates surrounding composition. As a writer in *The Tatler* asserted, 'a great Part of the learned Clergy of *Great Britain* . . . deliver the most excellent Discourses', but this excellence was often obscured by the 'Coldness and Indifference' of the delivery itself.[18] And many of the efforts of eighteenth-century elocutionists were focused primarily upon the business of delivery. Indeed, in his broad survey of public address from 1530 to 1828, William Phillips Sandford states that it is the 'emphasis upon *pronunciatio* [the term used by Cicero in *De Oratore* to refer to matters of performance] which distinguishes the [eighteenth-century] elocutionary movement from

---

[14] *Collected Works of Oliver Goldsmith*, ed. A. Friedman, 5 vols. (Oxford: Clarendon Press, 1966), vol. III, p. 151.

[15] Isabel Rivers discusses the contrasting 'scholarly, ornate, individual styles . . . and the popular, plain, collective style of Wilkins and Tillotson' in *Reason, Grace, and Sentiment: A Study of the Language of Religion and Ethics in England, 1660–1780, I: Whichcote to Wesley* (Cambridge: Cambridge University Press, 1991), pp. 37–8.

[16] John Wilkins, *Ecclesiastes, Or, A Discourse concerning the Gift of Preaching: As it falls under the Rules of Art*, 4th edn (London, 1753), p. 128.

[17] *Ibid.*, p. 133.

[18] *The Tatler* 70 (20 September 1709), in *The Tatler*, ed. Donald F. Bond, 3 vols. (Oxford: Clarendon Press, 1987), vol. I, p. 484.

every other school of thought in the history of the teaching of public speaking'.[19] Sheridan certainly prioritised delivery as the key to gaining the attention of an audience. The 'church service', he argued, 'according as it is either well or ill administered, must excite great emotions, or set people to sleep' (*BE*, p. 92), and his work and that of other elocutionary writers was spurred by a drive to prevent the latter and to introduce into British culture a mode of performance which *would* inspire great emotions and would consequently inspire in the British people a sense of religion, national duty, and sound civic practice. James Burgh (1714–75), who wrote a long and detailed manual on *The Art of Speaking* (1761), shared Sheridan's emphasis upon delivery. Burgh declared that of the several skills that make up a good orator he would concern himself only with that 'most important in the art, viz – *delivery*, comprehending what every gentleman ought to be master of respecting *gesture*, *looks*, and command of *voice*'.[20]

In promoting new modes of delivery – particularly *emotionally affecting* modes of delivery – elocutionists were effectively aiming to overturn what was often noted as a national trait. Sheridan imagined the plight of a painter searching Britain for a model of eloquence from which to copy: 'As to the pulpit', he quipped, 'I believe I need hardly mention that he would find little or no assistance there, unless it were for pieces of still life' (*BE*, p. 440). Goldsmith, having witnessed preachers in France, similarly regarded uninspiring oratory as a peculiarly British phenomenon, and in fact it was common to contrast the gesticulatory reticence of the British with the more exuberant use of gesture on the continent and particularly in France.[21] The Scottish philosopher Adam Smith, author of works concerning sentimental moral philosophy and rhetoric, and himself a notable public speaker as a lecturer, remarked in an address of 1763 that

Foreigners observe that there is no nation in the world which use so little gesticulation in their conversation as the English. A Frenchman, in telling a story that was not of the least consequence to him or to anyone else, will use a thousand gestures and contortions of his face, whereas a well-bred Englishman will tell you one in which his life and fortune are concerned, without altering a muscle in his face.[22]

---

[19] Sandford, 'Public Address', p. 143.
[20] Burgh, *Art of Speaking*, p. 2.
[21] See Goldsmith's 'A Sublime Passage in a French Sermon', in *Works of Oliver Goldsmith*, vol. III, pp. 49–51.
[22] Adam Smith, *Lectures on Rhetoric and Belles Lettres*, ed. John M. Lothian (London: Nelson, 1963), p. 192.

The good breeding of this inanimate Englishman described by Smith is significant – somatic reticence is seen to be a quality of the polite classes, and it is with these classes that elocutionary discourse is largely concerned. Eighteenth-century writing on elocution typically strives to redefine what it means to be 'well-bred' by imagining a body which is at once 'polite' and emotionally expressive; it aims to animate the body with passions and to reconfigure the cultural framework within which the body is read so as to encompass emotional display within the accepted terms of polite behaviour. The 'reform' of oratory in eighteenth-century Britain, in fact, can very often be taken to mean the *emotionalisation* of oratory – the transformation of the medium (stimulated by the latitudinarians) from a patrician, scholastic discipline to a more accessible and democratic form of discourse, involving regular appeals to the emotions of the audience. It is in this light that we must read criticism of British orators as dull. The complaints typically land upon *unemotional* orators – upon speakers who have not assimilated within their delivery a faith in 'the passions' as a socially beneficial force.

It is fundamentally the art of managing the passions with which tracts and treatises on eloquence are concerned as they set about moulding British orators into persuasive public performers. The passions were perceived in the eighteenth century as natural components of human physiology which had the potential to cement – but also to disrupt – harmonious social relations. As Alan T. McKenzie has written: 'For the writers of the eighteenth century, the passions constituted an inherent and essential component of human nature, one that had always been there. They produced instability, both psychological and social, but their definitions, components, and complications were preternaturally stable, offering invaluable possibilities of combination and development, possibilities both syntactic and moral.'[23] In various Enlightenment projects – not only those concerning elocution – the passions were subject to analysis and categorisation, and the signs by which they were understood to show themselves on the body were identified and described. René Descartes (1596–1650) had analysed the passions in an influential treatise on *Les Passions de l'âme* (1649), rapidly translated into English as *The Passions of the Soule* (1650). Descartes describes six 'primitive' passions of 'wonder, love, hate, desire, joy and sadness'.[24] More specific, particular passions are regarded in this work as

[23] Alan T. McKenzie, *Certain Lively Episodes: The Articulation of Passion in Eighteenth-Century Prose* (Athens: University of Georgia Press, 1990), p. 19.
[24] *The Philosophical Writings of Descartes*, trans. Joseph Cottingham, Robert Stoothoff, and Dugald Murdoch, 2 vols. (Cambridge: Cambridge University Press, 1985), vol. I, p. 353.

derivative distillates of these primary colours of emotional character.
Among other works, including several on elocution and acting,
Descartes's treatise informed a popular illustrated handbook concerning
the outward signs of the passions for the use of painters by Charles Le Brun
(1619–90), director of the French Royal Academy. The *Conférence de M. Le
Brun sur l'expression générale et particulière* (1698) – translated into English
in 1701 and 1734 – supplied simplified, schematic methods of representing
the passions in the visual arts. For Le Brun, the body is a text upon which
passionate change is almost always legible; the body's power of expression
'marks the Motions of the Soul, and renders visible the Effects of
Passion . . . for the most part, whatsoever causes Passion in the Soul,
makes some Action in the Body'.[25]

British eighteenth-century commentators on public performance typically proceed from the same understanding of the passions' visibility, and
they argue that an engagement with the passions in performance should
hold a greater interest for an audience and achieve a more profoundly
persuasive effect than any 'dry' speech which calls merely upon reasoned
argument to make its case. So, for example, John Ward (1679?–1758),
whose *A System of Oratory* (1759) offers detailed, classically informed
considerations of the multifarious aspects of composition and delivery,
described the passions as essential animators of the mind: 'the passions are
to the mind, what wind is to a ship, they move and carry it forward; and he
who is without them, is in a manner without action, dull and lifeless'.[26]
The passions of '*Joy* and *Sorrow, Love* and *Hatred, Emulation* and
Contempt' and others, which are categorised and analysed in Ward's and
other accounts with various degrees of detail, specificity, and acuteness of
taxonomic division, are laid down as the emotional ground shared by all
humanity.[27] Upon this ground, elocutionists argued, a literal *sympathy* –
a harmony of feeling – might be created, so as, through emotional com-
munion, to create complicity between speaker and audience. The potential
for sympathetic infection was seen as inherently physiological, with the
transference of passions occurring as a physical event – a representation
which is reflected in the spatial metaphors of 'moving' and 'transport' used

[25] *The Conference of Monsieur Le Brun, Chief Painter to the French King, Chancellor and Director of
the Academy of Painting and Sculpture; Upon Expression, General and Particular. Translated from the
French* (London, 1701), pp. 2–3. The 1734 translation appeared as *A Method to Learn to design the
Passions.*
[26] John Ward, *A System of Oratory, Delivered in a Course of Lectures Publicly read at Gresham College,
London*, 2 vols. (Hildesheim: Olms, 1969), vol. I, p. 157.
[27] *Ibid.*, vol. I, p. 159.

to describe e*motion*al change, and, indeed, in Ward's image of the ship. By exploiting the expressive potential of the body, elocutionists argued, speakers could make their passions *contagious*: 'as every one is differently affected himself', Ward writes, 'he is capable to make the like impressions upon others, and excite them to the same motions, which he feels himself'.[28]

Of the many types of somatic sign, then, elocutionists were concerned with those representing emotional change. They were working within the science of 'pathognomy' and exploring the social benefits that might be generated by that science. The pathognomic sign is literally the *gnomon* of *pathos* – the index of feeling – and its manifestations are transient looks and gestures. Reading pathognomic language is to attend to the body's mutable, shifting surface – as Barbara Maria Stafford has written, the 'pathognomist's oblique pursuit of ephemeral looks was . . . a kind of physiological angling. Like the sophist, he fished not for essence or character but for the myriad "airs" of animate things.'[29] With their roots in unconscious bodily processes, pathognomic signs are distinct from institutionalised gestures, such as waving, and also from the gestures of contrived bodily languages, such as the sign language used by deaf people. And in that pathognomic signs are fleeting, they are distinguished from the signs of physiognomy, which are understood to be legible points among the body's *fixed* features: the shape of the skull, the layout and features of the face, and so on – the type of somatic vocabulary which also concerns phrenology. For most of the eighteenth century, pathognomy and physiognomy were not fully distinguished as separate sciences, and 'physiognomy' was sometimes used to refer to the science of transient signs.[30] A remark in Richardson's *Sir Charles Grandison* (1753–4) suggests such usage to be distinctly French: a character refers to 'the grace which that people [the French] call *Physiognomy*, and we may call Expression'.[31] Yet 'physiognomy' is used in just this sense in an English work of six years earlier: James Parsons's *Human Physiognomy Explain'd: In the Crounian Lectures on Muscular*

---

[28] *Ibid.*, vol. II, p. 361.

[29] Stafford, *Body Criticism*, p. 123.

[30] As Shortland has shown, it was only in the late eighteenth century, with the work of Johann Casper Lavater (1741–1801), that physiognomy was really consolidated and defined as a science – physiognomy and pathognomy were 'almost always mixed up or inadequately differentiated before Lavater, and his creation of physiognomy as a "new science" is largely due to having separated it from pathognomy' ('Power of a Thousand Eyes', p. 389). Lavater's theory of physiognomy is expressed in *Physiognomische Fragmente* (Leipzig, 1775–8), first published in English in 1792.

[31] Samuel Richardson, *The History of Sir Charles Grandison*, ed. Jocelyn Harris, 3 vols. (London: Oxford University Press, 1972), vol. I, p. 12. Subsequent references are to this edition and are given in the text.

Motion (1747). This is a study of muscular motion, which seeks to demonstrate and categorise the responses of the muscles to passionate stimuli, and it can readily be placed in the tradition of Le Brun.[32] It is conceived as an aid to painters to enable them to depict various passions through the close observation of facial muscles, and, as such, it is a work of pathognomy. Writers of elocutionary works are *occasionally* concerned with physiognomy in its modern sense: in *The Actor*, for example, John Hill includes recommendations for the general appearance that performers should possess in order to be suitable in particular roles. But the predominant concern of elocutionists, like that of James Parsons, lies in the body's capacity *to move* – that part of the body's complex, multi-layered system of signing which was understood as natural, but at the same time was open to being manipulated and performed.

Alongside the body's visual pathognomic language, a type of *auditory* pathognomy is invoked throughout the works of the elocutionary movement, and *tones*, looks, and gestures appear as a set of expressive devices to which the public speaker and actor should constantly pay attention. Despite appealing to a different sense, the tonal qualities of delivery are ranked by elocutionists alongside the body's visual signs, and are recognised as possessing a similar capacity for conveying the passions. In *A System of Oratory*, in fact, Ward deems pronunciation and action to be virtually inseparable, and he considers the voice and body together: 'pronunciation or action may be said to be, *a suitable conformity of the voice, and the several motions of the body in speaking, to the subject matter of the discourse*'.[33] Like gesture, tone is regarded in elocutionary works as a pathognomic force which is integrated with verbal discourse but which, to some extent, is also a language of its own. This becomes particularly clear in discussions of extremes of passion, such as extreme grief, which, as Sheridan puts it, causes the word to give way to 'sobs, groans, and cries'.[34] These sounds, for Sheridan, are tone in its purest and most eloquent state, distanced from the vehicle of the word, which can constrict the powerful flow of passions.

---

[32] James Parsons, *Human Physiognomy Explain'd: In the Crounian Lectures on Muscular Motion* (London, 1747). On the relationship between the work of Parsons and Le Brun, see West, 'Polemic and the Passions'.

[33] Ward, *System of Oratory*, vol. II, p. 314.

[34] Thomas Sheridan, *A Course of Lectures on Elocution: Together with Two Dissertations on Language; and Some other Tracts relative to those Subjects* (London, 1762; repr. Menston: Scolar Press, 1968), p. 102 (hereafter *Lectures*, with page references given within the text).

Such is the general framework concerning the passions within which most elocutionary writing of the eighteenth century was conducted. What is, of course, paradoxical about the work of the elocutionists is that they celebrate a language which is theorised as both 'natural' and unconscious but then also set out instructions regarding its application. When we witness the *prescription* of 'nature', the cultural investment of the didactic project comes to the fore, and this investment is further exposed when we observe that elocutionists presented *different* inflections of the body's natural language. All elocutionists invoke nature, but *en bloc*, elocutionary tracts reveal that a body deemed properly eloquent was no stable or universally accepted construction. The two quotations with which I prefaced this chapter – separated by over a century and by vastly differing attitudes to what action might properly be performed in public – provide bold testimony to the mutability of authoritative body images. John Bulwer's classically based, mid-seventeenth-century *Chirologia* promotes a body which claims dignity through the stately limitation of its movements, and immoderate or busy action is condemned as absurd. James Burgh's mid-eighteenth-century *The Art of Speaking*, on the other hand, provides blueprints for the expression of the passions which are spectacularly dramatic and receptive to a huge repertoire of the body's available movements. Burgh may be describing passions in abstract contexts rather than giving close instruction, but passages such as that on '*Grief*' none the less form his basis for teaching '*delivery*, comprehending what every gentleman ought to be master of'. Burgh's mid-eighteenth-century gentleman has at his disposal a vocabulary of gesture which, a century earlier, would have carried him far beyond the bounds of Bulwer's sense of propriety. This is a necessarily simplified comparison, but it illustrates well the poles of a debate between 'classical' and 'non-classical' eloquence that involved much eighteenth-century writing about the body, and was played out upon the stage.

In what follows in this chapter, I shall expand upon the debate between competing body images to show that while a classically derived model of eloquence was never eliminated from elocutionary discourse, it was significantly challenged by a 'sentimental' mode representing an innovative conception of politeness.[35] It is worth pausing to note that in exposing this

---

[35] In *The Fate of Eloquence in the Age of Hume* (Ithaca and London: Cornell University Press, 1994), Adam Potkay argues that similar contestation surrounded eighteenth-century literary styles. 'Eloquence', for Potkay, denotes classical style, and its 'fate' resides in the challenges posed by a modern 'polite' style, which produce in the period an 'ongoing tension between the ideals of

debate, I am putting forward a view of eighteenth-century oratory quite
different from that advanced in Rolf Lessinich's 1972 study of the period's
preaching. Emerging from a 'spirit of the age' school of historiography,
Lessinich's study seeks to present writing on oratory as a smooth-surfaced
discourse, and it insists that the 'theory of preaching . . . remained virtually
unchanged from the beginning to the end of the neoclassic era'.[36] Lessinich
downplays the dynamics of elocutionary writing, and criticises James
Downey's study of sermons from the period because it stresses 'the indi-
viduality of the sermons more than their conformity' and shows 'particular
techniques and beliefs before enquiring into the characteristics which
distinguish the sermons of the Age of Reason from those of the
Metaphysical or baroque era'.[37] Unlike Downey, Lessinich finds conformity because he seeks it – his aim is to present a stable, coherent theory of
preaching for the 'Age'. Such an approach leads to misrepresentation, but it
also, I believe, misses the potential which is latent in the dissimilarities and
contestation within elocutionary writing, for it is through such points of
tension that underlying value systems and ideologies become most visible.
By exploring how reformers sought to *change* the behaviour of the body, we
gain insights into the upheavals and tensions at work in a society that itself
was changing as the influence of a growing bourgeois class encroached
upon traditional aristocratic forms of authority.

The challenge to classical somatic ideals by advocates of sentimental
forms of expression will be seen in the discussions of Sheridan and of
eighteenth-century acting, but we can explore this 'sentimentalisation' of
the public body firstly by considering the treatment in Britain of a French
work on oratory – Michel Le Faucheur's *Traitté de l'action de l'orateur* –
which, like Bulwer's *Chirologia*, used classical sources to authorise an image
of the eloquent speaker wherein emotionalism is heavily framed by signs of
dignity and social elevation. Translated into English early in the century,
Le Faucheur's popular work was important in its own right, and its success
suggests that British booksellers were able to use this ready-made manual
on eloquence to capitalise both upon anxieties concerning inadequate
speakers and upon growing interests in developing polite behaviour. But
this *Traitté* is also significant because of the manner in which later works –
particularly James Fordyce's *An Essay on the Action Proper for the Pulpit*

---

ancient eloquence and modern manners' (p. 6). It should be clear that my own use of 'eloquence' is
not tied to a classical formation, as in Potkay's account, but refers to expressiveness in a broader
sense.
[36] Lessinich, *Elements of Pulpit Oratory*, p. xi.
[37] *Ibid.*, p. x.

(1753) and the works of Sheridan – responded to and reinflected the type of elocutionary doctrine it advanced.

MICHEL LE FAUCHEUR'S *TRAITTÉ DE L'ACTION DE L'ORATEUR*

'*A Genteel regular* Movement of the Body, *without doubt, goes a great way in the Character of a* Publick Orator', declared the English translator of what would turn out to be a highly influential source for the British elocutionary movement.[38] Given the reputation of the French as a race of gesticulators, it is perhaps unsurprising that the work he had translated should have been imported from France. Its author, Michel Le Faucheur (1585–1657), was a Protestant clergyman who, originally from Geneva, made his career in Montpellier, Charenton, and Paris, and his *Traitté de l'action de l'orateur, ou de la prononciation et du geste* appeared in France, shortly after his death, in 1657.[39] This treatise, as will be seen, by no means teaches the exuberant gestures for which the French were known, but Le Faucheur none the less insists upon the centrality of somatic eloquence in good oratory, and so prioritises an aspect of preaching which, according to many accounts, was commonly neglected in Britain. Indeed, unlike the classical works it draws upon – principally Cicero's *De Oratore* and Quintilian's *Institutio Oratoria* – Le Faucheur's *Traitté* is not concerned with the aspects of oratory relating to composition, so that its focus lies primarily upon non-verbal techniques for appealing to the passions of audiences: '*It treats of* Pronunciation *and* Gesture *in particular, which are the very Life and Soul of* Rhetorick' ('Translator's Preface', n. p.). Ciceronian rhetoric, as laid out in *De Oratore*, was divided into the five arts of *inventio, dispositio, elocutio, memoria,* and *pronuntiatio,* of which the last refers to performance (*elocutio* in these terms refers to compositional style).[40] Le Faucheur pays only slight attention to the first four arts, an emphasis which, as I have noted, came to be followed by many subsequent British elocutionists.

---

[38] *An Essay upon the Action of an Orator; As to his Pronunciation & Gesture. Useful both for Divines and Lawyers, and necessary for all Young Gentlemen, that study how to Speak well in Publick. Done out of French* (London, 1702?), 'The Translator's Preface' (n. p.). It is from this edition that I quote throughout, with page references given in the text. Neither the translator nor the publication date is known, but Howell makes a convincing case for a 1702 dating (*British Logic and Rhetoric*, pp. 165–8).

[39] An outline of Le Faucheur's life together with bibliographical details concerning the *Traitté* and its translations are found in Howell, pp. 162–8. Drawing on Howell, Lynée Lewis Gaillet provides a short account of Le Faucheur and the *Traitté* in Moran, *Rhetorics and Rhetoricians*, pp. 70–4.

[40] Marcus Tullius Cicero, *De Oratore*, Loeb Classical Library, vols. 348–9 (Cambridge, MA: Harvard University Press; London: Heinemann, 1942), *passim*.

The *Traitté* – a substantial work, filling over two hundred closely printed duodecimo pages in the English edition – proved to be popular both in French and in subsequent translations. There were at least seven further French editions before the end of the seventeenth century, and in 1690 it was made more available to an international market with its translation into Latin. It was first published in English, probably in 1702, by Nicholas Cox under the title *An Essay upon the Action of an Orator; As to his Pronunciation & Gesture. Useful both for Divines and Lawyers, and necessary for all Young Gentlemen, that study how to Speak well in Publick.* This expanded title serves to puff the work, but importantly it also impresses upon potential buyers early in the century the correspondence between polite status and 'speaking well' – the possession of skills in delivery is an attribute (indeed, a *necessary* attribute) of respectable professionals and gentlemen. A second edition of the same translation appeared in London in 1727 with the title altered and expanded to *The Art of Speaking in Publick; or, An Essay on the Action of an Orator; As to his Pronunciation and Gesture. Useful in the Senate or Theatre, the Court, the Camp, as well as the Bar and Pulpit. The Second Edition Corrected. With an Introduction relating to the Famous Mr. Henly's present Oratory.* Of the famous Mr Henley I shall have more to say later – it suffices to observe here that Cox's second edition of the treatise is deployed with a view to making profit from a lively public interest that Henley was stimulating in the subject of oratory at the time. Otherwise, this second edition promotes a more generalised sense of the usefulness of speaking well: originally the work aimed principally 'to instruct *Youth* and assist those that are bred up to *Divinity* or the *Law*' (p. 16), but this new title urges a widening of the applicability of Le Faucheur's teaching so as to encompass politicians, actors, courtiers, and soldiers. Clearly this is largely a marketing ploy to entice more potential buyers, but, together with the revised main title (the 1727 version is not simply for proclaimed 'orators' but for that greater number of people who engage in 'Speaking in Publick'), it suggests an expansion of that section of the public for whom matters of elocution are, or should be, of interest. By the time a third edition was published in 1750 by Charles Hitch, several competing works had appeared in the marketplace, and a new title aims to establish the authority of Le Faucheur's tract by invoking its classical heritage: *An Essay upon Pronunciation and Gesture, Founded Upon the Best Rules and Authorities of the Ancients, Ecclesiastical and Civil, and Adorned with the Finest Rules of Elocution.*

Le Faucheur's fundamental purpose is to develop orators' powers of persuasion, and his inscription of a respectable, eloquent body is central to that project. Oratory, for Le Faucheur, is a key to social order; it is a pedagogic tool to be wielded paternalistically by those invested with political and religious authority so as to spread and enforce the tenets of Christian belief, sympathy and justice. And in order to be persuasive, Le Faucheur maintains, the orator must move the passions. Through a vast collection of examples and anecdotes, mostly derived from Cicero and Quintilian, Le Faucheur asserts the efficacy of gesture and of correctly modulated pronunciation in affecting the passions. Early rhetoricians, he writes, discovered that 'the *Sensitive Appetite* and its *Affections* had a wonderful Ascendant over the *Understanding* as well as the *Will*'; they found 'our *Passions*... [to be] most wrought upon by present *Objects* and what strikes in at our *Senses*' (p. 2). Consequently, in Le Faucheur's doctrine, the senses are prioritised over the understanding in an interpretation of human faculties which, written before any influence from Lockian philosophy, does not follow theories of the understanding as informed through sensual means. For Le Faucheur, the passions are affected by 'present *Objects*', which have the solidity to affect the senses, whereas the understanding is informed by an insubstantial idea. Applied to verbal utterance, it is the semantic 'idea' of a word which influences the understanding, while the passions are affected by a word's form and the qualities it is lent through physical production: vocal texture, pitch, loudness, and so on, plus all the gestural accompaniments provided by the speaker's body. The orator himself becomes a 'present *Object*', and in this capacity, which is sensually received by his hearers and spectators, is in a position to appeal directly to the passions of those he addresses.

The bodily language of the passions, for Le Faucheur, is universally comprehensible, and hence it is celebrated as the vehicle of international social commerce: 'by *Gesture*, we render our *Thoughts* and our *Passions* intelligible to *all Nations*, indifferently, under the Sun. 'Tis as it were the *common Language* of all Mankind' (p. 171). And this language is a language *of nature* – one which acquires a visible authority by virtue of its supposed foundation in nature. Regarding gesture, Le Faucheur writes that '*all Affectation* is *odious*... it must appear purely *Natural*, as the very *Birth* and *Result* both of the *things* you express and of the *Affection* that moves you to *speak* them' (p. 174). It should be stressed that where Le Faucheur (or, more accurately, his translator) uses 'appear' at this point, he is not promoting an *imitation* of nature; gestures should 'appear purely *Natural*' by *being* purely natural consequences of real emotion. The good orator, Le Faucheur argues, should have a personal emotional investment in the matter of which he speaks, and from this basis the feelings appropriate to the discourse will dictate their own signs and be displayed through the body without the need for any conscious 'acting out' of passions. 'The *Orator*. . . ought first of all to form in himself a *strong Idea* of the *Subject* of his *Passion*; and the *Passion* it self will then certainly follow in course; ferment immediately into the *Eyes*, and affect both the *Sense* and the *Understanding* of his *Spectators* with the *same Tenderness*' (p. 189). Exemplifying this principle, Le Faucheur writes of how a lawyer, if genuinely touched by the case for which he is pleading, 'will then easily show the *inward motion* and *concern* of his *Soul* by his *Pronunciation*, and by adjusting his *Voyce* to every one of those *Passions* that may affect the hearts of People with *Regard* and *Compassion*' (p. 98).

With regard to bodily action, Le Faucheur advises that the orator should use those gestures 'which arise naturally from the *Subject* of his *Discourse*' (p. 209), and these involve the body in its entirety: its general postures, head movements, arm movements, use of the hands, and so on. Unsurprisingly, he declares the face to be the most emotive of the body's parts, and in particular promotes the expressive potency of the eyes. 'As for your *Eyes*', he recommends, 'you must always be casting them upon some or other of your *Auditors* and rolling them gently about from *this side* to *that*, with an *Air* of *Regard* sometimes upon *one Person* and sometimes upon *another*' (p. 183). Eye contact, for Le Faucheur, is the channel by which passions are most effectively made contagious. If an orator feels anger, he suggests, it will inevitably be manifested in the eyes, and, thus displayed, the same passion will be contracted by spectators: 'this *Fire* of your *Eyes* easily strikes those of your *Auditors*, who have *theirs* constantly fixt upon *yours*; and it must needs set them *a-blaze* too upon the same *Resentment* and *Passion*' (pp. 184–5). As both a signifier and a receptor of feeling, the eye, the *Traitté* suggests, has the power to create social bonds – it is the means by which speakers and spectators can become conjoined within a union of mutually felt passion.

For Le Faucheur, the most emotive sign of which the eye is capable is that of the tear, and he dwells at length upon its expressive potential. In its unquestionable physicality the tear signals an extreme of emotion, and Le Faucheur insists that the witnessed tear will inspire the same strong emotions within spectators: '*Passions* are wonderfully convey'd from *one person's Eyes* to *another's*; the *Tears* of the *one* melting the *Heart* of the *other*, and making a *visible sympathy* between their *Imaginations* and *Aspects*' (pp. 189–90). Le Faucheur, then, does not seek to sculpt stoic orators, and his celebration of tearfulness reveals the investment his doctrine holds in a degree of emotional overflow. Indeed, Le Faucheur's *Traitté* can readily be seen as an early contribution to the softening of stoicism, which, as Barker-Benfield argues, is 'so apparent in English letters from Shaftesbury's *Characteristics* of 1711 and Addison's *Cato* of 1713 to Hume's "The Stoic", of 1742'.[41] In this early translation of the *Traitté*, we see aspects of the eighteenth-century culture of sensibility in embryonic form, but while Le Faucheur celebrates emotionalism, the idealised language of nature he promotes is none the less heavily and obviously marked by cultural or ideological pressures relating to, for want of a better term, 'classical decorum'. Le Faucheur's implied orator is instructed to allow the occurrence of natural emotional display, but is simultaneously fed a conscious sense of just how far nature can decently be put on public display. If the orator is to move – in both senses of the word – then, for Le Faucheur, he must do so within well-defined strictures of propriety and stateliness.

Discussing facial gestures, Le Faucheur instructs that 'you must take the greatest care imaginable of your *Countenance*, that nothing may appear *disagreeable* in it; for 'tis the *Part* most expos'd and in *view*, and your Auditors have their *Eyes*, if possible, continually fix'd upon't' (p. 182). What exactly constitutes the 'disagreeable' for Le Faucheur is here teasingly undefined, but elsewhere it is given more relief. 'Your *Eye-brows*', he writes, 'must neither be altogether *immoveable*, on the one hand, nor fickle or too full of *Motion*, on the other: And you must not raise them *both* up at every turn, as many People do upon any thing they speak with *eagerness* and *contention*; nor *lift-up* the *one* and *cast down* the other' (p. 192). Such rules seek to construct stateliness by discouraging busy, frantic gesture. Others are more concerned with somatic concealment, and the pressures of decorum are in clear evidence when Le Faucheur addresses the management of the mouth: 'As for your *Lips*, you must take care not to *bite* 'em, nor to *lick* 'em with your *Tongue*; as I have seen some People do sometimes: Which is very *Ungenteel* and *Unmannerly* in an *Orator*' (p. 193). Gentility, for Le Faucheur, involves a denial of the body's fleshliness; unlike other commonly visible body parts with their discreet coverings of skin, the tongue very obviously betrays the wet, organic character of embodiment and is regarded as best kept out of sight. Le Faucheur shapes his ideal orator here according to what Mary Douglas has dubbed the 'rule of distance from physiological origin'. Douglas describes how the concealment of the body's organic processes can function as a 'natural way of investing a social

[41] Barker-Benfield, *Culture of Sensibility*, p. 67.

occasion with dignity', so that 'social distance tends to be expressed in distance from physiological origins'.[42] Thus Le Faucheur seeks to formalise the orator's body and to invest it with distinction. The orator imagined by Le Faucheur is a visibly emotional being whose passions should penetrate the crowd; at the same time, though, that orator should be a dignified and impressive figure with a body signifying an elevation *above* the crowd.

Along with the limitations imposed upon facial movement, Le Faucheur insists upon a rigidly circumscribed repertoire of arm and hand gestures. Movement of the hands is, for Le Faucheur, an essential adjunct to speech: 'Upon all great Great *Motions,* the Action of the *Hands* is particularly *necessary,* to answer the Heat and Passions of the *Figures* that are made use of in a *Discourse*' (p. 199). And yet, following a classical rule of oratory, he argues that only the right hand – the hand of power – should be used for gesturing: 'You must make all your *Gestures* with the *right Hand;* and if you ever use the *left,* let it only be to accompany the *other,* and never lift it up so *high* as the *right.* But to use an *Action* with the *left Hand* alone is a thing you must avoid for its *indecency*' (pp. 196–7). He does allow that there might be exceptions to this general rule, when the use of the left hand cannot be avoided: 'when *Jesus Christ* commands the faithful Servant to cut-off his *right Hand,* if it offend him; I would represent that *Action,* if 'twere my Business, with the *Gesture* of the *left,* because there's no other to do't; for the *right Hand* cannot cut-off *it self*' (p. 197). The *Traitté* betrays no sense of irony in the use of this rather absurd example, and Le Faucheur's lengthy explanation of why such an exception is justified suggests the gravity with which the right-hand rule is advocated. This strictness may well be a legacy of the association of the 'sinister' hand with dishonesty and deception, but significantly it is in terms of 'decency' that the correct gestures are described.

This desire for decorum leads Le Faucheur to advise against certain specific gestures which would visibly lower the status of the orator: 'You must never *clap* your *Hands,* nor *thump* the *Pulpit,* nor *beat* your *Breast;* for that smells of the *Juggler* and the *Mountebank,* and 'tis good for nothing' (p. 196). The good orator projected by the *Traitté* has a stateliness from which these crude or violent gestures would detract, and Le Faucheur's cautions against vulgarity, extremes of force, and clownishness are matched

---

[42] Douglas, *Natural Symbols,* p. 12. Norbert Elias similarly connects the idea of 'civilisation' with the masking of parts and functions of the body in *The Civilizing Process,* trans. Edmund Jephcott, vol. I, *The History of Manners* (New York: Pantheon, 1978); vol. II, *Power and Civility* (New York: Pantheon, 1982).

by strictures laid down upon the scale of gestures. If the orator should 'lift-up the *Hand*, it ought not to be higher than the *Eyes*, and but very little *lower*' (p. 200), and, as though the hands can only be managed when in sight, the orator is told: 'You ought not to *stretch-out* your *Arms*, sideways, farther than half a Foot at most from the Trunk of your Body: Or, else you will throw your *Gesture* quite out of sight, unless you turn your *Head* aside to see it; which would be very *ridiculous*' (p. 201). The general rule is to limit gesture in order to guard against extravagance: 'your *Gesture* ought to be very moderate and modest; not bold, vast and extensive, nor indeed too frequent neither, which would make such a violent Agitation of the *Arms* and the *Hands* as would not become an *Orator*, and as if he were *chasing away Flies*' (p. 203).

These restraints, which presumably must be observed at least *semi-consciously* by the orator – for if they were part of a natural order of somatic language, he would need no telling of such limits – suggest, of course, that natural feeling is not the *primum mobile* behind Le Faucheur's language of gesture. The *Traitté* displays a tension between the conflicting claims of nature and decorum as motivators of the body's language – a tension which might best be accounted for as part of the drive towards social ordering represented by Le Faucheur's plan as a whole. In a project designed to encourage techniques of mass persuasion for the purposes of effective religion and stable social stratification, a propriety of nature itself seems to be being advanced. Social ideals and nature are being brought together in the act of persuasion through natural, but controlled, gesture; as the speaker might smooth out social irregularities by persuading a body of people before him to be of one mind, so he imposes a public order upon his own body by restraining it within rules of propriety. The human body and the 'body politic' are not connected here merely by virtue of traditional metaphor, but are linked by a shared subjectivity to processes of restriction and definition. Le Faucheur, in fact, is explicit in his intention that orators following his instructions will edify their congregations 'not only with their discourse and Style, but in some measure also by the decency of their *Speaking* and the Fineness of their *Action*' (p. 18). Properly trained, the body of Le Faucheur's orator should function as an elevated emblem of an emotionally attentive society.

Le Faucheur's doctrine, then, involves distinct and not obviously compatible processes for the production of bodily signs, and it identifies dignified somatic restraint as a fundamental quality of proper eloquence. It proposes that the speaker should 'feel the passion' to prompt an automatic emotional display, but it also overwrites this 'natural' eloquence with strict rules of bodily diction, which I have suggested constitute a system of 'classical decorum'. In short, the *Traitté* advises the orator both *to feel* and *to imitate*, and it provides descriptions of the type of gestures that should be imitated.

Subsequent tracts on oratory and acting reveal the emergence of competing attitudes to the classical form of somatic regulation advocated by Le Faucheur. Certainly one of those attitudes was veneration, and the *Traitté* served as a model for several later works concerning both oratory and acting. The earliest direct plundering of the English translation of the *Traitté* appeared in 1710 in Charles Gildon's account of '*The Action and Utterance of the Stage, Bar, and Pulpit*' included within his *Life of Mr. Thomas Betterton* (of which more later).[43] In 1715, Le Faucheur's classical strictures appeared again, compressed into the anonymous *Some Rules for Speaking and Action; To be observed at the Bar, in the Pulpit, and the Senate, and by every one that Speaks in Publick*. This popular pamphlet was based almost entirely upon the *Traitté*, and it reproduces Le Faucheur's recommendation that the orator should at the same time follow both nature and a list of rules.[44] A similar use of the *Traitté* appears again in the much-reprinted *An Essay on Elocution; or, Pronunciation* (1748) by John Mason. This essay is principally concerned with correct modulation of the voice, but it concludes with a short section giving advice on gesture which is based closely upon Le Faucheur's instructions.[45]

But not all eighteenth-century commentators on public performance could approve a form of eloquence governed by strict classical rules. Indeed, for the Reverend James Fordyce (1720–96), the very idea of applying rigid rules to a 'natural' practice was distinctly dubious.

JAMES FORDYCE'S *AN ESSAY ON THE ACTION PROPER FOR THE PULPIT*

If Wilbur Samuel Howell objects to a tract on elocution, it is a fair bet that the work in question presents some form of challenge to classical rhetoric – and it is no coincidence that the work I turn to now has incurred Howell's

---

[43] Howell identifies this as the earliest reworking of Le Faucheur (*British Logic and Rhetoric*, p. 182).

[44] The influence of Le Faucheur is very obvious, with many passages reproduced verbatim (see Howell, *British Logic and Rhetoric*, pp. 191–2). A third London edition of the pamphlet had appeared by 1716, there were two further by 1750, and a Dublin edition was printed in 1751.

[45] The essay was reprinted in 1748, 1751, 1757, 1761, and 1787.

particular distaste. I have already noted the championing of classical rhetoric that lards Howell's otherwise informative *British Logic and Rhetoric*; such partiality is conspicuous in the approach Howell adopts to *An Essay on the Action Proper for the Pulpit*, an eighty-six page treatise which appeared anonymously in 1753, but which has since been attributed to James Fordyce.[46] This work, for Howell, is a painfully 'superficial treatise on delivery rather than a profound discourse on rhetoric'. That description may not be altogether inaccurate, but I would suggest that it is precisely this 'failure' that makes the essay worth exploring. The work becomes significant when, rather than fume over its reluctance to follow classical authorities on rhetoric, we explore it as a potential gauge of cultural upheaval.[47]

The author to whom this treatise is attributed has become quite a familiar figure in studies of eighteenth-century literature and culture. James Fordyce is best known as an author of conduct literature, particularly his popular *Sermons to Young Women* (1766), the condemnation of which by Mary Wollstonecraft has contributed to Fordyce's gaining a reputation as a sentimentally inclined patriarch.[48] That Fordyce should also have been

[46] The essay has previously been attributed to John Mason; Howell provides good evidence for the erroneousness of this, but does not attribute the essay to Fordyce (*British Logic and Rhetoric*, p. 209). I am accepting here the attribution of the essay to Fordyce in the British Library catalogue and the ESTC, but, while I make some connections between the essay and Fordyce, I have not based my conclusions on the assumption that Fordyce was the author.

[47] Howell, *British Logic and Rhetoric*, p. 210. Howell shows similar despair when confronted by the efforts of Sheridan. The writings on oratory by Cicero and Quintilian, Howell writes, should reveal 'to anyone that ancient rhetoric...was much more than the study of voice and gesture; yet Sheridan saw only this one part of the total picture, and became certain that what he saw was all there was to see. No trace of self-doubt betrays itself in his rambling, repetitious, dogmatic argument' (pp. 227–8); 'the rhetorical system sponsored by Sheridan...was not only blighted by its having been a misreading of the rhetoric of ancient Greece and Rome, but it was foredoomed to become a leading influence in reducing rhetoric to a lowly estate in the English and American academic communities of the twentieth century' (p. 243).

[48] Wollstonecraft's comments on *Sermons to Young Women* are of relevance to this study, for they cast Fordyce as a producer of an artificial sentimental language capable of being performed: 'there is a display of cold artificial feelings, and that parade of sensibility which boys and girls should be taught to despise as the sure mark of a vain little mind...This is not the language of the heart, nor will it ever reach it, though the ear may be tickled' (*A Vindication of the Rights of Woman*, ed. Miriam Brody (Harmondsworth: Penguin, 1992), p. 196). Following Wollstonecraft's attack (and perhaps because of it), Fordyce has served as a reference point for conservative patriarchy in recent feminist literary history (see, for example, Janet Todd, *The Sign of Angellica: Women, Writing, and Fiction 1660–1800* (London: Virago, 1989), pp. 122–3). Fordyce's significance as part of the Scottish Enlightenment is explored in John Dwyer, *The Age of the Passions: An Interpretation of Adam Smith and Scottish Enlightenment Culture* (East Lothian: Tuckwell Press, 1998), pp. 121–9. For Fordyce's broader writing on matters of conduct, see his *Addresses to Young Men* (1777), *The Character and conduct of the Female Sex, and the advantages to be derived by young men from the society of virtuous women* (1776), and, with its oxymoronic title, his sermon on *The Folly, Infamy, and misery of unlawful pleasure* (1760).

concerned with shaping pulpit oratory suggests a location of this type of interest within a broader paternalist programme to define and regulate patterns of social behaviour. The urge to improve public address is no segregated, specialist matter here; rather, in the corpus of Fordyce's writing, it sits fittingly alongside concerns with everyday, public, and domestic modes of conduct. Doubtless, though, Fordyce addressed the subject of oratory because he had a deep personal engagement with it in practice. Fordyce was a Scottish Presbyterian minister who gained renown as a preacher in Scotland before moving to London, where his reputation for powerful oratory continued to thrive. It is significant that as a preacher he satisfied mainstream Anglican tastes and that his status as a dissenter did not diminish the broad appeal of his public appearances and his printed works.[49] David Garrick is said to have praised Fordyce's oratorical skills and attended his sermons more than once.[50] In turn Garrick's own eloquence is eulogised in Fordyce's essay: Garrick 'seems . . . upon the Stage to have a kind of despotic Empire over the Human Passions, not over those alone of the more *refined* Hearers, but those too of the more *vulgar*' (p. 16). The expression of this respect for Garrick is, in itself, a sign of the modernity of the essay. Fordyce is not hostile to using certain classical examples to support his points, but by also applying 'familiar examples' from literature, the theatre, and the visual arts, he lends the work accessibility and shows its engagement with contemporary culture. As well as attracting Garrick's praise, Fordyce became well known to Samuel Johnson (1709–84): 'though Johnson loved a Presbyterian the least of all', writes Boswell, 'this did not prevent his having a long and uninterrupted social connection with the Reverend Dr. James Fordyce'.[51]

The attitude to the rules of 'classical decorum' expressed in *Action Proper for the Pulpit* is significant – and not altogether straightforward. The essay, in fact, includes a paragraph reiterating rules such as: 'the hands should never be raised higher than the eyes . . . the *left* hand should never be employed to express any thing by itself, but only in concurrence with the *right*; that the latter being the hand of *power* . . . should therefore be *chiefly*

---

[49] Presbyterianism generally brought with it little alienation from 'mainstream' culture, and the distinctions between Presbyterianism and Anglicanism were slight. As Roy Porter writes, 'Dissenters tended to be a good deal more strait-laced in lifestyle than their Anglican brethren, but their worship – especially Presbyterians' – became equally moderate, anti-enthusiastic and morality-minded' (*English Society in the Eighteenth Century*, p. 179).

[50] For this and other details of Fordyce's life, see the *Dictionary of National Biography*, ed. Leslie Stephen, 66 vols. (London, 1885–1901), vol. XIX, pp. 433–5.

[51] James Boswell, *Life of Johnson*, ed. R. W. Chapman (Oxford: Oxford University Press, 1980), p. 1388.

employed by the Orator' (pp. 68–9). Howell perks up when he discusses this part of the essay, claiming that it 'turns quite practical' and 'echoes Le Faucheur repeatedly', but the status of these instructions is misconstrued if they are read in isolation from their fuller context in the essay.[52] Fordyce does not so much *echo* Le Faucheur here as *cite* his strictures as an *alternative* approach to elocutionary didactics. He introduces the passage stating that 'The *Connoisseurs* in this Art are of opinion, that' such rules should be observed (p. 68) – he demonstrates that these rules are separate from his own school of instruction, and he is by no means clearly attributing them to a higher authority. 'Connoisseur' was not necessarily a positive term in this period: Johnson's *Dictionary*, published two years after the essay, defines 'connoisseur' as 'A judge; a critick; it is often used of a pretended critick', and this pejorative edge is apparently present in Fordyce's usage.[53] Certainly he rounds off his short reiteration of classical rules by stating his worry that 'the Appearance of *Study* or *Design* in these or any other circumstances of a Preacher's Deportment in the *Pulpit*, would absolutely spoil the whole; just as *that* Carriage in *Company*, which looks not easy and unaffected, loses all its grace, how proper and exact soever it may be otherwise' (p. 69).

Action Proper for the Pulpit expresses a suspicion of the effects that specific guidelines for bodily action might have upon the appearance of a speaker (a suspicion shared by Sheridan and by Aaron Hill in his early acting theory). But the essay fully embraces the other strand of Le Faucheurian doctrine concerning the natural visibility of the passions and the potential of their display in the forging of social relations. An effect of the essay, then, is to liberate from the frame of classicism an idea of bodily performance which is at once emotional and polite.

Fordyce positively relishes the spectacle of feeling, and he presents it as a linchpin of virtuous society. Within everyday discourse, he suggests, a delicate language of feeling offers spectatorial and moral pleasures of the most intense kind:

It is not, perhaps, one of the least entertainments we receive from Conversation with our Friends, to observe whilst they are speaking to us the various turns of their Features, the various Radiations of their Hearts, in their Eyes; to observe these glancing with all the bland Lightening of an Animated Tenderness, or melting into the mild Suffusions of Sympathy, or beaming with the cordial Smiles of Congratulation, or darting forth the very Flame of Virtue. Is it possible, on such

---

[52] Howell, *British Logic and Rhetoric*, p. 212.
[53] Samuel Johnson, *A Dictionary of the English Language*, 2 vols. (London, 1755), vol. I, 'Connoisseur'.

occasions, not to catch the lovely Contagion, not to feel the Soul of Friendship rising on *our* Part, the correspondent Glow of Sentiment excited, and the breast heaving with reciprocal Emotion? Surely we may reckon these amongst the finest Sensations of Humanity. (pp. 72–3)

As a component of polite conversation, Fordyce suggests, the body functions as both a sign and propagator of virtue, and his essay seeks to promote this same capacity of the body so as to animate pulpit performance. 'Is not the case somewhat similar', he continues, 'when we have access to hear a Preacher whose *Countenance* in the Pulpit is a sort of bright *Mirrour* to his *Mind*, in which we discern the successive Images of Truth and Virtue, that rise up there?' (p. 73). If the pulpits of Britain were peopled with visually eloquent men of feeling, the essay suggests, Christianity – in a most compassionate form – could be properly fostered throughout the land.

Fordyce builds his doctrine, then, upon a firm conviction that true virtue and religiosity can take on *an appearance* – that the body can visually mediate and disperse moral qualities. 'What I would be understood to speak of here and all along', he writes as he introduces his topic, 'is simply those *Natural* and *Moral* Impressions which it is in the power of one *Man* to make upon another' (p. 4). And later he becomes explicit upon the power invested in the public speaker's body to transform religion into a persuasive spectacle:

If *Religion* be indeed that Lovely Form her Ministers represent her, it cannot sure be any disadvantage to her, to have her Image reflected from *their* Deportment *in* the Pulpit, as well as *out* of it. When they seem all possessed, expanded, exalted with those beautiful and sublime Perceptions which *she* inspires; when their Countenances brighten and their Eyes glow with her sacred Spirit . . . is it possible for the Auditors, if they have any remains of Ingenuity, not to be charmed into Love, or awed into Veneration? Do they not become in this instance *Spectators*, as well as *Auditors?* . . . RELIGION, RELIGION herself appears in some sort *visible* to Mortals. (p. 25)

From such passages it becomes clear why Fordyce produces, in Howell's words, a 'treatise on delivery, rather than a profound discourse on rhetoric'. Developing the latitudinarian promotion of accessible preaching, he celebrates the power of a sermon to affect the passions and identifies in the moving spectacle of religious oratory the key to public persuasion; for Fordyce, *delivery itself* is more affective and persuasive than the finer points of a sermon's composition. For illustration of the power of spectacular religion, he refers to Raphael's representation of *St Paul Preaching in Athens*, which he and many of his readers would have known through popular engravings of the painting. '[N]one will wonder at the silent, deep

Attention and Rapture, which appear in St. PAUL'S Hearers at *Athens*', he writes, 'who considers that truly Divine Orator, as he is there drawn by the Painter, looking with such a Face of Inspiration and impetuous Ardour, and seeming to pour forth a whole Tempest of sacred Eloquence, accompanied with the boldest and most majestic Action it is possible to imagine' (p. 26). The image not only represents the appearance of St Paul's body inspired with religion, but also shows the *affective power* which that appearance holds over an assembly of witnesses. It illustrates Fordyce's principle that

Mankind are unspeakably more influenced by their *Eyes* and their *Ears*, than by their *Understandings* alone; that they judge both of Men and Things chiefly from Appearance and from Feeling; that they are Then most apt to be convinced and touched, when the Person who addresses them seems to be so *himself*, that almost every Sentiment and Passion have certain Accents, Looks, and Gestures appropriated to them by Nature, which, from the intimate Connexion She hath established between the Body and the Mind, serve to express that Sentiment or Passion, as their genuine *Language*, or rather to exhibit and make them visible, as their immediate *Image*, or very *Picture*. (pp. 4–5)

Thus, for Fordyce, the proper impetus of eloquent gesture is genuine feeling, and the essay celebrates those orators who deliver 'Serious and Affectionate Addresses to the People, coming from their *own* Hearts, and directed to *theirs*' (p. 31). Working within a Cartesian physiological paradigm, Fordyce argues that if a passion is truly felt, then the mechanism of nature will do all that is necessary to manifest that feeling through the body. An orator 'warmed' by a passion will find that his 'Soul will diffuse itself through all the Powers of the Animal Machine: every Wheel will be wound up to its just pitch; and every Motion will come off free and clean' (p. 63).

Upon these principles Fordyce develops his training for the public speaker – training which involves not the learning or internalisation of particular forms of gesture, but the nurturing of virtuous passions such that persuasive expressions will be naturally marked upon the body. '[B]y cultivating a quick and strong Sensibility to the best Interests of Mankind', Fordyce tells his students of eloquence, 'you will acquire in a greater Degree a certain flowing Tenderness, or benevolent Meltingness of Nature; which, when supported by real Sense and Spirit, I have always observed to soften and dissolve an Audience, beyond any thing whatever' (p. 84). For Fordyce, the primary qualification of an effective orator, then, is the possession of 'a WARM AND WORTHY HEART' (pp. 78–9).

Fordyce's proper preacher is a lachrymose figure. Like Le Faucheur's *Traitté*, Fordyce's essay suggests that the most effective bodily signs are those of the eye, as it 'is principally the *Eyes* which must be the *Index* of the Soul' (p. 74). And again, it is the tear which is presented as the most emotive of the eye's available signs: 'a Tear, – yes, a manly Tear, may be shed by Compassion over the frailties of human Nature and Miseries of Mankind, forced out by a big-swollen Heart: I would never have you ashamed of it. It is the Tear of Virtue. It becomes the *Christian* Orator well: JESUS wept' (p. 84). Shed as a consequence of true feeling, the tear becomes Fordyce's most highly charged symbol of virtue, and with the justification of Christian morality and Christ's example, it becomes a suitable symbol for the display of a compassionate character.[54] In this celebration of the tear, we witness a furthering of Le Faucheur's anti-Stoical promotion of emotionalism in the pulpit, but we also see a self-conscious modelling of the signs and behaviour appropriate to masculinity. Fordyce takes into account that among his male readers there may be those for whom the shedding of tears is a shameful act – an act unbefitting those constructions of masculinity which preclude displays of such 'weakness'. But upon any reader who draws an association between emotional susceptibility and non-masculinity, Fordyce urges a new apprehension whereby the tear is freely recognised as entirely appropriate to manliness. In this treatise on action that is *proper* for public display, Fordyce presents the idea of a 'manly Tear' so as to *authorise* emotionalism in male behaviour; his understanding of the visibility of virtue and of compassionate Christianity indeed demands that he should authorise such display. Fordyce's proper preacher should still strike a dignified pose – 'Seriousness . . . must reign throughout: A certain ingenuous Modesty, supported with a manly Firmness of Utterance, will give both a Charm and a Dignity to the whole' (p. 53). But this mid-century ideal of eloquence – with its 'flowing Tenderness' and 'benevolent Meltingness of Nature' – is less conspicuously *elevated* above the spectatory than those competing models which are constructed in relation to classical decorum.

The assimilation within Britain of Le Faucheur's *Traitté* – with three editions of the English translation, and several deferential plunderings – suggests the great importance of oratory and of theatrical displays of power during this period. The reinflection of classical oratory represented by *Action Proper for the Pulpit* suggests that, by the mid century, traditional

---

[54] The elevation of Christ as a model of heroism had been an ongoing strand in the emergence of sentimentalism. A forceful text in this tradition is Richard Steele's *The Christian Hero; or, An Argument Proving that no Principles but those of Religion are Sufficient to make a Great Man* (1701) – Steele promotes Christ and St Paul as heroic models instead of traditional models such as Cato and Caesar (see Hammond, *Professional Imaginative Writing*, pp. 178–9).

ideals of patrician eloquence required modification if they were to be of relevance to modern society. The authorisation of non-classical emotionalism in the symbolisation of modern politeness will be seen again in the work of Sheridan and in the transformation of eighteenth-century stage practice, but before considering these areas, we can further delineate the emerging image of polite eloquence by examining certain types of body that were widely deemed to be *impolite*. Could emotionalism be pushed too far? If politeness found expression through physical displays of feeling, how was it distinct from 'enthusiasm' and all the dangers that were commonly associated with it? The writer in *The Tatler* quoted earlier recognised '[h]ow far Eloquence, set off with the proper Ornaments of Voice and Gesture, will prevail over the Passions, and how cold and unaffecting the best Oration in the World would be without them'. But he also warned that 'as too little Action is cold, so too much is fulsome'.[55] Fordyce was similarly concerned to note that 'when the Preacher rises to the utmost Contention and Vehemence, it must still be under great conduct: he must run into no undue transport' (p. 64). But at what point did an emotionally expressive body cease to embody politeness, and what types of process demarcated and authorised boundaries between polite and impolite eloquence?

[55] *The Tatler* 70 (20 September 1709), ed. Bond, vol. I, pp. 483 and 485.

CHAPTER 2

Bodies on the borders of politeness: 'Orator Henley', Methodist enthusiasm, and polite literature

The Manner of the *Itinerants'* holding-forth is generally very *boisterous* and *shocking*, and adapted, to the best of their Skill, to alarm the Imagination, and to raise a Ferment in the Passions, often attended with screaming and trembling of the Body. The Preacher now grows more tempestuous and dreadful in his Manner of Address, stamps and shrieks, and endeavours all he can to increase the rising Consternation, which is sometimes spread over a great Part of the Assembly in a few Minutes from its first Appearance. And to compleat the Work, the Preacher has his Recourse still to more frightful Representations; that *he sees Hell-flames flashing in their Faces*; and that they *are now! now! now! dropping into Hell! into the Bottom of Hell!* This boisterous Method seldom or never fails to set them screaming; and very often they grow distracted.

Theophilus Evans (1757)[1]

UNRULY BODIES

The development of polite discourse in eighteenth-century Britain, I have been suggesting, involved a positive valorisation of somatically displayed passions; the body animated by passions performed a symbolic function, standing as an accessible emblem for a society in which conspicuously patrician forms of expression were becoming less relevant or less tenable as the middle classes began to claim an increasingly significant share in public life. But the body image expressive of politeness was also given definition through the *rejection* of forms of somatic performance that visibly undermined values aspired to within the developing society. An offensiveness found in particular kinds of bodily gesture has already been glimpsed in the decorous programme of Le Faucheur – grotesque acts of lip-licking and

---

[1] Theophilus Evans, *The History of Modern Enthusiasm, from the Reformation to the Present Times*, enlarged 2nd edn (London, 1757), p. 119.

displays of the tongue prompted in that writer a shudder of offence that made his own insistence on public physical 'containment' all the more urgent. The classical decorum of Le Faucheur lost value as a blueprint of politeness as more tolerant models of eloquent behaviour emerged, but there remained space outside such tolerance where particular public bodies would continue to provide offence and thus continue to provide a tangible 'other' against which the defining lines of polite bodies could be bolstered. Peter Stallybrass and Allon White provide a useful description of how public identities are created partly through processes of negative definition: 'The public sphere is neither pure ideation nor something which existed only in and for itself: it is, like any form of identity, created through negations, it produces a new domain by taking into itself as *negative introjections* the very domains which surround and threaten it. It thus produces and reproduces itself through the process of denial and defiance.'[2] Through such a process – the identification and condemnation or critique of what was deemed impolite – eighteenth-century politeness gained coherence; polite eloquence was constructed partially in defiance of seemingly impolite modes of utterance. Here I want to examine such negative models as were presented to eighteenth-century British culture by a prominent individual preaching in London, John Henley, and by a major religious movement, Methodism. In related ways, both Henley and the Methodist movement became widely apprehended as dangerous alternatives to all that was proper, intelligent, sociable, and truly religious, the potential corruption of each of which quality, it is no exaggeration to state, could be read upon the body. Through 'eccentric' preaching Henley and the Methodist movement each posed innovations to patterns of presenting the body in public, and they each pushed the body's expressive potential to an extreme that was variously condemned as excessive, manic, violent, impolite, and positively dangerous to the health of individuals and society. The single body of Henley and the many bodies of leaders and followers of Methodism did more than reveal tongues or lick lips, as they demonstrated with their whole bodies a passion in speech that was deemed by many to overstep the bounds of acceptable, sane behaviour. Occupying the borders of polite society – indeed, located on these borders precisely because of the offence they posed to the empowered institutions of the established church and the law – both Henley and the Methodists drew wide attention to the business of eloquence, and contributed

---

[2] Peter Stallybrass and Allon White, *The Politics and Poetics of Transgression* (Ithaca, NY: Cornell University Press, 1986), p. 89.

creatively through their alterity to the more centred developing discourse of polite eloquence.[3]

But it was not purely through alterity that these marginalised figures contributed to the construction of polite eloquence; nor was their cultural position straightforwardly outside mainstream social institutions and public places. Henley, who styled himself a reviver of the ancient art of elocution, may have been condemned for eccentricity throughout his career as a preacher, but he attracted sufficient public appreciation (albeit mixed with curiosity) to sustain himself and his preaching house for nearly thirty years. And preaching in the busy Lincoln's Inn Fields area of London, he was by no means geographically marginalised. His position in the public sphere seems to have traversed cultural acceptance (the public were willing to pay to maintain this eccentric) and rejection (he was constantly criticised and satirised), in the process of which vacillation, Henley, if effecting nothing more constructive, fired a strong interest in public delivery as a serious public issue worthy of earnest consideration and debate. When Pope, in a dismissive portrait in *The Dunciad*, wrote mockingly of Henley as 'Preacher at once, and Zany of thy Age!', he recorded and fortified the sense of Henley's eccentricity, but at the same time he acknowledged the major cultural impact that this zany had made.[4]

In the case of the Methodists, a constructive contribution to polite elocutionary discourse was more obviously made. Spatially, the Methodists were more literally marginalised: the main stronghold of their support lay in rural areas, and since they were denied the use of conventional preaching houses, they were driven, often beyond the borders of settlements, to practise field preaching and worship in tabernacles. But despite legal and physical alienation, Methodism had an important impact upon the cultural centres from which it was pushed, where the condemnation of Methodism was by no means straightforward. In non-Methodist writing about Methodism – and about 'enthusiasm' in particular – there is often, as we shall see, a complex compound of disgust and desire. While condemning the bodily excesses of 'inspired' religious practices, writers are often obliged to acknowledge the effectiveness of passionate Methodist

---

[3] On the legal status of Methodist gatherings and practices, see David Hempton's chapter on 'Methodism and the Law in English Society, 1740–1820' in *The Religion of the People: Methodism and Popular Religion c. 1750–1900* (London and New York: Routledge, 1996), pp. 145–61. Early Methodism, Hempton writes, 'teetered on the brink of legal irregularities' (p. 147).

[4] Alexander Pope, *The Dunciad* (bk III, line 202) in *The Poems of Alexander Pope, Volume V: The Dunciad*, ed. James Sutherland (London: Methuen; New Haven: Yale University Press, 1943; repr. 1965), p. 175.

preachers and to concede that a qualified adoption of some of their techniques would be advantageous to establishment religion. Indeed, certain primarily critical writers, such as Richard Graves, encourage a controlled incorporation of elocutionary techniques from the religious and geographical peripheries occupied by Methodists into the politically (but not necessarily oratorically) empowered establishment institutions.

So neither Henley nor the Methodists were wholly 'othered', but both found themselves located *on*, and not beyond, the borders of politeness, as the challenges they made to emergent notions of polite behaviour were variously responded to with disgust or partially favourable interest. Responses to eccentricity or enthusiasm thus constitute a revealing component of polite discourse – they are utterances wherein we can witness not only the conflicting ideologies surrounding the human body, but also the complex rhetorical strategies of cultural contest and formation.

ORATOR HENLEY

In the first sermon delivered at his London preaching house in 1726, John 'Orator' Henley announced that his intention in setting up this new establishment was 'to recover the spirit of the antient preachers, and assert the honour of the English pulpit'. 'Above all', he went on, 'what shall most strongly engage our attention, shall be the beautiful, and long neglected science of rhetoric and elocution.'[5] Henley was embarking upon a new career as an independent preacher after several years of service within the established church.[6] After taking Holy Orders in 1712, he had worked both within the church and as a Grub Street writer for more than a decade. He resigned his Suffolk living in 1725, and the next year he founded 'The Oratory' as an independent academy for the delivery of sermons and lectures, with a principal purpose, as he made clear in his opening address, of reforming the manner in which such public presentations should be performed. A list of lecture subjects for the first two years of the Oratory's existence, which Henley published with other transactions, reveals that this emphasis was maintained: ten of the lectures delivered in the first five months were directly concerned with aspects of delivery. These included lectures on 'The general Principles of Speaking', 'The general Principles of Action', and the 'Antient History of Action' and remarks on the

---

[5] John Henley, *The Appeal of the Oratory to the First Ages of Christianity* (London, 1727), pp. 33 and 38.
[6] As any modern study of Henley must be, my analysis here is informed by Graham Midgley's engaging biography, *The Life of Orator Henley* (Oxford: Clarendon Press, 1973).

elocutionary rules of Quintilian, together with specific discussions of 'The
Action of the Eye and Features' and of 'The Action of the Hands'.[7] There
was, then, a reflexivity about the activities of Henley's Oratory, from which
was regularly broadcast information concerning the broadcast of information. Performing before his audiences and addressing the subject of how
eloquence should be achieved, Henley sought both to demonstrate and to
state the manner in which he believed the body should behave in public.

He aspired to great breadth in the applicability of his ideas regarding
bodily conduct, delivering a 1728 lecture on eloquence 'in the Senate, at the
Bar, in the Pulpit, and in all remarkable places, States, and Circumstances
of Humane Life; the Theatrical, in all Men . . . Action Religious, Political,
Athletic, and Ridiculous . . . being a universal Censure on Action, and a
Proof that all Life is Playing something, but with different Action'.[8] Like
James Boswell, then, whose social 'performing' I considered earlier, Henley
was keenly aware of the rhetorical dimension of social interaction, and his
work was directed towards the refinement of the different rhetorics – verbal
and somatic – which mediated human life in its various discursive situations. And Henley intended that the reach of his topic should be matched
by the range of people to whom his lectures would be useful. In laying out a
'Plan of the Oratory', Henley's first stated objective was to 'supply the want
of an university, or universal school in the capital, for the equal benefit of
persons of all ranks, professions, circumstances and capacities'.[9] These
egalitarian ends met with some success, and, despite his charging for
admission, Henley's Oratory proved to be popular among the lower
classes. 'The backbone of Henley's congregation', Graham Midgley writes,
'was the lower- and middle-class tradesman, often liberally sprinkled with
the butchers of Newport and Clare Markets, enlivened now and again by
visitors from Oxford and Cambridge or by rowdy gangs of young lawyers
from the Temple, and graced by more illustrious visitors who came to see
and hear for themselves this much talked-of celebrity.'[10] Henley, then,
rapidly aroused class-crossing attention to both eloquence and himself, as is
further suggested by the second edition of the translation of Le Faucheur's
Traitté, which, as I noted, was published in 1727, with its introduction
'*relating to the Famous Mr. Henly's present Oratory*'. In less than two
years a largely obscure country divine was transformed into '*the Famous

[7] John Henley, *Oratory Transactions. No II. To be occasionally publish'd* (London, 1729), p. 1.
[8] *Ibid.*, p. 12.
[9] *Ibid.*, p. iii.
[10] Midgley, *Orator Henley*, p. 79.

Mr. Henly, which figure of renown had, with personal elevation, carried the business of elocution to the forefront of public debate.

Henley may have declared his elocutionary ideals to be 'the spirit of the antient preachers', but he went about publicising his reformatory desires through a wholehearted embrace of modern techniques for penetrating the public sphere. He ably exploited the print trade, so that the day-to-day business of the Oratory was spread well beyond the walls of the academy itself and into the channels of circulation for pamphlets and magazines. Henley had published and edited various works before opening the Oratory, including letters in *The Spectator*, poetry, translations, editions of the works of Philip Sidney and the Duke of Buckingham, and works of history. The range of this early writing suggests in Henley the professional opportunism that was typical of many jobbing authors of the period; a more ambitious literary project, however, clearly engaged the personal interests that Henley was later to develop through his work at the Oratory. *The Compleat Linguist, or an universal grammar of all the considerable tongues in being* was published in nine parts between 1719 and 1723, offering grammars of Spanish, Italian, French, Greek, Latin, Hebrew, Chaldee, Arabic, and Syriac; a tenth part, *An Introduction to English Grammar*, followed in 1726. By that time Henley had started to use print to strengthen and promote the Oratory's work, and until his death in 1756 he continued to publish works relating to the activities of his establishment. An early *Guide to the Oratory*, subtitled '*an historical account of the new sect of the Henleyarians*' (1726?) suggests the strain of self-promotion and slight whimsicality that runs through these many works, which include numerous sermons, dissertations, and lectures, and several *Transactions* and *Miscellanies* recording the Oratory's events.[11]

Alongside print culture, Henley exploited another feature of early modern Britain that has become a central focus of interest in recent studies of the period: the public's willingness to pay for new kinds of diversion.[12] The establishment of the Oratory is a striking example of the innovative creation in early eighteenth-century Britain of new social spaces the structural basis of which was commercial, and its progress epitomises in many ways the typical development of a multitude of (particularly urban) public

---

[11] A bibliography of Henley's published writing appears *ibid.*, pp. 290–1.
[12] For recent scholarship, a seminal work on the commercial character of eighteenth-century culture is Neil McKendrick, John Brewer, and J. H. Plumb, *The Birth of a Consumer Society: The Commercialization of Eighteenth-Century England* (London: Europa, 1982). Brewer develops this study of purchased pleasures in *Pleasures of the Imagination*; the theme is also central to Langford's *Polite and Commercial People*.

institutions. Henley's first Oratory was a spacious loft room in London's Newport meat-market district, and the room had been used unchanged as a religious meeting house for various groups long before Henley's occupancy in 1726. Henley's known innovations were twofold: he added two rostra for the staging of disputations, and he altered the entrance to allow for the charging and controlling of admission.[13] In short, he made the venue more theatrical and he commercialised the business, transforming the delivery of sermons and speeches into a commodified public spectacle. Like Jonathan Tyers, the entrepreneurial proprietor of Vauxhall Gardens and all-round cultural salesman, Henley was clearly adept at tapping the resources of the paying public and was alert to strategies for appealing to people's imaginations and, in turn, their pockets.[14] His second Oratory in Lincoln's Inn Fields, where he remained for the rest of his career, was more theatrical still. He had significant alterations carried out on this larger venue, again to control the paid admission and again to create a sense of spectacle: the orations were delivered from a monumental two-tier pulpit 'covered with velvet and gold fleurs-de-lis above, the whole edifice topped with a large sounding board'.[15] As he preached from the middle of this dramatic construction and to a paying crowd, Henley's attempts to revive the ancient art of oratory were configured within a distinctly modern commercial setting. Admittedly, he was not always commercially successful, and was sometimes obliged to engineer schemes and devices to attract and sustain audiences – for example, he developed complicated Oratory membership schemes, and made the topics of his lectures more generally appealing (Midgley states that by 'the end of 1728 . . . sober and orthodox subjects . . . had started to give way to more burlesque and satirical commentaries on current affairs').[16] But the Oratory's endurance nevertheless suggests not only the doggedness of Henley's pursuit of his cause but also the public's potential to be made interested in that cause. Henley recognised the need to use *entertainment* to attract audiences, and so transformed dramatic preaching into a diverting cultural product.

In turn, the brand of eloquence put forward from Henley's pulpit – particularly as it appeared via his own preaching practices – shows the influence of a setting where entertainment was a priority. 'Discursive space',

[13] Midgley, *Orator Henley*, p. 73.
[14] On Tyers's commercialisation of Vauxhall and its influence upon other ventures, see Brewer, *Pleasures of the Imagination*, pp. 65–7.
[15] Midgley, *Orator Henley*, p. 75.
[16] *Ibid.*, p. 115.

to quote Stallybrass and White again, 'is never completely independent of social place and the formation of new kinds of speech can be traced through the emergence of new public sites of discourse and the transformation of old ones.'[17] Thus within the commercial and theatrical setting of the Oratory – most unlike the official state-instituted platforms used by the ancient orators whom Henley admired – Henley's self-declared brief, based on the eloquence of classical tradition, became transformed. Indeed, Henley can be seen to have overwritten a classical body image with a more dramatic and animated approach to gesture. He expressed a veneration of the ancients comparable with that of Le Faucheur, but he digressed from these models both in the doctrine laid out in his writing and in his own performances. It has been suggested, in fact, that Henley was strongly influenced by the work of Le Faucheur or its offspring, but his writing represents a reinflection of Le Faucheur akin to that of *An Essay on the Action Proper for the Pulpit.*[18] His elocutionary doctrine can be gauged from his sermon *The History and Advantages of divine Revelation, with the Honour, that is due to the Word of God; especially in regard to the most Perfect Manner Of delivering it, form'd on the antient Laws of Speaking and Action: Being an Essay to restore them.* Here he explains how non-verbal expression should be governed:

In proper speaking and gesture, the nature of the thing spoken, strongly imprinted on the mind, and present feeling of the orator, is the only guidance; and as things are, in their own nature, various, they necessarily require a variation of the voice, and of the deportment, that is conformable to each of them: and the precise fitness of one certain sound and movement of the whole person, even to a line of the countenance, to one certain thing, most properly and perfectly express'd, and the consequent unfitness of any other, to it, are as demonstrable, as any proposition in the Mathematicks.[19]

There are no specific instructions for gesturing since the '*only* guidance' comes from the orator's 'feeling' about the thing. Yet the language determined in this way has signs which are so precisely defined that the right or wrong sign can be demonstrated with the certainty of a mathematical sign. For Henley, this was the way to speak 'properly and perfectly'. But, importantly, not all of those who witnessed Henley could agree with his notion of bodily propriety.

---

[17] Stallybrass and White, *Politics and Poetics of Transgression*, p. 80.

[18] Howell writes that Henley was influenced 'no doubt by the popularity of such treatises as' Le Faucheur's *Traitté* and those works based upon it (*British Logic and Rhetoric*, p. 194).

[19] Published in 1725, the sermon is reprinted in *Oratory Transactions. No II*, from which I quote (p. 17).

In his pulpit, Henley's bodily actions were, according to most accounts, lively, bold, theatrical, and odd. Midgley writes that 'it was Henley's uninhibited and increasingly eccentric application of these ideas [concerning eloquence] which produced sensational and theatrical excesses and which outraged the eighteenth-century sense of religion and pulpit decorum'.[20] Anecdotes of his performances give an impression of the provoking way in which Henley practised what he preached. One observer, writing in the *Weekly Journal*, reports:

About the usual hour of the Orator's entering the public scene of action, a trap-door gave way behind the pulpit, as if forced open by some invisible hand; and at one large leap the Orator jumped to the desk, where he at once fell to work . . . but to come to his oration, which turned on the important subject of Education antient and modern, I had entertained hopes of meeting with something curious at least, if not just, on the great theme he had made choice of; though, instead of it, I heard nothing but a few common sentiments, phrases, and notions, beat into the audience with hands, arms, legs, and head, as if people's understandings were to be courted and knocked down with blows, and gesture and grimace were to plead and atone for all other deficiencies.[21]

This writer clearly arrived at the Oratory with predetermined expectations regarding pulpit decorum which were violated by Henley's appropriation of a dramatic mode of utterance for the presentation of a sober topic. From the opening description of the stage machinery by which Henley, like a pantomime genie, suddenly appeared before his crowd, the author brands the preacher with a type of clownish theatricalism which is deemed both inappropriate and ineffectual for conveying the 'important subject' of the oration. Indeed, Henley is shown to neglect this subject through his attention to the somatic elements of his performance. Hoping to hear reasoned argument, this shocked and disappointed writer discovers in Henley's performance a violent physical affront – an offensive, bodily assault upon the audience, in which Henley's every limb and feature is guilty of excessive gesture. Elsewhere Henley was also harshly criticised for *what* he said in his pulpit, but reports such as this show that the offence Henley posed to standards of reason and politeness derived, in large part, from what spectators witnessed him doing with his body. As another writer complained in the *Grub Street Journal*, 'Is not the most consummate Impudence exerted in all his words, actions and gestures, and diffused

---

[20] Midgley, *Orator Henley*, p. 99.
[21] Quoted from the *Weekly Journal* in J. P. Malcolm's *Anecdotes of the Manners and Customs of London during the Eighteenth Century* (London, 1808), p. 238.

over his whole person?'[22] In Henley, such accounts suggest, observers recognised an *embodiment* of impoliteness.

By presenting orations in such a controversial fashion, Henley sustained a position as 'a constant talking point in London for thirty years'.[23] Most of the talk and of the writing about Henley was, like the description in the *Weekly Journal*, deeply critical. Pope produced an extended critique for *The Dunciad* (1728–43), which formed one of many uses of Henley as a butt in satirical poetry. In *The Birth-Day of Folly* (1755), a 'heroi-comical poem' by George Alexander Stevens, Henley appears 'as void of wit as grace', and this extended piece of mockery focuses, in large part, upon bodily absurdities and improprieties:

> The mighty master of the sev'nfold face:
> Lo! bronz'd in matchless impudence he stands,
> And spreads to heav'n his high-directed hands,
> Tremendous with his broad, black eye-brows bent,
> As if on some infernal plot intent.[24]

Stevens also brought satire of Henley to the stage in his *Distress upon distress* (1752), and Henley appeared in a similarly uncomplimentary light in prose fiction of the period. In *Joseph Andrews* (1742), for example, Fielding makes a dismissive satirical reference to 'Henley himself, or as great an Orator (if any such be) . . . in his *Rostrum* or Tub'.[25] Henley was also the subject of both earnest and satirical writing in articles in such periodicals as Edward Cave's *Gentleman's Magazine*, which printed a scathing obituary of Henley in 1757 (including, within a catalogue of his failings, his 'antick gesture').[26] In 1731 that magazine had printed a short verse which encapsulates the key objections that were made to Henley's performances:

> When from gilt Tub sublime in Masquerade
> *Tully* reviv'd the *unknown* God display'd,
> Clare-Butchers mixt with Saints of *Drury-lane*,
> Astonish'd heard the learned lofty Strain,
> Which, like the Theme, th'*Athenian God* unknown
> Still left, but manifested plain his own.[27]

---

[22] *Grub Street Journal* 67 (15 April 1731).

[23] Midgley, *Orator Henley*, p. viii.

[24] George Alexander Stevens, *The Birth-Day of Folly: An Heroi-Comical Poem* (London, 1755), pp. 9–10. Among other poets to deride Henley were Richard Savage, Robert Lloyd, and Walter Harte.

[25] George Alexander Stevens, *Distress upon distress* (Dublin, 1752), pp. 53–4; Henry Fielding, *Joseph Andrews with Shamela and Related Writings*, ed. Homer Goldberg (New York and London: W. W. Norton, 1987), p. 184.

[26] *Gentleman's Magazine* 27 (April 1757), 181.

[27] *Gentleman's Magazine* 1 (April 1731), 154.

Depicting a carnivalesque scene, with a motley audience drawn from the lower orders (workers from Clare Market and, it is implied, prostitutes from the ill-reputed Drury Lane district), the writer condemns Henley for egocentricity and implies the fakery of this masquerading preacher. What Henley is positively shown *not* to be creating through his eloquence – and the constitution of the audience is a key point here – is 'Gentlemen', and Henley's attractiveness to 'low' crowds was clearly a problem for those involved in such a magazine as Cave's, which explicitly sought to construct and arbitrate between models of polite, gentlemanly identity. Henley, from such a perspective, had not reformed eloquence but had abused it, and had wrested it from the province of polite culture only to reconfigure and debase it among categories of people excluded from that increasingly powerful culture. Despite what Henley *said* about proper eloquent conduct, spectators perceived in him no 'natural' language of feeling but saw rather theatrical showmanship and buffoonery, and the prolonged critique that activities within the Oratory inspired served to transform the image of Henley's body into a public reference point for somatic impoliteness.

THE BODY IN ANTI-ENTHUSIASM

Henley's apparent subversion of decorum was in many ways echoed by eighteenth-century 'enthusiastic' Methodist preachers, who were likewise criticised for frantic tirades and extravagant bodily expression, and yet, at the same time, attracted large followings, particularly from among the lower classes, and within rural and industrialising areas. As David Hempton writes, the movement 'took strongest root in marginal areas, scattered settlements and new industrial environments where the traditional social cement was weakest'.[28] Methodism capitalised on the fragility of Anglican power in these communities, and employed a vehement style of preaching, which, like that of Henley, presented a challenge to the unemotive delivery associated with the Anglican church. With conspicuously powerful audience responses to such preaching – as described, for example, in the epigraph to this chapter – the emergence of Methodism in the late 1730s radically intensified and complicated eighteenth-century elocutionary discourse. In fact, eloquent Methodist preachers, of whom George Whitefield is the supremely famous and successful example, presented arbiters of politeness in religion and society with a certain problem.

---

[28] Hempton, *Religion of the People*, p. 149.

With its associations with 'enthusiasm', Methodism was condemned as a source of madness and social depravity, and yet the effectiveness of its agents of dispersal could not be denied. Whitefield, it is estimated, would sometimes attract as many as thirty thousand listeners, and with such manifest popularity Methodist preachers seemed to possess the very tools that many establishment preachers were lacking.

The negotiation of this difficulty – that a Methodist could be at once pariah and exemplar – is an issue for writers of, broadly, two types of text: firstly, works which seek to transform oratory through a reformulation of patterns of polite eloquence (in this category we can see several essays by Oliver Goldsmith which I discuss later, alongside more developed works such as Sheridan's *Lectures on Elocution*); and secondly, texts written in opposition to Methodism which, while condemnatory overall, are obliged to recognise the increased religious observation inspired by the leaders of the movement. In the latter type of text, which emerged largely from the Anglican community, anti-Methodism can function, as it does in Richard Graves's *The Spiritual Quixote*, as a stimulus for an introspective self-critique. For writers of both kinds of text, the body is a crucial site of contestation, and the degree to which it should be allowed to display passion for the purposes of persuasion becomes a point for debate in the formulation of polite behaviour. Such opposition to enthusiastic preaching provides a bold demonstration that the eloquent body defined by eighteenth-century arbiters of politeness was a strictly circumscribed construct.

Alongside the relatively tempered considerations of Methodism provided by such writers as Sheridan, Graves, and Goldsmith, there was also a culture of stauncher anti-enthusiasm. Indeed, by the time of Methodism's foundation, a tradition of anti-enthusiasm had already arisen in response to the several nonconforming religious groups which, from the mid seventeenth century, had identified faith through the inspiration of the body. The most recent group, and one with whom the Methodists were often compared and associated, were the French Prophets, who had come to London in 1706 and had preached and attracted followers until their decline in the 1730s. Hillel Schwartz describes these *inspirés* as characterised by '[s]haking, falling, choking and convulsions', and, as the Methodists would be, the French Prophets were regularly charged with enthusiasm and condemned for their wild delivery.[29] In the mid century, the Methodists

---

[29] Hillel Schwartz, *The French Prophets: The History of a Millenarian Group in Eighteenth-Century England* (Berkeley: University of California Press, 1980), p. 19. Schwartz discusses at length the theatricalism of the French Prophets' preaching (pp. 251–7).

effectively became a new target in a tradition of opposition to religious movements with claims to a mystical form of inspiration.

The culture of opposition to Methodism was intense, and it found expression through both violence and cultural discourse. Particularly in the first twenty years of the movement, Methodists were assaulted with taunting and mob violence, often incited and organised by the clergy or gentry of the district they were disturbing.[30] Methodists were ostracised, sometimes losing their homes or jobs; several preaching houses were demolished and individuals were beaten and, on a few occasions, killed.[31] Alongside such physical violence, the culture of literary attack was both lively and expansive: a recent bibliography of eighteenth-century anti-Methodist publications lists 934 publications between 1738 and 1800, of which 598 were new titles and 336 reprints and new editions, and there were more expressions of anti-Methodist feeling than those of these specialist works.[32] In terms of the number of its adherents, Methodism was actually *not* a huge movement during this period.[33] Such thorough efforts to nip the movement in its bud suggest that its apparent threat was unduly magnified, a distortion which can be attributed to the association with the enthusiasm of earlier sectarian groups, and the belief that enthusiasm could spread like a contagious disease. In fact, while the number of early Methodist members may have been relatively small, its steady increase during the century could easily reinforce such an impression.[34]

'Enthusiasm' is certainly the central complaint within many anti-Methodist texts, or it functions as an accessible handle for a programme of broader opposition. The term was used in the eighteenth century, often very loosely, to mean an excess of religious zeal associated with a belief in inspiration directly from the Holy Spirit. Johnson defined it in his *Dictionary* as a 'vain belief of private revelation; a vain confidence of divine favour or communication . . . Heat of imagination; violence of passion'.[35] Enthusiasm, then, was seen to be a type of passion, but it was a *destructive*

---

[30] See John Walsh, 'Methodism and the Mob in the Eighteenth Century', in G. J. Cuming and D. Baker (eds.), *Popular Belief and Practice*, Studies in Church History 8 (Cambridge: Cambridge University Press, 1972), p. 216.

[31] *Ibid.*, p. 213.

[32] Clive D. Field, 'Anti-Methodist Publications of the Eighteenth Century: A Revised Bibliography', *Bulletin of the John Rylands University Library of Manchester* 73 (1991), 159–280.

[33] Porter writes that there 'were only 24,000 Methodists in 1767 and 77,000 by 1796' (*English Society in the Eighteenth Century*, p. 177).

[34] Hempton describes Methodism's 'period of sustained rapid expansion from about 1740 to about 1840' in *Methodism and Politics in British Society 1750–1850* (London: Hutchinson, 1983), p. 12.

[35] Johnson, *Dictionary*, vol. I, 'Enthusiasm'.

type, and it carried implications of mad behaviour and social disruption. As Henry D. Rack puts it, enthusiasm 'was the bugbear of decent and ordinary Anglicans'.[36] Its association with bodily deviance derived from the involuntary physical convulsions sometimes felt by both leaders and followers of religions based on inspiration; this physical uncontrol was attributed by detractors to madness, but by supporters, to the pangs of the New Birth. Both Whitefield and John Wesley recorded in their published journals regular occurrences of their followers falling into convulsions.[37] Wesley described how during a sermon 'one, and another, and another sunk to the earth; they dropped on every side as thunderstruck'; at another, '[m]en, women and children wept and groaned and trembled exceedingly'.[38] Wesley, in fact, remained relatively moderate in his preaching,[39] but the greater intensity and fervour of Whitefield's delivery was seen to be capable of causing severe physical disturbances, with his first sermon alleged to have sent fifteen people mad.[40] Methodism, then, was a religion that brought to the body a loss of control, and the leaders of the movement were active in celebrating and publicising uninhibited expressions of emotion as signs of true faith.

There were, of course, theological objections to Methodism (although Wesleyan Methodism maintained that it presented no innovation to

---

[36] Henry D. Rack, *Reasonable Enthusiast: John Wesley and the Rise of Methodism* (London: Epworth Press, 1989), p. 275.

[37] Such phenomena are discussed in R. A. Knox, *Enthusiasm: A Chapter in the History of Religion* (Oxford: Clarendon Press, 1950), pp. 520–35; and, together with an outline of theories of causation, in Rack, *Reasonable Enthusiast*, pp. 194–7.

[38] Cited in Knox, *Enthusiasm*, pp. 521 and 534.

[39] When Wesley gave advice on delivery to John King, a preacher in America, he recommended him to 'Scream no more . . . Speak as earnestly as you can, but do not scream. Speak with all your heart, but with a moderate voice' (cited in T. B. Shepherd, *Methodism and the Literature of the Eighteenth Century* (London: Epworth Press, 1940), p. 54). That Wesley should borrow extensively from Le Faucheur's *An Essay upon the Action of an Orator* for his own *Directions concerning Pronunciation and Gesture* (Bristol, 1749) further suggests the relative moderation of his preaching. This is a short pamphlet which condenses Le Faucheur's advice, reproducing many passages verbatim. Wesley retains Le Faucheur's combination of elocutionary methods by insisting that the orator should feel the passion whilst also giving specific advice on certain gestures. I am not aware of Wesley's use of Le Faucheur having been identified before, and so it may be useful here to indicate where comparable passages can be found. On pronunciation, cf. *Directions*, p. 5 with *Essay*, p. 71; on managing the face, cf. *Directions*, p. 10 with *Essay*, p. 182; on eye movement, cf. *Directions*, p. 11 with *Essay*, p. 183; on restricting force in manual gesture, cf. *Directions*, p. 11 with *Essay*, p. 196. There are many more instances of borrowing. Rack suggests that the moderation recommended in Wesley's manual was 'in the heat of revival . . . unlikely to be observed' (*Reasonable Enthusiast*, p. 345).

[40] Knox, *Enthusiasm*, p. 524. Whitefield became a far more controversial figure than Wesley, and was the focus of more criticism. Examining specifically satirical attack, Albert M. Lyles indicates the tendency to target Whitefield over Wesley in *Methodism Mocked: The Satiric Reaction to Methodism in the Eighteenth Century* (London: Epworth Press, 1960), p. 112.

Church of England doctrine), and opponents argued that Methodism led to atheism and sensuality, and that the idea of being chosen for salvation could be and was interpreted to sanction acts of vice. By 'dangerously dividing communities into the saved and the lost', Hempton writes, 'the Methodists were allegedly responsible for undermining ecclesiastical discipline, social stability, communal harmony and public morality'.[41] The aspect of Methodism that attracted perhaps most criticism was the idea of justification through faith alone, which appeared to sanction the neglect of good works. What is apparent from many anti-Methodist texts, however, is that the social disruption caused by a preacher's arrival in a parish and horror at some of the consequences of Methodist conversion were the cause of more immediate alarm. Enthusiasm would have presented little threat to the social order contained within a handful of quiet eccentrics, but when the enthusiast was seen to possess the persuasive power to spread apparent lunacy, a far more troublesome problem was presented.

Thomas Green, a Leicestershire vicar, attacked enthusiasm in his expansive *A Dissertation on Enthusiasm; shewing The Danger of its late Increase, and the great Mischiefs it has occasioned, both in ancient and modern Times* (1755). His writing, his preface declares, was motivated by his long having had his parish disturbed by divisive religious groups, and with recent proof of the dangers of enthusiasm in 'a person, who in a fit of despair stabbed himself to the heart, after he was become a follower of those new teachers'.[42] Green cites other examples of suicides and an attempted matricide, and he expresses repulsion from the Methodist reports of physical aberrations:

The accounts of those strange and astonishing disorders amongst the *Methodists*, given by their own writers, cannot even be read without a kind of horror or pain and uneasiness; such as the frightful screamings, yellings, tremblings, swoonings, convulsions, despairing agonies, nay horrid blasphemies, and variety of grievous tortures both of body and mind, which are said to be common amongst them.[43]

For Green, these are '*great Mischiefs*' indeed, and his own notion of good religion clearly demands that faith should involve no such loss of bodily control. The enthusiastic body is one that overflows – it is defined by what it releases into the world, its screams and yells, its wild shakes and tremors. As such, it is clearly comparable with the sentimental bodies that became more fully authorised within polite culture, with their overflowings of

---

[41] Hempton, *Religion of the People*, p. 146.
[42] Thomas Green, *A Dissertation on Enthusiasm* (London, 1755), p. vi.
[43] *Ibid.*, pp. 94–5.

tears and their swoons. Indeed, it is has been suggested that eighteenth-century Methodism and sensibility were basically two sides of the same coin – 'is not sentimentalism a secular mode of Methodism?', asks Melvyn New rhetorically – and there are certainly close affinities between the movements, which both place great store in the passions made visible as signs of virtue or true faith.[44] But in somatic terms, the Methodist enthusiast is typically a more vehement and violent performer than the delicate idols of sentimentalism. As will be seen later, a heroic body for Samuel Richardson will 'tremble' and 'swoon', but it will not 'yell', and it will certainly not emit the 'horrid blasphemies' that Green, who is not opposed to emotionalism in general, finds among the Methodists. The somatic eloquence celebrated within such polite cultural products as the Richardsonian novel retains a degree of the physical 'containment' that such writers as Thomas Green clearly endorse.[45]

Green's response to Methodist enthusiasm was by no means isolated. Fearing the spread of enthusiasm, Theophilus Evans (1693–1767), a vicar of St David's in Brecon, was similarly horrified by the spectacle of bodies out of control, and his response to Methodism was underpinned by similarly austere notions of what is decent behaviour for a body in public. In his influential and polemical *The History of Modern Enthusiasm* (1752) Evans condemned enthusiasm through detracting description of a range of non-conforming sects with claims to religion through inspiration, and the body is a prime focus in his attack. This extensive history describes a continuum of groups from the fanatical sects of the interregnum through Quakerism, the French Prophets, and Methodism, and all are charged with undifferentiated enthusiasm. Methodism, for Evans, is simply 'the *Revival* of several Enthusiastick Notions, and mad Pranks, among the several

---

[44] Melvyn New, review of Mullan, *Sentiment and Sociability* in *The Scriblerian* 23 (1991), 249. In a similar vein, Barker-Benfield argues that 'it is reasonable to suggest that Methodism (and probably evangelism generally) and the cult of sensibility were two branches of the same culture' (*Culture of Sensibility*, p. 273). Likewise Madeleine Forell and Janet Todd make connections between the appeal 'to the heart' in both Methodist works and those of sensibility, and they argue that the 'place and nature of the cult of sensibility in the Wesleyan revival is revealed in Charles Wesley's hymns' (*English Congregational Hymns in the Eighteenth Century* (Kentucky: University of Kentucky Press, 1982), p. 3).

[45] This will become more apparent in Chapter 5, but it is worth noting here how the vocabulary of sentimental fiction typically tethers the heroic, moved body within bounds that are transgressed by enthusiasts. Should the novel of sentiment's preference for heroic 'cries' over more violent 'yells', 'roars', 'bellows', 'bawls', 'howls', 'screeches', and 'shrieks' not become apparent from close reading, that such a hierarchy is in place can be confirmed by automatic word-searches of Richardson's works, and of the 'novel of sentiment' more broadly, via Chadwyck-Healey's *Literature Online*.

Sectaries of the last Century; such as their Crying out, Screaming, Roaring, Groanings, Trembling, Yelling, Convulsions, Swooning, Blasphemies, Curses', and so on.[46] As a work of admonition, *The History of Modern Enthusiasm* is not concerned with documenting theological nicety, but rather depicts enthusiasm as a singular and monstrously deviant force, manifesting itself in offensive bodily behaviour. Evans's own writing, he claims, is 'the best Preservative against the Growth of Enthusiasm' (p. xi), and he endeavours to avert readers from this destructive force, and to debunk many of the grounds on which its dissemination is based.

Enthusiasm, for Evans, is an *excess* of passion. If contained within certain bounds, he suggests that it can be advantageous, and he describes a 'Natural Enthusiasm' which is necessary in the production of good poetry or oratory: 'An Heat, a Fire, that does warm the Mind, and makes the Imagination glow', and which serves to 'enliven and invigorate an Oration' (p. 2). It becomes a threatening power when it eclipses other faculties: the 'Spirit of *Enthusiasm* is a very dangerous Ingredient when it once gets the Dominion over a Man's Temper, and is become the *Governing* Principle' (p. xi). Such domination leads, Evans insists, to madness, and he calls upon the authority of the sane to justify the verdict, saying of the Methodists that 'they must and do own, that they have been looked upon as *mad* (on account of their wild and frantick Actions) by Friends and Relations, by indifferent Persons, by regular Physicians, the most proper Judges by the World in general, and have been sent to *Bedlam*, and adjudged there to be Persons distracted' (p. 127). Significantly, judgement is founded here upon *spectacle*: the Methodists are *looked upon* as mad; their 'frantick Actions' symbolise disorder and, from the perspective of *regular* and *proper* witnesses, the anti-social force they represent is best contained within the walls of the madhouse. For the maintenance of a regular and proper society, Evans's work suggests, symbolically antagonistic spectacles must be repressed or conspicuously condemned.

Evans is unrelenting in his attack upon the enthusiastic body. He finds the 'Manner of the *Itinerants'* holding-forth' to be 'generally very *boisterous* and *shocking*', and is repulsed by the 'screaming and trembling of the Body' and the 'stamps and shrieks' of such speakers (p. 119). Regarded as the agents of madness and disorder, the leaders of Methodism are roundly condemned by Evans, and, in particular, he discredits Whitefield (p. 111). But through all his opposition and disgust, Evans is hard-pressed to deny

---

[46] Evans, *The History of Modern Enthusiasm* (1757), pp. 128–9. I refer to this edition throughout, giving references within the text.

the fact that these figures are persuasive performers. At a typical Methodist meeting, he writes, the

most solemn Performance would be an artful Management of the Holder-forth to scare his Audience with some shocking Expression, as, *that Hell flashes in their Faces; that Satan stands ready to snatch them away:* And then he would repeat three or four Times, with a peculiar Tone, the awful Word, *Damn'd! Damn'd! Damn'd!* This loud Repetition of the Word *Damn'd,* with such an Emphasis in the Pronunciation, would fright the Children and make them cry; this would affect the tender Mothers, and set them screaming also: And thus the whole Congregation by Sympathy would catch the Infection, and the Scream would become general, which they fancied, like the *French* Prophets, to be the Work of Conviction. (p. 115)

There are unwitting effects in such passages of castigation. Debunking mysticism demands that while Methodist speakers are condemned, they are at the same time acknowledged as possessing effective oratorical skill. The tone used may be 'peculiar', but it ensures an enraptured, attentive, and sympathetic crowd, and the effects of such delivery occur with a striking immediacy. By no means can Evans approve such performances, for they clearly offend his sense of somatic propriety. But from his position of opposition he is actually admitting the power of Methodist oratory; he is exposing a potential in such oratory which elsewhere was more creatively exploited by, among others, Oliver Goldsmith and Richard Graves.

NEGOTIATIONS OF METHODISM IN POLITE LITERATURE

For Oliver Goldsmith, enthusiasm was no monstrously mad contagion that threatened to unhinge a recognisably ordered society, but was rather a valuable sign of emotional sincerity which, when displayed by an orator, held the capacity to enliven a performance and arouse the attention of the audience. Strongly expressed emotions, for Goldsmith, were not alien to polite behaviour. In essays published in 1759 and 1760 in the *Critical Review*, *The Bee*, the *Weekly Magazine*, and the *Lady's Magazine* – magazines self-consciously engaged in the production of polite society – Goldsmith addresses the subject of public eloquence and argues for the appropriateness of powerful displays of the passions within polite public performances.[47]

---

[47] These essays are respectively: 'A System of Oratory' (a review of John Ward's 1759 work of that title), in *Works of Oliver Goldsmith*, vol. I, pp. 167–70; 'Of Eloquence', vol. I, pp. 476–83; 'A Sublime Passage in a French Sermon', vol. III, pp. 49–51; 'Some Remarks on the Modern Manner of Preaching', vol. III, pp. 150–5.

Having recently concluded a continental tour, he found the existing 'polite' oratory in Britain to be a peculiarly lifeless affair. In a revealing essay on 'A Sublime Passage in a French Sermon' he contrasted France and Britain, describing 'that strange phlegmatic method in which our congregations behave while hearing a sermon: the more polite the audience always the more drowsy; near the court it is perfect lethargy, citizens only seem to doze, the audience are alive only at the Tabernacle or Moorfields'.[48] As a topographer of politeness, the contemporary formulation of which he clearly seeks to question, Goldsmith describes a movement outwards from the nation's supposed hub of polite values, and this journey through increasingly low-class identities reveals a related increase in audience attentiveness, and with it the implication of preferable religious observation. With the arrival at the Moorfields, Goldsmith has left the town and the established church, and has reached the preaching ground of the Methodists, among which conceptually and physically marginalised group he recognises effective eloquence at work. His essays on this subject represent an effort to negotiate a partial acceptance of the Methodists' controversial preaching techniques by a community of polite magazine readers. In this way the essays are engaged in both the construction and the advertisement of an emotionally moved body as an emblem of politeness.

The foundation of effective eloquence for Goldsmith is the speaker's genuine belief in the subject of the oration – the principle of modern, 'natural', unclassical oratory, which by that time, as we shall see, was being expressed forcefully and frequently by Thomas Sheridan. Sharing much of Sheridan's thinking, Goldsmith writes in *The Bee*: 'Nature renders men eloquent in great interests, or great passions. He that is sensibly touched, sees things with a very different eye from the rest of mankind. All nature to him becomes an object of comparison and metaphor, without attending to it; he throws his life into all, and inspires his audience with a part of his own enthusiasm.'[49] Enthusiasm is contagious here but not dangerously so, and, apparently untroubled by the term's controversiality, Goldsmith incorporates it into a passage inscribed with hallmarks of polite sensibility: 'nature' and the capacity to be 'sensibly touched'. It has been shown that in producing his remarks upon oratory Goldsmith made use of Voltaire's entry on 'Eloquence' and D'Alembert's on 'Elocution' in the *Encyclopédie* (1755).[50] Given Goldsmith's position at the time as a hectically busy

---

[48] *Works of Oliver Goldsmith*, vol. III, p. 49.
[49] *Ibid.*, vol. I, pp. 476–7.
[50] See Arthur Friedman's n. 2, *ibid.*, vol. I, p. 476.

aspiring author, his use of this source may resemble a convenient journalistic shortcut, but it was not only for expediency that he exploited the *Encyclopédie*. Goldsmith's unfavourable review of Ward's classically grounded *A System of Oratory* reveals both his informed understanding of the subject and his strong allegiance to a modern mode of oratory unbound by the rule of classical precedent. To transform British eloquence Goldsmith recognised a need for some impetus from outside contemporary polite society. Ancient Rome or Athens were inadequate here – indeed, it was the already-assimilated oratory of classical cultures that seemed to Goldsmith to be restraining 'natural' eloquence. A more productive impetus was offered by the example of the French, and, as I have been suggesting, by the native 'outsiders', the Methodists.

Goldsmith engages self-consciously with the Anglican suspicion of enthusiasm, writing in *The Bee* of the 'spruce preacher' who 'reads his lucubrations without lifting his nose from the text, and never ventures to earn the shame of an enthusiast'.[51] He attempts to depreciate the image of the carefully prepared sermoniser, and to endow 'enthusiasm', a term he uses repeatedly, with new value among his reading community. As the fuel of persuasion Goldsmith admires 'those rapturous enthusiasms, those irresistible turns', and he insists that these must emerge not through any contrived artistry but from the feelings prompted by a true belief in the matter of the sermon.[52] And he becomes explicit on the exemplary possibilities offered by Methodists: 'When I think of the Methodist preachers among us, how seldom they are endued with common sense, and yet how often and how justly they affect their hearers, I cannot avoid saying within myself, had these been bred gentlemen, and been endued with even the meanest share of understanding, what might they not effect!'[53] Developing this for the *Lady's Magazine*, he suggests that 'Even Whitefield may be placed as a model to some of our young divines', if 'to their own good sense' they will join 'his earnest manner of delivery'.[54]

In presenting such value in controversial public figures, who in other outlets were being satirised or condemned as agents of social decay, Goldsmith negotiates a complex relationship with his reading community. His endorsement of Methodism is firm, but always qualified with a careful distancing of his sympathy from any Methodist deviation from 'common

---

[51] *Ibid.*, vol. I, p. 480.
[52] *Ibid.*, vol. I, p. 477.
[53] *Ibid.*, vol. I, p. 481.
[54] *Ibid.*, vol. III, p. 154.

sense' – presumably the aspects of the faith associated with witchcraft and superstition (the belief, for example, that the bodies of the unconverted were inhabited by Satan). And significantly, considering the polite literary outlets of these essays, he transforms good sense into an issue of class: the Methodists lack sense because they have not 'been bred gentlemen'. As Langford has demonstrated, in the eighteenth century superstition was commonly associated with the lower classes and the 'Celtic fringe', and the construction of polite identity involved an 'elimination of superstition', which 'had to do with class, and with economic progress'.[55] So when Goldsmith defines the parameters of his approval of Methodism, he is not only clarifying the potential usefulness of the movement, but at the same time inscribing the relationship between his authorial identity and his implied readership with a sense of their shared class position. Declaring his allegiance to 'common sense', the author asserts a gentlemanly status and hails his readers as having been similarly well bred, and it is from this position of implied complicity with his readers that Goldsmith endeavours to promote a potentially challenging view of what it means for a body to be polite.

Goldsmith is questioning the practices of polite culture. In these anonymously published essays he adopts an authorial persona by which he ingratiatingly secures a place within polite culture, but from this position he articulates a detached critique of local society. With his background in Ireland and a long period of travel on the continent, Goldsmith develops a writing identity in London which is absorbed by his adopted culture but which does not shed the critical perspective provided by the foreign. In fact, although he writes about Irishness he rarely mentions his own, and, developing an image of a grandly toured English gentlemen, he regularly invokes his continental experiences when advancing ideas with which to renew British culture.[56] Goldsmith's urge to transform society is sometimes boldly explicit – in an essay of 1760 in the *Royal Magazine*, his pseud-onymous author 'H. D.', who identifies himself variously as British and English (but not Irish), wishes: 'could I teach the English to allow strangers to have their excellencies; could I mend that country in which I reside, by improvements from those which I have left behind'.[57] He suggests that

---

[55] Langford, *Polite and Commercial People*, p. 283. Langford cites the 1736 repeal of the Witchcraft Act as an index of changing attitudes to popular superstition.

[56] In the pseudo-Chinese letters that comprise *The Citizen of the World* (1760–2), Goldsmith exploited his foreignness in an alternative fictional direction; here again, though, it is partly Goldsmith's semi-detachment from society that underlies the narrative position.

[57] *Royal Magazine* (June 1760), in *Works of Oliver Goldsmith*, vol. III, p. 68.

there is an insular xenophobia in the English which will need to be over-come before any 'foreign' improvements might be allowed to cross ingrained cultural borders. And his writing on eloquence suggests that such entrenchment is maintaining questionable 'polite' oratory, the flaws in which he endeavours to expose as he illuminates the alternatives offered by Methodism.

So when Goldsmith remarks that 'the more polite the audience always the more drowsy', he is either using 'polite' with irony, or as nothing more than a class tag which is drained of its adjectival meaning. Being 'polite', if it is to imply following desirable civic practice, does not include, Goldsmith suggests, the neglect of religion, and he states that dull preach-ers are 'basely found to desert their post' if they fail to inspire religion.[58] He focuses particularly upon speakers who address the poor – that group 'who really want instruction' – and he suggests that should such speakers be clinging to an unemotive yet 'polite' mode of address, they are failing to carry out their social duties as the messengers of God.[59] The poor should be addressed, Goldsmith argues, 'not by the labours of the head, but the honest spontaneous dictates of the heart', and if an establishment institu-tion like the Anglican church is to be effective *throughout* the social hierarchy – a possibility upon which the popularity of Methodism cast doubt – then it should recognise the need to adopt new modes of address.[60] Overall, then, Goldsmith is imagining a reformulation of what it means for the body to be polite in public. Reserved delivery, Goldsmith argues, may display great self-control and it may allow the sophistication of a speech to be noticed (although perhaps not comprehended), but this is not effective civil practice and hence it should be transformed into something more emotively and effectively eloquent.

Goldsmith's attitude to Methodism was potentially controversial, but it was not unique, and we find a comparable engagement with Methodism in *The Spiritual Quixote; or, The Summer's Ramble of Mr Geoffry Wildgoose* (1773), a work in which Richard Graves deployed the popular and palatable literary vehicle of the quixotic narrative for the purposes of cultural critique. Graves (1715–1804), a longevous Anglican clergyman who pro-duced various prose and verse pieces from his parish in the west of England, began this lengthy, digressive 'comic romance' in 1757, and it was finally

[58] *Works of Oliver Goldsmith*, vol. I, p. 480.
[59] *Ibid.*, vol. I, p. 480.
[60] *Ibid.*, vol. I, p. 481.

published in 1773. With a second edition and a Dublin edition the following year, it became one of Graves's more prominent texts, and he capitalised on its success, appearing in later works as 'the Editor of *The Spiritual
Quixote*'. He was prompted to write the work by the disturbance of his
parish by an itinerant preacher, but he had already had sufficient personal
contact with Methodism to be aware of its intentions and irritated by its
consequences. John Wesley had been a visitor to the Graveses' family home
in 1729, and Graves was further acquainted with the leaders of Methodism
while at Oxford, where, it has been speculated, he may for a short time have
been a member of the Wesleys' Holy Club.[61] Graves was also on intimate
terms with Charles Wesley, and his brother was a fluctuating convert to
Methodism for about a decade and indeed became an itinerant preacher
until a final recantation in 1746.[62] Graves's own attitude towards
Methodism remains a matter of some speculation, but there are good
reasons for attributing to him the ambivalence more certainly ascertained
in *The Spiritual Quixote*.[63]

For the most part *The Spiritual Quixote* is an anti-Methodist satire
ridiculing the excesses and wrong-headedness of its protagonist, Geoffry
Wildgoose, who, when converted to Methodism, begins a career as an
itinerant preacher – it is 'an attempt to expose the ill-judged zeal of a frantic
Enthusiast', the prefatory material announces.[64] However, within the
satirical framework, there is also a creative analysis of Methodism which
is not wholly disapproving of the movement and which identifies, as does
Goldsmith's writing, particular value in the rousing oratorical practices of
its preachers.[65] One issue that becomes important within the work, then, is
the distinction between what is proper and improper behaviour for a
performing body. Like Goldsmith, Graves valorises a body image that is
both emotional and polite by indicating the exemplary possibilities
revealed by Methodist preaching; at the same time, though, his narrative's

---

[61] See Clarence Tracy, *A Portrait of Richard Graves* (Cambridge: James Clark, 1987), pp. 41–7; and
Nicholas Lyons, 'Satiric Technique in *The Spiritual Quixote*. Some Comments', *Durham
University Journal* 35 (1974), 268–71.

[62] See Tracy, *Richard Graves*, p. 41; and Lyons, 'Satiric Technique', p. 270.

[63] As Tracy does (*Richard Graves*, p. 83).

[64] Richard Graves, *The Spiritual Quixote; or, The Summer's Ramble of Mr Geoffry Wildgoose*, ed.
Clarence Tracy (London: Oxford University Press, 1967), p. 3. Subsequent references are to this
edition and are given in the text.

[65] Commentaries on *The Spiritual Quixote* have disagreed over the nature of its satire. Michael
Rymer has argued that Graves presented a wholehearted attack on Methodism in 'Satiric
Technique in *The Spiritual Quixote*', *Durham University Journal* 34 (1973), 54–64. Others,
including me, have found the critique more qualified (see Lyons, 'Satiric Technique', *passim*; and
Tracy, *Richard Graves*, p. 47 and *passim*).

sustained satire of enthusiasm has the effect of demarcating limits for polite emotionalism. And, again like Goldsmith, Graves undertakes a subtle narrative negotiation with polite readers to enable the expression of this selective approval.

The quixotic narrative was a literary form well suited to this project. When Graves began writing *The Spiritual Quixote*, there was a concentration in England of interest in and imitation of Cervantes' *Don Quixote* (1604/14), so he was working with a formula that had gained considerable recent approval as an entertaining but instructive type of writing. This mid-century preoccupation with quixotism, Brean Hammond has argued, emerged from an impulse, initiated largely by Henry Fielding, to forge a type of writing which was 'serious' but which at the same time could accommodate desirable narrative features (slapstick, satire, exciting plots) excluded from the influential formula for fiction provided by Richardson. Often contrasted with Rabelais, Cervantes was generally assimilated within eighteenth-century England as a polite author, and this eased the appropriation of his writing, which offered gratification unavailable from the more static, domestic, conversation-dominated fictions of Richardson.[66] Certainly Graves, while clearly aiming to entertain his readers, was keen to point out the serious purposes to which his own Cervantic work might be applied. *The Spiritual Quixote* contains a putative author figure, who writes a preface arguing for the practical value of this type of literature:

I can see no more harm in a Fable of this kind (if properly conducted) than in any other either mythological or parabolical representation of the truth. Nay, I am convinced that Don Quixote or Gil Blas, Clarissa or Sir Charles Grandison, will furnish more hints for correcting the follies and regulating the morals of young persons, and impress them more forcibly on their minds, than volumes of severe precepts seriously delivered and dogmatically inforced. (p. 3)

Graves pairs *Don Quixote* with *Gil Blas* (1715–35), Le Sage's French version of Spanish picaresque (published in an English edition in 1749), and holds these works up *with* but *separately from* the most monumental of Richardson's works, suggesting his awareness that these represent different types of writing although they share the common feature of being instructive. And while he recognises (and reinforces) the generic distinction that Hammond illuminates,

---

[66] 'Mid-century reinscriptions of *Don Quixote* were important', Hammond argues, 'since they enabled a form of fiction that, while it still qualified as "serious" on the criteria that were evolving in the period, nevertheless provided the readerly satisfactions that... it appeared to be Richardson's express purpose to deny' ('Mid-Century English Quixotism and the Defence of the Novel', *Eighteenth-Century Fiction* 10 (1997–8), 261).

Graves does not restrict his own work to either of the instructive traditions on offer – a fable of *The Spiritual Quixote*'s kind can be related to either pair of examples, he implies, and the work is indeed something of a hybrid of the two traditions. It is framed by the Cervantic formula and, with a nod towards Fielding's preface to *Joseph Andrews*, is identified on its title-page as '*A Comic Romance*', but its conspicuous Cervantic origins and credentials should not obscure the investment the work also has in the Richardsonian tradition. Structured around a journey, *The Spiritual Quixote* is rich in Fieldingesque humour and offers a succession of satiric and sometimes very slapstick comic scenes (Wildgoose's enthusiastic harangues, for example, are responded to with judgemental volleys of dung). But the work also contains many lengthy passages typical of sentimental writing. A long, digressive story of a Mr Rivers, for example, abounds with devices typically found in the fiction of sensibility: thwarted love, threatened virtue and consequent illness, and tearful scenes of separation. Rivers himself is something of a man of feeling, and, providing a fairly explicit register of genre, he and his wife are given assistance from 'a near relation to Sir Charles Grandison (who has since made so great a figure in the world)' (p. 222). Considering such generic diversity, it would seem that Graves sought to egg his moral omelette with whatever ('serious') narrative precedents he had to hand. But the mixed literary heritage of the work also has a further significance in that, while the Cervantic device is the means of Graves's cultural critique, *The Spiritual Quixote* ultimately approves a model of bodily performance in line with the sentimental eloquence popularised through Richardsonian fiction.

    In addition, for a project displaying before a polite readership not only the bodily excesses of enthusiastic preachers but also their exemplary qualities, the figure of the quixotic hero was, in many ways, an ideal device. For one thing, the role of Quixote – a giant among literary madmen – provided a comfortably fitting costume for the figure of the enthusiast, who, as has been seen, was being inscribed in the establishment imagination as mad and, in some cases, treated as such in Bedlam. Already, in 1738, an article in the *Gentleman's Magazine* had described enthusiasm as 'Religious Knight-Errantry', and the correspondence between Quixote and the enthusiast, as popularly perceived, injects a plausibility into much of the narrative.[67] Wildgoose's story is set in motion by a series of events comparable with many a genuine Methodist conversion: he becomes dissatisfied with the orthodox church and, under the influence

---

[67] *Gentleman's Magazine* 8 (February 1738), 89.

of various sectarian texts (counterparts to Don Quixote's romances), he is attracted to Methodism and begins to preach the New Birth. Emulating George Whitefield (whose initials he shares), Wildgoose resolves to become an itinerant preacher, and he finds his own version of Sancho Panza in one Jerry Tugwell, an earthy commonsensical cobbler, who joins him as a travelling companion. Their journey generates numerous comic encounters and opportunities for Wildgoose to preach, the latter bringing both converts and regular persecution by angry crowds. Importantly, so far as this novel's 'body work' is concerned, therefore, this application of the Cervantic formula generates many scenes *dramatising public performance* – episodes where Wildgoose's performing body is depicted in action, being witnessed and judged by onlookers.

There is a further quality of quixotic madness, though, which makes the Cervantic formula more apt still as a vehicle for the useful instruction that Graves (or, at least, the putative author who greatly resembles Graves) is keen to point out in his narrative. Graves urges the opening of polite eloquence to the controlled influence of the Methodist example, and he advances this cultural work by exploiting an ambivalence in how the quixote's madness might be viewed in relation to conventional, authorised practice. A central tension of *Don Quixote* involves the confrontation and confusion between madness and the law.[68] *Don Quixote* shows contemporary law in conflict with the quixote's 'mad' chivalric codes of honour, but it provides no straightforward direction as to which system is finally preferable. Readers are faced with negotiating the ambiguous and uncertain status of his difference – as Susan Staves has put it: 'Is Don Quixote a buffoon whose delusion reveals only his insane pride and the total absurdity of the literature which has provoked his quest? Or is he an exemplary figure who refuses to be sullied by the filthy reality of a fallen world?'[69] In Graves's transposition of *Don Quixote*, there is a similar tension in the depiction of Wildgoose, who wavers between appearing as a risible, deluded fool and as an admirable exemplar.

The Spiritual Quixote presents a type of vacillating satire, then, and one of its principal themes is the relation between passion and propriety in the pulpit. Early in the work, as Wildgoose becomes disenchanted with the established church, he declares Anglican worship to be 'a tedious piece of

---

[68] See Hammond, 'Mid-Century English Quixotism', pp. 266–7; and Douglas, *Uneasy Sensations*, pp. 116–29.

[69] Susan Staves, 'Don Quixote in Eighteenth-Century England', *Comparative Literature* 24 (1972), 194.

lip-labour, without the least edification' (p. 25), and, for him, the reform of
religion is a matter not so much of theology but of the *physical presentation*
of that theology. Indeed, there are moments when Wildgoose's words read
almost like an elocutionary handbook. Discussing contemporary religion,
he insists that

the fault is not in the service, but in those who perform it. The most pious
sentiments will affect us but little, when delivered by the lips of those who appear
to have no religion in their hearts; and loll on their elbows, and stare about for
objects of amusement; as if their devotions were a fatigue and confinement to
them. (p. 177)

Wildgoose is advanced in his quixotic pursuits by this point in the novel,
but there is no mad enthusiasm in such statements as these. Rather, the
character functions here as a mouthpiece for the increasingly mainstream
eighteenth-century argument that for oratory to *be effective* it must *appear
affective*, and that orators who do not visibly appeal to the passions will
have little command over their congregations. Like the elocutionists discussed in the previous chapter, Wildgoose understands passionate
exchange to be vital to public address, and he shares the view that the
body is integral to such communication. From the outset, he is

sufficiently sensible of the difference between mere talking, and preaching in a
fanatical manner. Where nothing was intended but informing the understanding,
the former alone might answer the end: but where the passions were to be moved
and the affections engaged, a more vehement action (approaching to gesticulation), a greater earnestness, and more impassioned tone of voice, were to be made
use of. (p. 26)

And throughout the narrative, Graves engineers opportunities for
Wildgoose to stress, in true sentimental fashion, that the body's gestures
must be employed in appealing to the passions – that 'the silent rhetoric of
tears . . . is often more pathetic than all the oratorical flourishes in the
world' (p. 125).

Alongside his abstract understanding of preaching techniques,
Wildgoose has the qualifications to put theory into effective practice. In
body Wildgoose is fundamentally a polite creature. He has 'in his person
and behaviour something naturally agreeable, an openness of countenance
and a simplicity of manners' (p. 14), and, prior to his departure from the
established church, he 'had always been remarkably decent in his behaviour
at the public worship . . . made his responses with an audible voice . . . [and
surpassed his neighbours] in his external deportment at church' (p. 17). As
the novel advances, we are reminded that Wildgoose has 'naturally a good

elocution, an harmonious voice, and an agreeable person' (p. 144), but these decent, polite qualities become obscured by his enthusiasm. Reading sectarian literature produces in Wildgoose 'that sort of phrenzy, which we ascribe to enthusiasts . . . whose imaginations are so entirely possessed by those ideas, as to make them talk and act like madmen, in the sober eye of merely rational people' (p. 20). And thus Wildgoose's eloquence, whilst undoubtedly persuasive, becomes the vehicle not of any polite discourse but of one imbued with madness. At times, Wildgoose is almost a caricature enthusiast, preaching 'with eyes fixed and foaming mouth' (p. 26), or haranguing on 'wrath and indignation, fire and brimstone with great zeal and vehement gesticulations' (p. 105). Elsewhere, Graves's descriptions of Wildgoose in action are more complex and suggest the contiguity of enthusiasm and sound, passionate eloquence. Preaching in Gloucester, Wildgoose is presented as having

something naturally agreeable in his countenance, and also a very musical tone of voice: and though, in the vehemence of his harangues, he had a wildness in his looks, proceeding from the enthusiastic zeal which possessed his imagination, yet that very circumstance gave a more pathetic force to his eloquence. And he himself appearing so much in earnest, and affected with the subject, it had a proportionable effect upon his audience. (p. 73)

Like Goldsmith, Graves is mediating the troubling implications of a form of eloquence which is highly persuasive but also passionate beyond reason. Fired with enthusiasm, Wildgoose appears mad – he has 'wildness in his looks' – but at the same time he is deploying a 'pathetic force' which successfully excites the interest and emotions of his audience. When, earlier, Wildgoose foams at the mouth, he is, to the 'sober eye' that Graves invokes, fairly obviously the object of satire, but passages such as this demand a more complex response, as Wildgoose can neither be fully approved as a sentimental preacher nor straightforwardly laughed at as a comic maniac.

Graves can by no means approve the mad excesses associated with enthusiasm. Wildgoose expresses madness through his body language, but he also proliferates it through his preaching. As Graves has Tugwell observe, Wildgoose 'does preach main well, that is certain; but as for *convarting*, methinks some of them are only *convarted* from bad to worse' (p. 319). He creates many converts in Wales, where the fact that it is principally his body that speaks madness becomes comically emphatic when we are told that those 'most affected . . . did not understand a word of English' – the narrator attributes this to 'the vehemence and apparent sincerity of the Orator, and the mechanical and infectious operation of an enthusiastic energy' (p. 269). In fact, Wildgoose's followers contract bodily eccentricities even more extreme than those shown by the preacher himself. A group of the Welsh converts wake Wildgoose and Tugwell with a nocturnal display of enthusiasm: 'the people had worked themselves up to such a pitch of religious phrenzy, that some were fallen prostrate upon the floor, screaming, and roaring, and beating their breasts, in agonies of remorse for their former wicked lives; others were singing hymns, leaping and exulting in extasies of joy, that their sins were forgiven them' (p. 294). That such violent bodily behaviour should be recognised as dangerous mania by readers is stressed through its friction with the worldly common sense of Tugwell, who declares that 'these Welsh people are all mad, I think; I never heard such rantipole doings since I was born; a body cannot sleep o' nights for 'em' (p. 295). They are bodies out of control, and their manic behaviour is presented as an anti-social force interfering with the lives of more orderly beings, such as Tugwell, for whom nights should be used for sleeping. For Wildgoose, however, these unruly displays are the 'symptoms of the New Birth!' (p. 295), and he actively celebrates such somatic eccentricity. When another harangue is interrupted by a man who has 'been almost mad ever since he had heard Mr. Wesley preach', Wildgoose is impressed: ' "Mad!" quoth Wildgoose; "I wish all that hear me this day were not only *almost*, but altogether as mad as this poor countryman. No," says he, "these are the true symptoms of the New Birth" ' (p. 281). By presenting these various responses, then, *The Spiritual Quixote* holds up alternative ways of reading the enthusiastic body. In the same way as Don Quixote mistakes windmills for giants, Wildgoose sees faith in the enthusiast where Graves would have his readers recognise madness.

But while Graves articulates this powerful critique of mania, he does not dismiss the vehemence of Methodists out of hand in the manner of Theophilus Evans and other ardent anti-enthusiasts. Rather, he uses his novel to set out a programme by which the example offered by the Methodists might be refined and, in a moderated form, incorporated within polite practice. The most explicit presentation of an approved model for bodily eloquence emerges from the conversations of the narrative's concluding scenes, in which Wildgoose is 'cured' of his enthusiasm through the wisdom of Dr Greville. This saviour is, in many ways, a pillar of polite society – an ideal figure for bringing about Wildgoose's reclamation and re-establishment within mainstream culture. He himself has his character written upon his body: he is 'a Clergyman, in whom the sacerdotal character appeared in its genuine dignity; not in an assumed solemnity of aspect, or formal grimace, and a pompous perriwig . . . but in a serious, yet affable, behaviour; the result of a sincere piety, sanctity of manners, and goodness of heart' (p. 432). And he holds firm principles that everything should be 'done decently and in order' and that 'no one has a right to break through the regulations of society, merely from the suggestions of his own fancy' (p. 449). Through the sober advice and guidance of this affable disciplinarian, Wildgoose becomes convinced of the errors of his enthusiastic ways, but whilst his Methodist exploits are generally discredited, his experiences none the less present ideas relating to bodily conduct with which Dr Greville can readily agree. Wildgoose discusses with his restorer the state of public preaching:

'I wish the Clergy would be a little more earnest in their delivery, and inforce their precepts with some little vehemence of tone and action; as I am convinced what an effect it would have upon the most rational Christians.

'I am sensible indeed, from what I felt when I first heard Mr. Whitfield, that too violent gesticulations are not agreeable to the modesty and reserve of an English audience; and there is certainly a difference between the action of the Pulpit and of the Stage. But, when a Preacher reads his sermon with as much coldness and indifference as he would read a news-paper, or an act of parliament; he must not be surprized, if his audience discover the same indifference, or even take a nap, especially if the service be after dinner.'

'Why, there is no doubt', replies Dr. Greville, 'but an empassioned tone of voice, a suitable gesture, and a pathetic style, have more effect upon the middling and lower ranks of mankind, for whose use sermons are chiefly intended, than the most rational discourse, delivered in a dry uninteresting manner. And this certainly is one great advantage which the Methodists and other fanatical Preachers have over the regular Clergy, in rousing so many indolent drowsy Christians to a sense of Religion.' (p. 463)

The Spiritual Quixote imagines a spectrum of possible bodily action, and between the poles of manic enthusiasm and soporific reserve it seeks to identify a mode of expression which is at once eloquent and polite. A body marked with 'too violent gesticulations' falls outside of Graves's polite realm; such a realm should be represented by bodies which, with greater modesty, display 'some little vehemence of tone and action . . . a suitable gesture, and a pathetic style'.

As the quixote is re-established within the Anglican church, Graves asserts the authority of the establishment system he represents, but he does so only after its flaws have been put on public display and after marginally sited ideas for its improvement have been posited. Wildgoose's story opens up an interrogation of the bodily behaviour that is appropriate to polite society, and textually approved practice is discovered either side of legally sanctioned borders – both at the heart of 'polite' (but improvable) society and at the Moorfields.[70] As in Cervantes' original, then, quixotism involves here a deviation from dominant ideology, and its cure represents a return to orthodox values, but, through the proposition of deviance, established norms are exposed both as flawed and as ameliorable through a selective application of the quixote's alternative world-view.

In fact, it is in such a way, I believe, that the unruly bodies I have been considering here served eighteenth-century politeness more generally (it is no surprise that enthusiasm should have been dubbed 'Religious Knight-Errantry' long before Graves's novel, and that John Henley should have been said to have 'No equal . . . 'Midst all the *Quixots* of divinity').[71] A body animated by *too much* passion – a violently expressive body or one suggest-ing madness – could never be fully endorsed, let alone imitated, by 'polite' spectators, for it appeared to symbolise values antipathetic to the culture they represented, which, however supportive of 'sympathy' as a basis for human relations, clearly preferred the passions to be held in check with conspicuous reason. But an unruly body could none the less captivate spectators with the alternative forms of performance it offered. In the case of Henley, such a body was able to fire a keen public interest in oratory and, by appearing impolite, was able to animate public discourse concerning the division between what *was* and what *was not* polite somatic conduct. Methodist enthusiasts served a similar function, but, more than Henley, they also offered positive attractions from within their alterity. Indeed, the persuasive passions of the enthusiast provoked a partial liber-ation of what polite bodies might actually do.

---

[70] It is worth while here to compare Goldsmith's remark: 'At present, the enthusiasms of the poor are opposed to law; did law conspire with their enthusiasms, we should not only be the happiest nation upon earth, but the wisest also' (*Works of Oliver Goldsmith*, vol. I, p. 482).

[71] *Gentleman's Magazine* 27 (April 1757), 181.

CHAPTER 3

Thomas Sheridan:
forging the British body

[A] new Book came into the World under the specious Title of
BRITISH EDUCATION: said to be wrote by THOMAS SHERIDAN . . .
Bless us, what a Cry was rais'd! Ladies that could not spare time
from the Card-table, even on *Sundays*, to read a Chapter in their
Bible, or afford half an Hour to consider how Affairs stand between
God and their Souls, yet contrived to snatch some Intervals for the
reading of Mr. *Sheridan's* Book.

Anon. (1769)[1]

NATIONAL BODIES

Graves and Goldsmith were writing their works during a period in which
the business of forging 'natural' eloquence among the subjects of Britain
had acquired a new degree of public prominence. Much of this interest in
matters of public eloquence was due to the sensational publication in 1756
of Thomas Sheridan's weighty and controversial *British Education*. This
was the first of several works in which Sheridan addressed elocution, and in
it he laid out the central contention of all his later writing, arguing that an
improvement in standards of oratory – including a reform of the manner in
which public bodies should perform – would significantly contribute to the
strength and stability of the nation.

When Sheridan thought about his nation, he had in mind 'Great
Britain' – a relatively new concept in his time, described by Linda Colley
in her celebrated *Britons: Forging the Nation 1707–1837* as 'an invented
nation superimposed . . . onto much older alignments and loyalties'.[2] This
new nation was by no means a naturally cohesive or coherent unit, but
following the political union of England and Wales with Scotland in 1707,

---

[1] Anon., *A True History of the Scheme for erecting a new Seminary for Education* (Dublin, 1769), p. 5.
[2] Linda Colley, *Britons: Forging the Nation 1707–1837* (New Haven: Yale University Press, 1992), p. 5.

influential notions of Britishness were fostered through various cultural enterprises and through the identification of practices and beliefs that Britain's diverse peoples could be said to have in common. Colley identifies particularly Protestantism, commercialism, and imperial advancement as areas of allegiance around which a sense of British identity could be felt by otherwise divided social groups. Sheridan's project was similarly involved in 'forging the nation', as he aimed to further the processes of patriotic construction by spreading a refined form of the English language throughout Britain, and by developing a programme of polite physical eloquence by which that English should be delivered in public. A standardisation and refinement of the way people spoke, Sheridan insisted, would strengthen the nation both as a unified domestic unit pervaded throughout its constituent parts by the inhabitants' sense of their shared Britishness and as a world power made stronger by an internally coherent identity.[3]

Eloquence, as imagined by Sheridan, was something already belonging to 'the most august body in the world, the people of Great Britain' (*BE*, p. v), but in a period he deemed degenerate, in which 'irreligion, immorality, and corruption are visibly increased, and daily gather new strength' (*BE*, p. 1), it was in need of rediscovery and anchorage through the proper education of the nation. The reform of eloquence, therefore, is accorded an absolute centrality in Sheridan's plans to improve the nation. *British Education*, the subtitle states, is

An Essay towards proving, that the Immorality, Ignorance, and false Taste, which so generally prevail, are the natural and necessary Consequences of the present defective System of Education. With An Attempt to shew, that a revival of the Art of Speaking, and the Study of Our Own Language, might contribute, in a great measure, to the Cure of those Evils.

And in the introductory material of the book, Sheridan further emphasises the vital importance of reformed eloquence within his project, summarising it as '*A design to revive the long lost art of oratory, and to correct, ascertain, and fix the English language*' (*BE*, p. vi). Driven with a sense that oratory was a fundamental key to social, moral, and intellectual change, Sheridan devoted the latter half of his life to 'fixing the language', attempting to

---

[3] Sheridan was not alone in his mission, and the fixing of a common language – partly effective, partly aspirational – was an important enterprise which contributed to the emergence of Britain as a conceivable nation. It is as part of this wider movement that Sheridan's work should be viewed. Colley touches upon language reform in the emergence of Britishness; it is given fuller treatment in Barrell's chapter on 'The Language Properly So-Called: The Authority of Common Usage', in *Equal, Wide Survey*, pp. 110–75.

body is important to all aspects of sensibility

standardise the pronunciation of English, nurturing the art of reading aloud, and developing the many aspects of public delivery relating both to the spoken word and to its ~~accompanying bodily gestures~~. Indeed, language reform became even more paramount in Sheridan's work than its location in the subtitle of *British Education* might suggest it was originally, and in later works, such as the *Lectures on Elocution* (1762), Sheridan's primary interests are displayed as the first object of attention.

Sheridan's patriotic interest in defining and spreading polite delivery drew significantly upon existing ideas of national differences, and he planned to reinforce these differences through the further promotion of British eloquence against that of other European powers, notably France. Appearing in a year in which the beginning of the Seven Years War massively aggravated the tensions between Britain and France (the countries had been at peace, militarily at least, since 1748), *British Education* capitalised upon and furthered a fierce dislike of things French in its drive to shape a notion of what it meant to be British.[4] Unlike Goldsmith, who saw embedded in French culture potential examples from which the British might learn, Sheridan asserted the true (if lost) quality of British identity in opposition to the corrupt practices of the French, which he regarded as all too pervasive. In a passage which wavers unsteadily between the metaphorical and the literal, he argued

Too long have the beauties of the British muse, like those of our ladies, been concealed, or spoiled, by foreign modes and false ornaments. The paint and patches of the French, the fantastical head-dress, the squeezing stays, and enormous hoop, only spoil the bloom of her complexion, the flowing ringlets of her hair, her easy shape, and graceful mein...Thus adorned like an harlot, she inflames the youth with wanton desires, and spreads the infection thro' the land. What hopes can there be of a robust and healthy offspring from such impure embraces? Let us endeavour to recover her from the tyrannical sway of fashion and prejudice, and restore her to her native rights. Let us leave to the fallow French their rouge and white paint, but let the British red and white appear in it's genuine lustre, as laid on by nature's own pencil. Let them torture the body into a fantastick shape, or conceal crookedness under an armour of steel; let them cover puny limbs, and a mincing gait, under the wide circumference of a hoop; but let the easy mein, the comely stature, the fine proportioned limbs decently revealed, and the unrestrained majesty of motion in the British muse, be displayed to sight in their native charms. (*BE*, pp. 365–6)

---

[4] Gallophobia, indeed, can be seen as a further strand in the emergence of Britishness, and Colley argues that casting the French as a threatening 'other' furthered a sense of British unity through opposition (*Britons*, pp. 1–7).

It is not always entirely clear when Sheridan is discussing 'the British muse' here and when he has turned his attention to more earthly bodies – it is almost as though he has to remind himself at the end of the passage of the metaphorical path on which he began. But that he should depict general- ised national differences through a metaphor of the body is revealing firstly of his obsessive preoccupations with that subject – almost all his works are in some way concerned with the language of the body. And that the metaphor should slip into literality is further suggestive of the crucial role that, as we shall see, Sheridan believed the individual eloquent body played in forming nations and in emblematising their most deep-seated values. The 'squeezing stays, and enormous hoop' – or, let us say, all that is somehow a constrictive or masking imposition upon what 'nature's own pencil' is supposed to have drawn – are symbolically representative, for Sheridan, of a nation that is lost to sophistication, but in the broader context of his writing, in which the eloquent body is fundamental to national glory, they are also a very literal cause of that nation's corruption (despite, of course, Sheridan's bitter awareness that, in terms of cultural influence beyond its borders, France was doing rather well). The British muse, in contrast, is imagined with her 'unrestrained majesty of motion' and with her natural reds and whites – as though the skins of British ladies were organically endowed with the flag of St George – so that Sheridan in effect claims the ability to be natural as a peculiarly British prerogative. And if that peculiar gift could be rediscovered and fostered, Sheridan argues, the nation would emerge as the greatest power in the world. 'Would not London', he asks rhetorically (before wishing poverty and a total loss of spirits upon the French), 'become the capital not of England, but of the world; and England be considered as a queen of nations?' (*BE*, p. 490).

He was, perhaps unsurprisingly, seen to be making exaggerated claims for what improved oratory might achieve. David Hume was not alone when he complained that Sheridan's lectures 'are vastly too enthusiastic. He is to do everything by Oratory.'[5] But despite the doubtlessly accurate apprehension that his interests were slightly hobbyhorsical, Sheridan was,

[5] In W. Benzie, *The Dublin Orator: Thomas Sheridan's Influence on Eighteenth-Century Rhetoric and Belles Lettres* (Leeds: Scolar Press, 1972), p. 25. The later elocutionist John Walker, author of *Elements of Elocution* (1781) – a tract largely based on James Burgh's work – concurred with Hume: 'His enthusiasm as to what oratory will do, may be too great: but he reads well' (Boswell, *Life of Johnson*, p. 1224). Lord Chesterfield argued much the same, writing in a letter 'Sheridan has lately published here an excellent book, entitled *British Education*. Warmed with his subject, he pushes it rather too far … but, upon the whole, it is both a very useful and entertaining book' (in Benzie, *Dublin Orator*, p. 5). Samuel Foote produced some of the more public criticism of Sheridan, satirising him in the plays *The Orators* (1762) and *The Mayor of Garret* (1764).

as we shall see, highly successful in broadcasting his claims for oratory throughout much of Britain and in penetrating deeply into its polite and fashionable cultural centres. While much of his work was certainly never more than aspirational, he became the best-known elocutionist of the mid century and, as such, he held a significant position in the business of constructing politeness. The hostile writer describing the initial reception of *British Education* (quoted in the epigraph to this chapter) dramatises responses to the work in such a way as to debase it: by proposing the text's appeal to a reading community of women and (worse!) card-playing women and (worse still!) card-playing women who overlook their bibles, the writer is positing Sheridan's work as an empty thing of fashion, devoid of any serious educational or moral content. At the same time, though, the writer is suggesting the very broad appeal that Sheridan's writing attracted, and also his ability to inspire new interest in education and elocution among groups of people not normally drawn to such matters. The same capacity – an ability to enfranchise new subjects in a culture in which the reformulation of language and of delivered speech is *an issue* – is also suggested by the appeal of his very popular public lectures. Indeed, Sheridan's cultural infiltration lends him a significance that is often over-looked in modern eighteenth-century studies, where he tends either to be obscured by his more famous dramatist son, Richard Brinsley Sheridan, or to be apprehended through the pointed phrases of Samuel Johnson.[6] 'Sherry is dull, naturally dull', is one of the more memorable remarks from Johnson's mostly dismissive statements regarding Sheridan.[7] Johnson's antipathy towards Sheridan, it is worth pointing out, arose partly out of jealousy. In 1762 there had developed, in Boswell's words, 'an irreconcileable difference' between the two, and while history tends to applaud Johnson in his spats and to grant him the upper hand of cultural authority, the root cause of this difference – the awarding by Lord Bute of an annual government pension of two hundred pounds to assist Sheridan in his work – is actually a further indication of the notice and support that Sheridan was attracting to the business of elocutionary reform.[8]

---

[6] Only two full-length studies of Sheridan have appeared: Esther K. Sheldon's *Thomas Sheridan of Smock-Alley* (Princeton: Princeton University Press, 1967) addresses his work in the Dublin theatre prior to his career as an elocutionist; W. Benzie's *Dublin Orator* outlines Sheridan's later work and provides summaries of the arguments contained in his published works on elocution and grammar. Benzie touches on Sheridan's patriotic concerns (p. 14), but does not develop a discussion of this aspect of his work. Sheridan's later work is also discussed in Wallace A. Bacon, 'The Elocutionary Career of Thomas Sheridan (1718–1788)', *Speech Monographs* 31 (1964), 1–53.

[7] Boswell, *Life of Johnson*, p. 320.

[8] *Ibid.*, p. 273.

There are other features of Sheridan's work that are of particular relevance for this study, in that his projections of polite eloquent bodies amounted to a commercialised development of the processes shown earlier in the rewriting and transformation of Le Faucheur's strictures regarding physical expression: Sheridan importantly advanced the sentimentalisation of the body. Asserting that naturalness was part of the British 'spirit', he proposed that the polite body should find its expression through natural feeling, and he laid down no strict rules for governing the body's manage-ment. I shall examine the details of Sheridan's ideal bodily eloquence later, but first want to consider the social and institutional conditions that enabled (and invited) its promotion in mid-eighteenth-century Britain. For like John Henley, but with more establishment approval than Henley ever attracted, Sheridan made much of his later living from promoting a sentimentalised model of polite eloquence, and this career in constructing politeness – something that would have been unsustainable without the exploitable resources of Britain's bourgeois classes – is revealing of the high status that such polite pursuits had acquired by the mid century.

SHERIDAN'S PUBLIC LIFE

Accounts of Sheridan's career – his education in Ireland and England, his close relationship to his godfather Jonathan Swift (himself an ardent language reformer),[9] his beginnings in the Irish theatre, his movements as an actor and theatre manager between Dublin and London, prior to his becoming an elocutionist who published busily on the subject and embarked on lecture tours across Britain – have been given already in the works of Esther K. Sheldon, Wallace A. Bacon, and W. Benzie, but a few material points from that narrative may here usefully illuminate Sheridan's role in mid-century polite culture. Sheridan's life was remarkably public. His work took him across a series of prominent public platforms – the prin-cipal theatres (Smock-Alley, Covent Garden, Drury Lane, Crow-Street, the Haymarket) and lecture halls in London, Oxford, Cambridge, Bath, Edinburgh, and other major cities – from which he endeavoured through example and through argument to transform the behaviour of the paying

---

[9] The influence upon Sheridan's work by Jonathan Swift, a close friend of Sheridan's father – another Thomas (1687–1738) – is suggested by Sheridan's recollection of Swift's inquiries into the education he was receiving at Trinity in Dublin: 'When I told him the Course of Reading I was put into, he asked me, Do they teach you English? No. Do they teach you how to speak? No. Then, said he, they teach you Nothing' (in Sheldon, *Thomas Sheridan of Smock-Alley*, p. 16).

public gathered before him. His published texts were certainly important and they provide a legacy of his work, but particularly in the case of the *Lectures on Elocution*, the printed matter should be recognised partly as a spin-off (with both commercial and educational ends) from his popular public performances.

Sheridan, in other words, aimed to transform British eloquence by exploiting the opportunities presented by the widespread interest in attending the theatre and fashionable lectures. Indeed, this intention is suggested by his own claims concerning his early work as an actor. According to an account he wrote some fourteen years after his acting debut in Dublin in 1743, his work in the theatre was pursued always with a view to developing educational work as an elocutionist. In *An Oration pronounced before a Numerous Body of the Nobility and Gentry* (1757), a speech delivered and published in Dublin the year after *British Education* had appeared, he declared that his becoming an actor was an obvious route towards gaining practical experience in the art of speaking. He further suggested that he remained in the theatre with hopes of setting up an academy for training promising actors so that the theatre 'would become an admirable Assistant to the School of Oratory, by furnishing to the young Students constant good Models and Examples in all the different species of Eloquence'.[10] Such declarations should be read with some caution, for they may have been the anxious justifications of a man conscious of a perceived lowly status as an actor and of the difficulties involved in transforming his trade into that of a respectable educationalist. But these comments nevertheless suggest Sheridan's apprehension that the existing institutions of eighteenth-century cultural life were open to change and manipulation and were ready to be appropriated for the purposes of cultural reconstruction. In this respect, the original setting of the Dublin *Oration* is also significant. The *Oration* was addressed, as Sheridan's title proudly states, to '*a numerous body of the Nobility and Gentry*'; this august group of listeners was '*assembled at the Musick-hall in Fishamble Street*' in order to hear of this '*new scheme of education*'. This use of one of mid-century Dublin's most fashionable venues firstly suggests Sheridan's expedient employment of a public space in order to accommodate new interests in redeveloping social practices. But with the record of the venue intact in the title of the published speech, it would seem also that, from this early stage, Sheridan wished to signal that his work was valuable not only for its

[10] Thomas Sheridan, *An Oration pronounced before a Numerous Body of the Nobility and Gentry* (Dublin, 1757), pp. 23–4.

reformatory ends but also as a type of entertainment for the polite classes.[11] And the latter appeal of his lectures is certainly evident from his subsequent successful tours of the fashionable centres of eighteenth-century British cultural life. That he should lecture by invitation in the universities of Oxford and Cambridge as he did in 1758 and 1759 (and indeed be awarded an honorary MA) testifies to the degree of establishment approval he gained, but that he should take his lectures to the more recreationally attuned scene of Bath points firmly to his parallel status as a fashionable entertainer.

Speaking to the Dublin gentry in 1757, Sheridan was attempting to establish a new educational academy, the 'Hibernian Society', devoted to qualifying young Irishmen 'in all the Accomplishments of a Gentleman to make a Figure in polite Life, and to assist him in acquiring a just Taste in the liberal Arts, founded upon Skill'.[12] Sheridan's focus here, as elsewhere, was upon making 'Gentlemen' – he gave some attention to women's education, and considered the advantages brought to the lower classes by the example of gentlemen, but he did not address lower-class education directly. Indeed, Sheridan's overall project hinged precisely upon crafting this 'Figure in polite Life' – upon refining the image and conduct of the publicly visible man, who would represent 'polite Life' and thereby disperse the mores associated with it. The academy Sheridan envisioned was to be an educational factory turning out human emblems of polite culture, and the scheme met with considerable enthusiasm. Soon after the Dublin *Oration*, Sheridan told Samuel Richardson (who was educating the nation in related polite ways through his three novels) that the Hibernian Society had a subscription list of 'upwards of two hundred names ... amongst which there are forty-eight Members of Parliament',[13] and, despite opposition to the plan expressed in several pamphlets, a Hibernian Academy for the education of Irishmen was opened, the same year as the Guinness brewery, in 1759. In fact, unlike the brewery, the academy declined after a few years – according to Benzie, its failure was largely due to attacks made upon it by private schoolmasters – but Sheridan's success as a lecturer continued.[14] After one course of lectures on elocution given in London in 1759, the *Public Advertiser* announced a second course following the public

---

[11] The Fishamble Street music hall was established in 1741 and was the setting for such events as the first performance of Handel's *Messiah* in 1742 (see Patrick Fagan, *The Second City: Portrait of Dublin 1700–1760* (Dublin: Branar, 1986), p. 60).

[12] Sheridan, *Oration*, p. 25.

[13] *Correspondence of Samuel Richardson*, vol. IV, pp. 173–4.

[14] Benzie, *Dublin Orator*, p. 18.

pressures upon Sheridan, 'being encouraged by the favourable reception which his first course of lectures met with, and being urged to it by the unanimous desire of the subscribers'.[15] And such pressure was not merely the puffing fiction of an advertiser. An account by Sheridan's wife, the play-wright and sentimental novelist Frances Sheridan, records the popularity of the lectures: describing a course given in London in 1762, she wrote

The Course of Lectures which Mr. Sheridan is now reading in the city is attended in a manner that shows the people more warm and earnest on the subject than can well be conceived; his auditory seldom consisting of less than five hundred people, and this is the utmost the hall will contain; many have been disappointed for want of room, and he is strenuously solicited to repeat the Course again immediately in the same place. This I believe he will comply with, though he is to give another Course next month at Spring-Gardens.[16]

Like Henley's lectures, Sheridan's were commercially as well as education-ally motivated, and the squeezed crowds described by Frances Sheridan were willingly paying considerable sums to attend these fashionable events. In his memoirs of Sheridan's son, John Watkins records the subscription fee of a guinea per head for the London lectures – a substantial amount which 'upwards of sixteen hundred' paid.[17] And the published version of the lectures was sold by subscription at half a guinea (in boards), with a list (declared as incomplete) prefacing the work of more than six hundred individuals who had signed up for copies at the public lectures. The list itself suggests the profile of Sheridan's audiences: they consisted predomin-antly of gentlemen, but there were also numerous clergy, and several military men and members of parliament; about 10 per cent of the subscribers were women. Sheridan maintained his standing among such a community, and in 1780 a similar body of subscribers was attracted to his *A General Dictionary of the English Language*.

Sheridan also had popular success in Scotland, and his interest in establishing a firm notion of Britishness across the regions of the politically united countries was furthered through his invitation in 1761 to lecture in Edinburgh. He was invited to Edinburgh by the Select Society, an organ-ised group of intellectuals and social commentators including many of the key figures of the Scottish Enlightenment. James Boswell, who eagerly took measures to improve his own pronunciation, records the summer of 1761,

---

[15] *Public Advertiser* (5 March 1759), in Benzie, *Dublin Orator*, p. 21.
[16] Samuel Whyte, *Miscellanea Nova* (Dublin, 1800; rept. New York and London: Garland, 1974), pp. 104–5.
[17] John Watkins, *Memoirs of R. B. Sheridan* (London, 1817), p. 79.

when 'Mr. Thomas Sheridan was at Edinburgh, and delivered lectures upon the English Language and Publick Speaking to large and respectable audiences'.[18] Sheridan's course was intensive: he lectured four times a week for four weeks, and presented a reduced course of the lectures for women. Later works of the Scottish Enlightenment are indebted to Sheridan's proposals for improved delivery – Hugh Blair, the first Professor of Rhetoric and *Belles Lettres* in Edinburgh, and the author of *Lectures on Rhetoric and Belles Lettres* (1783), acknowledges in a footnote to a lecture on 'Pronunciation, Or Delivery' that 'On this whole subject, Mr. Sheridan's Lectures on Elocution, are very worthy of being consulted; and several hints are here taken from them.'[19] Sheridan was welcomed in Scotland, or at least by its élite metropolitan community, largely because of the training he offered with regard to accent. During this period, there was, as Benzie puts it, 'a stigma attached to the "vulgar" Scottish accent and to Scotticisms in written English', because of Edinburgh's position as a world centre of intellectual and cultural activity and 'the need for Scots MPs to make themselves understood in London after the Union'.[20] Such a desire among Scots to Anglicise their vocal character is shown by the example of the Scottish lawyer Alexander Wedderburne (later Lord Loughborough), whose transformation of his accent constituted for Boswell an almost Ovidian metamorphosis. Wedderburne provided, Boswell suggested, 'animating encouragement to other gentlemen of North-Britain to try their fortunes in the southern part of the Island', where, with an adjusted manner of speaking, the opportunities to fulfil professional ambition were far greater than north of the border.[21] Sheridan himself recorded other examples of successful Anglicisation. In an essay on 'Rhetorical Grammar', which prefaced his *General Dictionary*, he recalled the interest his Edinburgh lectures had inspired, remembering an 'ardour ... for obtaining a just and polished delivery ... among the young gentlemen of Scotland'. He cites the 'extraordinary instance' of Lord Aylmoor, who, without setting foot outside Scotland, nevertheless developed an Anglicised

[18] Boswell, *Life of Johnson*, p. 273. In the same work Boswell writes of how he had 'taken some pains to improve my pronunciation, by the aid of the late Mr. Love, of Drury-lane theatre, when he was a player at Edinburgh, and also of old Mr. Sheridan' (p. 469).
[19] Hugh Blair, *Lectures on Rhetoric and Belles Lettres*, ed. Harold F. Harding, 2 vols. (Carbondale and Edwardsville: Southern Illinois University Press, 1965), vol. II, p. 205. Blair's debts to Sheridan, and those of George Campbell, are discussed briefly in Edward P. J. Corbett's and James L. Golden's introduction to *The Rhetoric of Blair, Campbell, and Whately* (New York: Holt, Rinehart and Winston, 1968), p. 14.
[20] Benzie, *Dublin Orator*, p. 23.
[21] Boswell, *Life of Johnson*, p. 274.

intonation by 'conversing with such Englishmen as happened to be there, and reading regularly with some of the principal actors'.[22]

With his success in Scotland, the fact that Sheridan should have *not* taken his lectures to Wales is a suggestive silence in his career that further illuminates the commercial framework within which such polite reform as he offered was conducted. He was by no means inattentive to that part of the nation, and apparently desired that the Welsh as much as the Scots should be enfranchised within his vision of a culturally and linguistically united Britain. In *British Education* he regretted the absence of an effective English dictionary before the appearance of Johnson's just a few months earlier, and he described the particular need for one in the linguistically diversified British lands:

there were three different nations, the Scotch, Irish, and Welch, who made up a considerable part of the British dominions, both in power and extent, who spoke in tongues different from the English, and who were far from being firmly united with them in inclinations, and of course were pursuing different interests. To accomplish an entire union with these people, was of the utmost importance to them, to which nothing could have more effectually contributed, than the universality of one common language. (*BE*, pp. 213–14)

Later in his own dictionary he included a short passage on Welsh pronunciation and on means by which the Welsh 'might get rid of their provincial dialect'.[23] But he did not actively advance or develop his project – one of English linguistic imperialism within a mixed nation – in Wales. The conditions in Wales were not ideal for Sheridan, who was not a reformer who would travel to voice his cause wherever it seemed to be pertinent. To begin with, most of the Welsh population in the eighteenth century were monoglot speakers of Welsh, and Sheridan was not a teacher of English, but a teacher of *refinement* in delivered English.[24] Furthermore, the Welsh communities were mostly rural, disparate, and relatively poor, and Wales 'had no universities or capital city like Edinburgh to serve as a focus for its cultural life'.[25] Hence there was no centre where Sheridan might attract a suitable paying audience. He was not a zealot for his cause to the extent of, say, John Wesley, who preached wherever he thought necessary and almost regardless of the type of reception he might receive (and who did go to Wales). Rather, Sheridan engaged himself in promoting eloquence

[22] Sheridan, *General Dictionary*, vol. I, p. 61.
[23] *Ibid.*, vol. I, p. 62.
[24] Colley states that what 'distinguished the Welsh was their language, a language that three out of four of them still spoke out of choice as late as the 1880s' (*Britons*, p. 13).
[25] *Ibid.*, p. 13.

within metropolitan communities where there already existed an interest in developing protocols of polite behaviour, together with a willingness among the public to pay for diversions addressed to that topic.[26]

FIXING THE LANGUAGE OF GENTLEMEN

Foregrounding Sheridan's commercialism and his opportunistic choice of lecturing venues should not, though, undermine the seriousness with which he approached his subject. He did not, as Henley did, vary the subject matter of his lectures or introduce burlesque techniques in a bid to sustain popularity (the fact that he toured between different regional audiences, unlike the London-based Henley, no doubt made his limited topic more repeatable and commercially viable). Rather, with his patriotic ends, he maintained his focus basically upon two closely interrelated themes: the fixing of the English language, and the refinement of how that language should be delivered in public.

In planning '*to correct, ascertain, and fix the English language*', Sheridan was following a long line of reformers who, since the early seventeenth century, had complained of the ductility of English or had developed projects to stabilise or fix its usage. Employing distinct but related strategies – 'universal language' schemes, 'improvement' schemes, attempts to establish standard grammar, lexicography – language planners had striven to define and institute linguistic standards which would overcome the variations and inconsistencies of English. Francis Bacon, in *The Advancement of Learning* (1605), had presented the instability of verbal communication as an impediment to knowledge, and following Bacon, early members of the Royal Society paid concerted attention to what Edmund Waller, in a 1645 poem *Of English Verse*, called the 'daily changing tongue'.[27] For the natural philosophers of the society, language reform was a necessary adjunct to the advance of scientific knowledge. Thomas Sprat wrote in his *History of the Royal Society* (1667) that it was 'a *Society* that prefers *Works* before *Words*', but the refinement and stabilisation of the language were none the less treated as essential to the collective

---

[26] My emphasis upon Sheridan's commercialism should not obscure the fact that the Sheridans were often in need of money – Frances Sheridan wrote largely in order to bring more money into the household (see Frances Sheridan, *Memoirs of Miss Sidney Bidulph*, ed. Patricia Köster and Jean Coates Cleary (Oxford: Oxford University Press, 1995, pp. x–xi).

[27] Francis Bacon, *The Advancement of Learning*, ed. Michael Kiernan (Oxford: Clarendon Press, 2000), p. 121 and *passim*; *The Poems of Edmund Waller*, ed. G. Thorn Drury, 2 vols. (London: Routledge, 1905), vol. II, p. 69.

achievement of scientific 'works'.[28] Bacon's work envisaged a perfected grammar, not subject to the corruptions of the vulgar, and projections of this type continued to be made and developed in the 'universal language' schemes of the seventeenth century, in works like George Dalgarno's *Ars signorum* (1661) and John Wilkins's renowned *An Essay Towards a Real Character and a Philosophical Language* (1668). Such endeavours were pursued not only by a scientific élite, and a socially and geographically broad culture of language reform existed in the work of schoolmasters such as Cave Beck, master of an Ipswich school, whose *The Universal Character* (1657) shares principles with works produced under the aegis of the universities or the Royal Society.[29]

Other reformers before Sheridan had advanced schemes less idealistic than those of the universal language planners. John Dryden, for example, regretted 'how barbarously we yet write and speak', and proposed that the English should establish a language academy, comparable with those in France and Italy, which would authorise and administer a standardisation of English.[30] No such academy was ever successfully established, but the print trade was harnessed to the cause of standard English and in published works, such as James Greenwood's *An Essay towards a Practical English Grammar* (1711), early prescriptive linguists endeavoured to institute a realisable standardisation of grammar. Jonathan Swift, who in the third book of *Gulliver's Travels* famously satirised the idealistic schemes of language planners, was similarly active in projecting plausible improvement of the language. In *A Proposal for Correcting, Improving and Ascertaining the English Tongue* (1712), Swift complained 'that our Language is extremely imperfect ... its daily Improvements are by no means in proportion to its daily Corruptions'.[31] Like Dryden, Swift admired the stability of 'the *Latin*

---

[28] Thomas Sprat, *History of the Royal Society for the Improving of Natural Knowledge*, ed. Jackson I. Cope and Harold Whitmore Jones (St Louis: Washington University Press; London: Routledge, 1959), p. 434.

[29] Murray Cohen argues that among linguists of the period 'the ones who have the greatest impact are schoolmasters. Often, these are provincial scholars who boldly offer the idea of a lifetime or compile the lessons of a life's work' (*Sensible Words: Linguistic Practice in England 1640–1785* (Baltimore: Johns Hopkins University Press, 1977), p. 6). James Knowlson provides an informative survey of language planning in *Universal Language Schemes in England and France 1600–1800* (Toronto: University of Toronto Press, 1975).

[30] John Dryden, dedication to *Troilus and Cressida*, in *Plays*, The Works of John Dryden, vol. 13, ed. Maximillian E. Novak (Berkeley: University of California Press, 1984), p. 222.

[31] Jonathan Swift, *A Proposal for Correcting, Improving and Ascertaining the English Tongue in a Letter to the Most Honourable Robert Earl of Oxford and Mortimer, Lord High Treasurer of Great Britain* (London, 1712), p. 8.

Tongue, in its Purity', and his proposal sprang from his seeing 'no absolute Necessity why any Language should be perpetually changing'.[32]

Probably the most ambitious single project of language stabilisation in the eighteenth century was Johnson's *A Dictionary of the English Language*. Completed in 1755, it appeared at a time when lexicographical works had already proved themselves popular. Alongside foreign-language diction- aries, rhyming dictionaries, and dictionaries explaining medical terms and terms specific to particular trades, dictionaries of the English language had begun to be produced for a popular readership from the late seventeenth century with works like Elisha Coles's *An English Dictionary* (1676) and *Cocker's English Dictionary* (1704), which was directed to the explanation of 'hard words'. Nathaniel Bailey's *Universal Etymological Dictionary* (1721) was particularly successful: by the time Johnson's *Dictionary* was pub- lished, Bailey's was in its sixteenth edition, and by 1789 it had reached a twenty-sixth. Another of Bailey's works suggests that popular dictionaries could also be deployed to further the type of cultural unification which Sheridan hoped to achieve through language reform. In his *Dictionarium Domesticum, being a new and compleat houshold dictionary for the use of city and country* (1736) Bailey yokes metropolis and province in the embrace of common language usage. So when Johnson produced his work, he was contributing to and vitalising a tradition of works which addressed public needs, and offered themselves for broad public consumption and applica- tion. Sheridan greatly admired Johnson's work, declaring that 'If our language should ever be fixed, he [Johnson] must be considered by all posterity as the founder, and his dictionary the corner stone' (*BE*, p. 376).

For Sheridan, the stabilisation of the English language was to be achieved through the careful education of the élite, whose polite linguistic and social practice should then function as a template for all classes. He followed the educational principles of Locke, whose *Some Thoughts Concerning Education* (1693) influenced his work, in promoting a society in which the example of 'the great and the good', with their privileged access to a fine education, should filter through the social hierarchy and thus vitalise the nation as a whole.[33] 'It must be allowed', Sheridan insists in *British Education*,

that the bulk of mankind have not leisure to be philosophers, or to see things in their causes. And yet the well-being of the state depends upon their actions being regulated by the rules of improved reason. They must therefore imbibe all their

---

[32] *Ibid.*, pp. 9 and 16.
[33] For Sheridan's debts to Locke, see, for example, *BE*, p. 15.

principles of knowledge, as well as conduct in life, from those who have opportunity and abilities to enquire into the sources of the moral duties, and the natural relations of things. (*BE*, p. 103)

He justifies the educational opportunities of an élite class as a national need, and he employs the figure of Lord Chesterfield to assert the social potential of the noble moral exemplar. He dedicates *British Education* to Chesterfield – presenting himself as 'a subject of Great Britain' addressing 'a patriot' (*BE*, p. v) – and he reminds the peer of his duty not only to maintain moral rectitude, but also publicly to display his character for the broader benefit of his countrymen.[34] It is in 'the interest and duty of the great and good', Sheridan writes, 'to contribute all in their power to have their characters and actions transmitted to posterity; whether it proceed from a laudable desire of fame, or from a principle of extending the good influence of their example' (*BE*, p. viii). Fame is laudable, for Sheridan, when it serves not the ego of the eminent individual, but the interests of the public of all classes. The publicly visible gentleman thus stands as the fountainhead of social practice, and his education 'is of all others the most important to the publick' (*BE*, p. 24). Gentlemen, for Sheridan, are 'born to be legislators, to be the bulwarks of our constitution, to fill up posts which require wisdom, conduct, and the most improved abilities, to animate and give motion to the whole body of the people, to be an example and model to all, the fountain of manners and source of principles' (*BE*, p. 25). And thus, 'if their education be defective, or bad, the whole constitution is affected by it' (*BE*, p. 25). *British Education* is therefore '*entirely calculated to* finish the education of a gentleman, *and to take it up only* where the university leaves it' (*BE*, p. xxviii).

Where education in language was concerned, Sheridan's emphasis was always upon the *spoken* word, and his desire to advance the political unity of Britain through fixing the *delivery* of English furthered the work of earlier linguists who had concerned themselves with speech.[35] At the

---

[34] Sheridan's choice of Chesterfield as dedicatee was motivated particularly by Chesterfield's own interest in elocutionary reform. Whilst governing Ireland, Chesterfield had proposed (without effect) that university lectures on the art of speaking should be presented (an idea Sheridan admires in *BE*, p. xi). Chesterfield later presented his own thoughts on eloquence in his *Letters to his Son* (1774).

[35] John Barrell has given attention to this aspect of Sheridan's work in a discussion of how 'throughout the century, and increasingly towards its end, the way people spoke was regarded as a matter of social, and of moral discipline; and just as magistrates were concerned to see the laws made in the metropolis enforced throughout the provinces, so writers on language practice were anxious to confirm the political unity of Britain by recommending the enforcement, throughout the country, of the laws of good usage and pronunciation, as derived from the custom of "the most polish'd speakers . . . residing in the Metropolis" ' (*Equal, Wide Survey*, p. 138).

beginning of the century, one A. Lane, a schoolmaster, had declared in his *A Key to the Art of Letters* (1700) that 'the first and principal thing in learning of any language, is to get the true Pronunciation of the words'.[36] This emerging notion of a singular 'true Pronunciation' reflects a drive to rationalise the living language – an ambition which was pursued more widely and vigorously as the century progressed. For example, in 1727 Nathaniel Bailey capitalised on the success of his *Universal Etymological Dictionary* and published a companion volume, *An Orthographical Dictionary, shewing both the orthography and the orthoepia of the English Tongue*. Such a dictionary performs a very different function from the 'hard words' or technical dictionaries being published thirty years earlier: it does not merely help a reader to comprehend a verbally complex text, but offers precise standards for the use of English in both written and spoken contexts. It advertises itself as a vessel containing *the* orthography and *the* orthoepia of English, authorising both the idea of linguistic standardisation and that standard itself.

Sheridan similarly strove to institute a standard usage, as he worked to instil a polite pronunciation across Britain's divided regions. Johnson questioned the authority of Sheridan to attempt such a project and pointed to the initial difficulty of identifying a standard mode of speech to set about standardising. '[W]hat entitles Sheridan to fix the pronunciation of English?', he complained. 'He has, in the first place, the disadvantage of being an Irishman: and if he says he will fix it after the example of the best company, why they differ among themselves.'[37] The latter problem – the diversity of modern polite utterance – was one Sheridan recognised, but he believed that it could be overcome by recovering the court language from the early century. Imagining a golden age of spoken English, Sheridan idealised a time

during the reign of Queen Anne, when English was the language spoken at court; and when the same attention was paid to propriety of pronunciation, as that of French at the Court of Versaille. This produced a uniformity in that article in all the polite circles; and a gentleman or lady would have been as much ashamed of a wrong pronunciation then, as persons of a liberal education would be now of mis-spelling words.[38]

---

[36] Cited in Cohen, *Sensible Words*, p. 47.

[37] Boswell, *Life of Johnson*, p. 470. Johnson gave some attention to pronunciation in his *Dictionary*: 'In settling the orthography, I have not wholly neglected the pronunciation, which I have directed by printing an accent upon the acute or elevated syllable', he wrote in the preface. With his accents, Johnson gave guidance regarding emphasis, but he did not attempt to standardise pronunciation *per se*.

[38] Sheridan, *General Dictionary*, vol. I, preface (n. p.).

Having been educated by speakers conversant with the conventions of the élite early in the century, he aspired to overstep the intervening period of linguistic 'decline' and to re-establish and universalise this polite standard. He hoped to fix 'anchors to our floating language, in order to keep it steady against the gales of caprice, and the current of fashion', but only when those anchors represented the noble example of the metropolitan gentleman.[39] His comments concerning spelling suggest that, by 1780, Enlightenment educational projects had created a culture in which great accuracy in written English had become firmly rooted as an attribute of modern polite identity. His work as an elocutionist contributed to the emergence of a comparable cultural position for spoken English, and despite the problems inherent in producing standardised pronunciation (as expressed by Johnson), Sheridan and others created and fed a lively public discourse concerning polite utterance.[40] From *British Education* to his *General Dictionary of the English Language*, Sheridan's works were all, at least in part, concerned with making the nation 'speak well', and his efforts were not without effect. Boswell – ever the advocate of Sheridan in the face of Johnson's critique – insisted that Sheridan 'had considerably improved the arts of reading and speaking with distinctness and propriety'.[41]

ELOQUENT BODIES AND THE PRODUCTION OF SOCIETY

Sheridan prioritised the spoken above the written word because he saw in speech a socialising power that was always unavailable to the writer. The language of the page, he argued, however well crafted, could never reproduce the energy and emotion of living speech. 'All writers', he wrote in his *Lectures on Elocution*, 'seem to be under the influence of one common delusion, that by the help of words alone, they can communicate all that passes in their minds. They forget that the passions and the fancy have a language of their own, utterly independent of word, by which only their exertions can be manifested and communicated' (*Lectures*, p. x). The

---

[39] *Ibid.*, vol. I, preface (n. p.).

[40] Among other works of the period which are concerned with pronunciation are: William Kenrick's *New Dictionary of the English Language* (1773), which included a system for showing how words should be accented; John Rice's *An Introduction to the Art of Reading* (1765); John Herries's *Elements of Speech* (1773); and John Walker's *A Rhetorical Grammar* (1785). Like John Rice, Sheridan also developed protocols in 'the art of reading' – an aspect of his work which is discussed in Richard Bradford, *Silence and Sound: Theories of Poetics from the Eighteenth Century* (London: Associated University Presses, 1992).

[41] Boswell, *Life of Johnson*, p. 273.

passions, indeed, were central to Sheridan's vision of a thriving and harmonious Britain – the individual's capacity to feel sympathy was the cement by which British society should be bonded. It is 'not necessary to society, that all men know much', he declared, but 'it is necessary that they feel much, and have a mutual sympathy, in whatsoever affects their fellow creatures' (*Lectures*, p. 101). And the passions could only be truly communicated, he insisted, by means of living speech. The 'true signs of the passions', Sheridan wrote, are not words themselves but the 'tones, looks and gestures' which accompany, or sometimes overwhelm, verbal utterance (*Lectures*, p. 100). From his earliest writing on elocution, Sheridan lauded speaking as

the immediate gift of God, who has annexed to it (when cultivated by man) powers almost miraculous, and an energy nearly divine. He has given to it tones to charm the ear, and penetrate the heart; he has joined to it action, and looks, to move the inmost soul. By that, attention is kept up without pain, and conviction carried to the mind with delight. Persuasion is ever it's attendant, and the passions own it for a master. Great as is the force of it's powers, so unbounded is their extent. All mankind are capable of it's impressions. (*BE*, p. 85)

For Sheridan, then, language was only truly effective when it emerged from a body – when verbal discourse was animated with non-verbal, somatic signs which transformed it into a vehicle of the passions. Through elegant pronunciation and an application of proper tones, delivered speech should make a strong appeal to the ear, but, Sheridan stressed, speech was also a *visual* medium. 'Nature', he argued in his *Lectures*, 'did not trust an article, so essential to the well-being of man [as language], to a communication by one sense only; she has also made it visible to the eye, as well as audible to the ear' (*Lectures*, p. 113). As such, the delivery of speech – not only the utterance of words but their production in association with the whole body's expressive repertoire – became a key theme in his work. And Sheridan's promotion of a language of the body contributed significantly to the construction of an eloquent body that was polite through the exhibition of distinctly sentimental virtues.

What Sheridan saw in proper, passionate speaking was nothing less than the means of creating civil society. His *Lectures*, he claimed, would show 'how the passions hurtful or dangerous to society may be suppressed, and those of the nobler and social kind, calculated to promote the general good, may be brought forward, invigorated, and carried into due exertion'. He would demonstrate furthermore 'how the powers of the imagination may be so regulated as to diffuse a general good taste thro' the nation; a point essentially necessary to promote some of the noblest ends that can be answered by the two other powers, those I mean of a refined understanding, and delicate sensibility' (*Lectures*, pp. xi–xii). And proper public delivery lay at the core of this scheme to reform Britain. The very occasion of a public speech – with individuals coming together to form an assembly, all focused upon the same performing figure – was an ideal opportunity for creating social bonds, but it was up to the speaker, Sheridan argued, to initiate the diffusion of communal emotion. An audience experiencing a truly effective speaker – one who 'blends the two languages [of ideas and of passions] properly' – will find that

the fancy, the passions, the understanding are all pleasingly agitated; each individual receives an additional delight, from the sum communicated to the whole auditory, reflected from eye to eye, during a charmed attention to the orator; poured out from breast to breast, when his silence permits them to give way to the fullness of their hearts. Perhaps there is no other situation in which the social disposition of mankind is so exquisitely gratified. They assemble at such meetings with satisfaction in their looks, from expectation of the delight which they are to receive; they part with mutual congratulations, on account of mutual benefit, and entertainment. Such an intercourse, frequently repeated, tends to eradicate all selfish passions, and to bring forward and invigorate all the fine emotions of benevolence, and the great duty of Christian charity ... [Such delivery] alone can tend to make us, what we were designed to be, social beings. (*Lectures*, pp. 182–3)

The speaker in this scenario functions as an agent of a visually transmitted emotional contagion; from the performance springs a mass exchange of sentiment as noble passions are passed 'from eye to eye' – significantly in moments of *silence* – with the result that the audience becomes fused in feeling. And by inspiring such collective emotional experiences, good speakers are capable, Sheridan argues, of cultivating socially conscious citizens – selfless beings animated by the sentimental virtues of benevolence and charity.

For Sheridan, therefore, appealing to the emotions was the fundamental duty of a public speaker – it was the foundation upon which all other aspects of an oration rested. 'The office of a public speaker', he wrote,

is, to instruct, to please, and to move. If he does not instruct, his discourse is impertinent; and if he does not please, he will not have it in his power to instruct, for he will not gain attention; and if he does not move he will not please, for where there is no emotion there can be no pleasure. To move therefore, should be the first great object of every public speaker; and for this purpose he must use the language of the emotions, not that of ideas alone, which of itself has no power of moving. (*Lectures*, p. 133)

Sheridan identified this language of the emotions as an inherent attribute of human physiology – a language which, by virtue of being a 'natural' aspect of embodiment, could be universally expressed and comprehended. Gesture is celebrated as part of a naturally settled linguistic system which is 'universally legible, without pains or study', and which 'contains in itself a power, of exciting similar, or analogous emotions' within its witnesses (*Lectures*, p. 113). The 'human countenance and limbs', he writes, are 'capable of an infinite variety of changes, suitable to the tones; or rather to the emotions, whence they both take their rise. To this purpose every nobler organ in man's complicated frame, and the whole animal œconomy contribute. The muscles, nerves, the blood and animal spirits, all are at work to shew internal commotion' (*Lectures*, p. 114). Unlike manufactured verbal languages, this language of the body is seen as the generous work of the 'Almighty artificer', and its signs are seen to be entirely natural consequences of the passions: 'As every passion has its peculiar tone, so has it, its peculiar look or gesture' (*Lectures*, p. 114). And thus the body, for Sheridan, was naturally capable of a vast range of very precise emotional expression. Considering the eyes and the hands, he asks

What inward emotion is there, which cannot be manifested by these? Do not the eyes discover humility, pride; cruelty, compassion; reflection, dissipation; kindness, resentment? Is there an emotion of fancy, is there a shade of ridicule, which they can not represent? . . . WITH respect to the power of hands, every one knows that with them, we can demand, or promise; call, dismiss; threaten, supplicate; ask, deny; shew joy, sorrow, detestation, fear, confession, penitence, admiration, respect; and many other things. (*Lectures*, p. 116)

In line with this understanding of gesture as a natural language, Sheridan's pedagogic technique is to urge speakers to become emotionally involved with the subject of their delivery, so that the signs of the passions are automatically produced: 'Let him speak entirely from his feelings; and they will find much truer signs to manifest themselves by, than he could find for them' (*Lectures*, p. 121). The other advice, which Sheridan offers repeatedly, is that speakers should avoid the affectation of emotional signs, for this, he insists, will inevitably be recognised and will suggest insincerity. '[A]ll constraint upon nature', he writes,

is instantly perceived, as it produces affectation, and of course destroys true feeling; for it is as impossible, where affectation takes place in the manner of delivery, or in the signs of inward emotions, that the feelings of the heart should be excited, as that two musical strings, not in unison, should vibrate to each other, when only one is struck. (*Lectures*, p. 120)

Sheridan is not, then, the type of instructor who lays down fixed rules for the body's expression; he advances no definite strictures regarding eloquent conduct in the manner of Le Faucheur. Indeed, Sheridan makes clear his view that 'no general practical rules . . . as would be of any efficacy, can be laid down in this respect' (*Lectures*, p. 118), and one consequence of this is that his writing on the body includes few attempts actually to describe the appearance of true somatic eloquence. His pedagogic approach renders such description redundant.

Yet despite arguing for the primacy of nature as the generator of somatic expression, Sheridan at the same time maintains that nature can be perfected by art. Like other eighteenth-century writing on elocution, Sheridan's works are marked with a tension between a conspicuous veneration of nature and an urge to refine it – a desire to make nature just slightly more civilised and polite. 'IN elocution', he writes, 'the two great articles are, force, and grace; the one has its foundation chiefly in nature, the other in art' (*Lectures*, p. 121). In this regard, Sheridan argues that mankind has been licensed by Nature to develop this 'grace' by refining the body's innate expressive capacity:

BUT tho' in this written language of nature, she [Nature] has given such forcible, and distinct characters, to all the animal passions of man . . . she has laid down the same law, with regard to the visible signs . . . as she has done with regard to the tones. In both she has furnished the means with equal liberality; but has left it to the invention and care of man, to make a right use of them, and apply them in suitable degrees. By the exertion of such skill and pains, it would be found that the visible language alone, which can be shewn in the features and limbs of man, is of itself sufficient, without other aid, to every purpose of social communication. (*Lectures*, p. 116)

It is the duty of mankind, he contends, to cultivate Nature's liberal gift of language so as to establish 'a right use' of the body and 'suitable degrees' of somatic expression. Sheridan may not convey a strong sense of what his ideal of bodily eloquence actually looks like, but, as in this passage, he regularly calls upon a series of telling terms and modifiers suggesting the manner in which he urges nature to be tailored. For Sheridan, a speaker's bodily eloquence should be 'suitable', 'refined', 'delicate', 'fine', 'graceful', 'proper', 'harmonious', or 'exquisite', so that the performance will 'delight' and 'please' an audience, and in the process will demonstrate – 'with propriety' – exactly what it means to be 'cultivated' and 'polite' and to possess 'good taste'. 'It is evident, in the use of the language of emotions', he writes,

that he who is properly moved, and at the same time delivers himself, in such tones, as delight the ear with their harmony; accompanied by such looks and gestures, as please the eye with their grace; whilst the understanding also perceives their propriety; is in the first class, and must be accounted a master. In this case, the united endeavours of art and nature, produce that degree of perfection, which is no other way to be obtained, in any thing that is the workmanship of man. (*Lectures*, p. 133)

Sheridan has clearly rejected the 'classical decorum' of the old school, but in forging a modern mode of eloquence he has by no means granted free rein to the orators he seeks to deploy as social emblems.

Some sense of what Sheridan implies by 'propriety', and the terms it rubs shoulders with, can be gauged from comments he made on Methodism. Like Richard Graves, Sheridan pursued interests which forced him to respond to the movement, and his attitude to Methodist enthusiasm illuminates to some degree the type of eloquent gesture recommended in his own writing. His responses, in fact, reveal a vacillating attitude to Methodism akin to that found in *The Spiritual Quixote*. In *British Education* he noted, with almost unqualified approval, 'the wonderful effects which have been produced by the wild uncultivated oratory of our methodist preachers' (*BE*, p. 91), and he acknowledged that 'in the eyes of a fanatick multitude' their 'canting and frantick gestures might be more forcible than the best regulated oratory' (*BE*, p. 153). Rather than banish the Methodists to the margins of British society, he locates 'our' preachers well within his and his readers' culture and appreciates the achievements of *uncultivated* delivery (in this fiercely Francophobic work, too much cultivation would carry the tinge of Frenchness, perhaps). But by the time of the *Lectures on Elocution* his approval has become more guarded. Careful to assert his own self-consciously rational perspective, he still recognises the effectiveness of enthusiastic oratory, describing the 'many flagrant instances in our methodist preachers, of the powers which words acquire, even the words of fools and madmen, when forcibly uttered by the living voice' (*Lectures*, p. xiii). But the power of such eloquence, he suggests, was limited, and while it could fire strong temporary effects, it would fail properly to spread true religion, which, from his earliest writing, he proposed was the real 'basis of our constitution, and pillar of our state' (*BE*, p. 53). The 'fancied operations of the spirit', he argued, could produce 'a certain cant, and extravagant gestures', but this 'sort of language of emotions...is well calculated to make enthusiasts, but not believers' (*Lectures*, p. 120). Shunning cant and extravagance, Sheridan promoted a more restrained form of bodily eloquence – one that was emotional but not manic, passionate but recognisably distinct from the eighteenth-century notions of madness, with which inspired religions were regularly associated.

Sheridan was certainly keen that speakers should display deep emotions, and, like elocutionists before him, he laid a particular emphasis upon the power of the eye to express socially beneficial passions. '[O]f all the organs', he declared, 'the eye, rightly called the window to the breast, contains the greatest variety, as well as distinction and force of characters. In rage it is inflamed, in fear it sickens; it sparkles in joy, in distress it is clouded' (*Lectures*, p. 114). And like James Fordyce, Sheridan was concerned to promote the eloquent effects of tears, and to show that, for the gentleman speaker, weeping in public should entail no sense of shame or emasculation. In Sheridan's thinking, in fact, such emotional 'weakness' is equated with political power:

Nature has indeed annexed to the passion of grief, a more forcible character than any other, that of tears; of all parts of language, the most expressive . . . not only to ease the burthened heart, but more powerfully to excite his fellow creatures to pity, and to relieve his distress. Thus at once affording balm to the afflicted, and inciting man to the exercise of their noblest quality, benevolence. (*Lectures*, p. 114)

Tears, then, are endowed with political potential – they are not only effective at the moment of their shedding, but powerful beyond that moment as instigators of social, moral action. It is typical of Sheridan, and typical of elocutionary writing more broadly, to consider such minutiae of embodiment and to argue for their importance as the underpinning of human society. Sheridan writes of 'the nation' and he writes of Britain in the wider context of international relations, but he remains ever aware that nations can never be abstracted from the mass of organic beings of which they are composed. For Sheridan, the language of these creatures is the stuff of which nations are built.

When we read Sheridan's published works now, it is difficult not to share the view of those contemporary critics who complained that his efforts 'to do everything by Oratory' were unrealistic, impracticable and obsessive. Yet at the same time as his idiosyncrasies stand out, his works display an interplay of familiar eighteenth-century preoccupations. Sheridan's plans to advance the nation and his attempts to inscribe the orator's body with communicable signs of civic virtue were far from unusual. In fact, it is almost as though what we find in Sheridan's impassioned publications is these prevalent preoccupations writ large, and it is this magnification that produces Sheridan's slight eccentricity. But however we might now regard his plans for national advancement, what cannot be overlooked is Sheridan's contemporary popular appeal. Johnson may have found 'Sherry' dull and his judgement may have endured, but Sheridan had attractions enough to sustain a significant and lifelong position in eighteenth-century public life. And from that position he was undeniably successful in drawing attention to the cause of elocutionary reform and in making the modes and manners of public delivery a significant issue within British cultural discourse.

CHAPTER 4

The art of acting:
mid-century stagecraft and the broadcast of feeling

The Time *shall come* – (nor far the destin'd Day!)
When Soul-touch'd *Actors* shall do more, than PLAY:
When Passion, flaming, from th'asserted Stage,
Shall, to taught Greatness fire a feeling Age...
Why was the *Actor stain'd*, by Law's Decree? —
Lost Time's *Recove'rer!* Truth's *Awake'ner*, He!
Passion's *Refiner!* – Life's *shoal Coast* survey'd –
The wise Man's *Pleaser*, and the good Man's *Aid*.
Precept, and Practice, in *One Teacher*, join'd,
Bodied Resemblance of the copied Mind.

Aaron Hill (1746)[1]

EIGHTEENTH-CENTURY THEATRES AND POLITENESS

Thomas Sheridan need not have looked beyond the theatre in order to pursue his mission as an elocutionary reformer and saviour of the nation. For by the mid eighteenth century the theatres in Britain had secured sufficient public respectability for dramatic entertainment to be widely apprehended as a powerful vehicle of useful instruction and social reform. The spectacle of acting itself might 'fire a feeling Age', averred Aaron Hill.

Such a view of the theatre's social function was relatively new when Hill made this claim in 1746. The court-centred theatres of the Restoration and late seventeenth century – with typically boisterous audiences, and repertoires rich in bawdy dramas – were hardly venues for teaching modern manners and ethics. For many commentators of that period who were concerned with the moral health of the nation, the theatres were dangerously decadent institutions promulgating lewdness and debauchery.

---

[1] Hill, *Art of Acting*, pp. 8–9.

Jeremy Collier, the arch anti-theatre conservative of the late seventeenth century, argued as much in his famously condemnatory *A Short View of the Immorality and Profaneness of the English Stage* (1698), and Collier's work was just part of a widespread campaign against theatrical entertainment that stretched well into the eighteenth century.[2]

Collier was opposed not to the theatre *per se* but to the contemporary abuse of what he saw as its proper purpose. 'The business of *Plays* is to recomend [*sic*] Virtue, and discountenance Vice', he wrote, but as he saw the situation around him, the theatres were 'in the Enemies Hand' – like 'Cannon seized they are pointed the wrong way'.[3] Among supporters of the theatre there grew up a campaign to seize those cannon back – to *civilise* dramatic entertainment – and through the promotional efforts of playwrights, theatre managers, actors, and commentators on drama, the cultural position of the theatre in Britain was radically transformed during the first half of the eighteenth century. Stallybrass and White have described how from the late seventeenth century the theatre underwent a 'cleansing process'; they demonstrate, for example, how the prologue to John Dryden's *Cleomenes* (1692) 'endeavours to coax and shame the unruly audience of aristocratic Beaux and vulgar groundlings into *keeping still* and *keeping quiet*, transforming them, precisely, into a deferential and receptive bourgeois audience'.[4] Such efforts began a process which was by no means rapid. Beginning his career some fifty years after Dryden's play, David Garrick, actor and manager of Drury Lane theatre, was similarly concerned with suppressing audience unruliness, with elevating the cultural standing of the theatre, and with turning it into a respectable, polite institution. Garrick was hugely influential in this respect and was

---

[2] In the first quarter of the eighteenth century there was intense controversy over the morality or otherwise of the stage. Between Collier's work and William Law's *Absolute Unlawfulness of the Stage-Entertainment Fully Demonstrated* (1726) there appeared at least eighty works which engaged in the debate (see the bibliography in Sister Rose Anthony, *The Jeremy Collier Stage Controversy, 1698–1726* (New York: Blom, 1937), pp. 300–7).

[3] Jeremy Collier, *A Short View of the Immorality and Profaneness of the English Stage* (London, 1698), pp. 1–2.

[4] Stallybrass and White, *Politics and Poetics of Transgression*, p. 84. The rise in the theatre's respectability is reflected not least in the changes in the type of drama that was popularly staged. Robert D. Hume has shown that a late seventeenth- and early eighteenth-century moralisation of the theatres is recognisable in, for example, a new foregrounding of characters capable of standing as clear moral exemplars (*The Development of English Drama in the Late Seventeenth Century* (Oxford: Clarendon Press, 1976), pp. 491–2). J. L. Styan also indicates that a 'consequence of the change from an aristocratic audience to a bigger, broader public composed more of middle-class merchants, professional men and their families was to curtail the bawdy content of the drama' (*The English Stage: A History of Drama and Performance* (Cambridge: Cambridge University Press, 1996), pp. 280–1).

recognised as such – in his epitaph by Edmund Burke he was eulogised for raising 'the character of his profession to the rank of a liberal art, not only by his talents, but by the regularity and probity of his life and the elegance of his manners'.[5] Such a civilisation of the theatres and of the actor's profession was never fully achieved in the period – theatres remained associated with prostitution, for example, and occasional riots occurred throughout the century – but there is nevertheless a marked difference, in terms of polite status, between the decadent patrician playhouses of the Restoration and the later more respectable bourgeois institutions.

Attending the theatre, then, became in the eighteenth century a legitimate, civilised diversion for the polite classes, and in this trans-formation we find another compelling case of the body being deployed in order to propagate politeness – both the perceived politeness *of* the theatres, and notions of politeness beyond them. The spectacle of the body on stage, performing according to innova-tive notions of proper theatrical expression, became, like the image of an orator, a means of emblematising polite society and of showcasing modes of polite self-representation – and as such, a polite body image was itself nourishing and sustaining a perception of the theatre as a polite, moral institution.[6] The first half of the eighteenth century saw the solidification of an idea of the theatre as a 'school of conduct' (something which was only a bleak aspiration for Jeremy Collier), and as part of this process, the spectacle of acting became invested with huge didactic potential as a fountainhead from which polite principles could be dispersed throughout the viewing public.

---

[5] The epitaph is reproduced in George Winchester Stone, Jr and George M. Kahrl, *David Garrick: A Critical Biography* (Carbondale: Southern Illinois University Press, 1979), p. 648. These biographers illuminate the civilising impulse underlying Garrick's manifold contributions to the theatre as an actor, manager, playwright, producer, and energetic, all-round doer. Leigh Woods similarly highlights Garrick's 'interest in the moral obligation of theater to its audience' and his 'ways of capitalizing on his own upright conduct as a private citizen' to promote such a project (*Garrick Claims the Stage: Acting as Social Emblem in Eighteenth-Century England* (Westport, CT and London: Greenwood Press, 1984), p. 14).

[6] My approach to the acting of this period, then, is in line with that outlined in general terms by Erika Fisher-Lichte: 'If we describe the European history of the human body in terms of the civilizing process, the question arises whether the history of acting might not also be investigated and explained in like terms. For the actors' bodies, as presented on the stage, are likewise culturally conditioned in accordance with the actual state of the civilizing process. Moreover, the particular mode of their presentation onstage may contribute to this ongoing process by representing and propagating new models of self-presence and self-presentation for audience imitation' ('Theatre and the Civilizing Process', pp. 22–3).

Sheridan's hope that the theatre might become 'an admirable Assistant to the School of Oratory' was realised to a significant extent – indeed, it became an assumption that actors' performances would influence the conduct of those who witnessed them. In a public *Letter to David Garrick* of 1769, one 'H. W.' commented upon how certain actors were exerting a damaging influence through their performances:

I must own it offends me to the soul to hear such wretches as Mossop, Smith, and others of equal contemptible abilities, spoken of by ignorant and undiscerning spectators as first-rate actors and models of elocution. Whilst such performers appear in capital parts, young persons should not be allowed to frequent the theatre, least they should catch a vicious pronunciation, and contract an ungraceful manner.[7]

For H. W., the respectability of the theatres is sufficiently well established for it to be simply assumed that performance has a didactic function and will influence those in attendance. The theatre appears as a seminary at which the young are likely to 'catch' or 'contract' patterns of behaviour, and the task for the author is not to question the theatre's role in social and somatic definition – that is taken for granted – but to arbitrate between worthy and unworthy models of eloquence and manners. The *Letter* is mounting a defence against the spread of the 'ungraceful'.

Addressed to Garrick, H. W.'s *Letter* appeals to the cultural authority of a man whose body was respected, throughout much of Europe, more than any other for its eloquent capabilities and refinement. For Joseph Pittard, the author of highly complimentary *Observations on Mr. Garrick's Acting* (1758), Garrick was the image of good taste: 'as *Poussin* is considered the Painter of Men of Taste', he declared, 'so in like Manner Mr. *Garrick* is the Player'.[8] Denis Diderot (1713–84) avowed that witnessing Garrick perform 'alone made it just as worthwhile to make the journey to England as all the remains of ancient Rome made it worth the journey to Italy'. The compliment follows a passage in which Diderot marvels at Garrick's breathtaking ability to express a succession of passions – wild joy, moderate joy, tranquillity, surprise, astonishment, sadness, despondency, fear, horror, and finally, despair – all within a few seconds of highly charged facial acting.[9] In Britain and beyond, Garrick was apotheosised for his physical eloquence, and through his mastery of his craft, together with

---

[7] *Letter to David Garrick*, pp. 30–1. I have been unable to identify H. W.

[8] Pittard, *Observations on Mr. Garrick's Acting*, p. 8.

[9] Denis Diderot, *The Paradox of the Actor* (1770–84), in *Selected Writings on Art and Literature*, trans. Geoffrey Bremner (Harmondsworth: Penguin, 1994), p. 120.

the well-publicised respectability of his private life, he attained a cultural position of extraordinary authority. It is this authority that H. W. invokes as the *Letter* aims to broadcast an agenda for the useful role of the theatre in a process of civilisation. The *Letter* makes clear that the actor's body, like that of the public speaker, could function as a site upon which notions of polite, eloquent behaviour could be modelled and authorised.[10]

In weighing up the merits of different contemporary actors, H. W.'s *Letter* is, in fact, intervening in a public debate concerning the forms and functions of theatrical expression which had been intensifying since the early years of the century. The subject of acting engaged numerous writers who sought variously to analyse actors' performances, to assess the virtues or problems inherent in alternative techniques, or to construct theories about and teach the acting process. In what follows here, I want to examine contributions to this debate in order to show how performers and commentators on stage performance consciously or unconsciously invested the actor's body with the power 'to civilise' and treated it as a textual space for the inscription of politeness. For many commentators, the propriety or otherwise of a performance style involved the degree to which it could claim to be 'natural', but 'natural acting' was a contested category, and actors and theorists of acting presented competing conceptions of what constituted a 'natural' and 'proper' manner of performing before the public. Particularly there was contestation (as in the discourse surrounding oratory) between 'classical' and 'non-classical' body images, and there can be seen within acting discourse a process – by no means smooth – of 'sentimentalisation' whereby classical body images were appreciably devalued and the acting body was newly inscribed as a vehicle of the passions without the guiding hand of classical decorum. It is a contest in which are crystallised important questions concerning the forms of polite self-presentation – questions which arguably received their most intense 'working out' during the middle years of the century, partly but not only because of Garrick and the responses his acting elicited. My main focus falls, therefore, upon mid-century acting discourse, and it will be useful to begin the account with a glimpse of the tensions between classical and modern acting styles as they came into frictional contact upon the mid-century stage itself – or at least as they were witnessed and remembered by the playwright and theatrical memoirist Richard Cumberland (1732–1811).

---

[10] Woods argues that Garrick's 'success on the stage lay largely in the extent to which his private concerns bodied forth in his acting, and to which these stood for values either assumed or subscribed to by the great majority of Garrick's audience' (*Garrick Claims the Stage*, p. 4).

ACTING STYLES IN CONFLICT

In his *Memoirs* (1806), Cumberland vividly recalls his boyhood experience of a performance at Covent Garden in 1746 of *The Fair Penitent* (1703), a highly acclaimed sentimental tragedy by Nicholas Rowe. The performance featured James Quin (1693–1766), the actor who had come to dominate the London stage in the 1730s and had impressed audiences, particularly in tragic roles, with his grand, classical style. Acting alongside him on this occasion was Garrick, some twenty-five years younger than Quin and the exponent of a conspicuously non-classical technique which, in the five years since his London debut as Richard III, had brought him enormous renown. Cumberland begins describing Quin:

[W]ith very little variation of cadence, and in a deep full tone, accompanied by a sawing kind of action, which had more of the senate than of the stage in it, he rolled out his heroics with an air of dignified indifference, that seemed to disdain the plaudits, that were bestowed upon him . . . I first beheld little Garrick, then young and light and alive in every muscle and in every feature, come bounding on the stage . . . heavens, what a transition! – it seemed as if a whole century had been stept over in the transition of a single scene; old things were done away, and a new order at once brought forward, bright and luminous, and clearly destined to dispel the barbarisms and bigotry of a tasteless age, too long attached to the prejudices of custom, and superstitiously devoted to the illusions of imposing declamation.[11]

Cumberland is certainly overstating a sense of total stylistic revolution here, and it is interesting to note his observations of his fellow audience members, many of whom 'seemed to *love darkness better than light*' and preferred 'the master of the old school . . . [to] the founder of the new'.[12] Nevertheless, the passage usefully and clearly marks the distinction between the stately, classical, declamatory style – one closely related to the classical style in oratory – and a modern style which rejects declamation as a mode of utterance and advances a more holistic use of the body to express emotion. Indeed, while Quin's deployment of his body – with his 'sawing kind of action' and 'air of dignified indifference' – is certainly vital to his stately performance, it might be said that the emphasis of such acting is not so much upon the bodily expression as upon the impressive vocal rendering of the script. The emphasis is certainly not upon *variety* of bodily expression, and Quin was criticised elsewhere for imposing a standard gloss of dignity upon all his roles at all times. '[T]ho' *Dignity* is finely maintain'd

---

[11] Richard Cumberland, *Memoirs of Richard Cumberland* (London, 1806), pp. 59–60.
[12] *Ibid.*, p. 60.

by the Weight of *majestic Composure*', wrote Aaron Hill in a 1735 article partly addressed to Quin (or '*Mr.* ALL-WEIGHT', as Hill calls him), 'there are Scenes, in your *Parts* where the *Voice* shou'd be sharp and impatient, the *Look*, disorder'd and agoniz'd, the *Action* precipitate and turbulent.'[13] Hill was expressing a desire to see a more varied articulation of the passions than was offered by grand declamation – a desire which would be satisfied by Garrick, who, as Cumberland's account suggests, brought to the stage an innovative style which can be said to have a deeper and more complex investment in the body as an expressive tool. Garrick did not treat acting as the grandiloquent presentation of the playwright's words (indeed, one might speculate upon whether 'little Garrick' might have been deemed absurdly Lilliputian had he seriously attempted grandiloquence); rather, the script served him as the foundation for a performance technique in which character was displayed, as Cumberland puts it, 'in every muscle and in every feature'.[14]

Cumberland's description of the female leads in *The Fair Penitent* reveals a similar clash of styles, and further suggests that the modern challenge to classical acting involved a significant devaluing of declamation and a new emphasis upon varied bodily action. Cumberland was unimpressed by the performance of Susannah Maria Cibber, who 'sung or rather recitatived Rowe's harmonious strain'. He complained that her speaking 'was so extremely wanting in contrast, that, though it did not wound the ear, it wearied it; when she had once recited two or three speeches, I could anticipate the manner of every succeeding one'.[15] In stark and pleasing contrast, for Cumberland, was the performance of Hannah Pritchard: 'an actress of a different cast, [who] had more nature, and of course more change of tone, and variety both of action and expression'.[16] It is striking that Cibber is remembered only as a voice – as a body she inspires no comment – whereas Pritchard is celebrated for both vocal and spectacular virtues. And performing with varied *action* and *expression*, it is Pritchard who gains the credit of having 'more nature'.

---

[13] *The Prompter* 92 (26 September 1735).
[14] Angela Smallwood discusses this shift in dominant performance techniques, suggesting that, with the advent of Garrick, 'the purely verbal component of theatre became less prominent and the performer's resources of non-verbal expression, tones of voice, looks, movements, were most successfully brought to the fore' ('A Study of the Representation of Character and Passion in the Novels of Fielding and Sterne, by Comparison with the Representation of these Subjects on the Stage and in Painting in the Period', unpublished D. Phil. thesis, University of Oxford, 1981, p. 61).
[15] Cumberland, *Memoirs*, p. 59.
[16] *Ibid.*, p. 60.

Cumberland's critical evaluations of these actors are clearly informed by his own allegiances to the modern, non-classical style, and it may be that, written nearly sixty years after the performance, the account is partially slanted by a false teleology, with the memoirist retrospectively vaunting the style that he knew would come to dominate the mid-century stage. The allegiances of the observer are significant here because it is arguably Cumberland's alienation from classical conventions that causes him to recognise, for example, 'more nature' in Pritchard than in Cibber. When accounts of eighteenth-century acting are read from a twenty-first-century perspective, it is tempting to follow Cumberland and to regard the non-classical style as more 'naturalistic' than the mode which, to a significant degree, it supplanted. But this should not obscure the fact that 'nature' – together with abundant quantities of 'feeling' and 'passion' – had earlier been perceived and applauded in classically inclined actors and actresses whose style, by the 1730s, was being censured for artificiality and mannerism. The history of eighteenth-century acting shows not so much a rise of naturalism as an ongoing contest between alternative versions of what was regarded as 'natural' behaviour for the body on stage. The acting of Garrick and Pritchard was 'natural' for Cumberland because it displayed a consonance with the culture that was shaping him as a spectator. The declamatory style, on the other hand, represented, as he puts it, 'a tasteless age' – an alien, past culture, unenlightened by his own notions of taste or of what it means to be polite. Quin's presence on the stage of 1746 is, for Cumberland, an anachronism – a remnant of a bygone culture, the residual energies of which should be extinguished if the theatre is to be in tune with modern society.

By Cumberland's time, in fact, classical acting was losing its relevance – and 'naturalness' – for many contemporary theatregoers. If we are to see classical acting in a context where it was more fully naturalised, we must look back to a period prior to the later performances of Quin; indeed, we must look back to a period before Garrick and other actors – notably Charles Macklin – had effectively triggered a 'paradigm shift' in performance style.[17] And in this regard it is worth considering the techniques and legacy of the celebrated Thomas Betterton (1635?–1710), whose stage career,

---

[17] As an innovator in performance techniques, Macklin is acknowledged primarily for rejecting declamatory delivery – both in his own acting practice and as a teacher – and for promoting a method of delivery based upon conventional speech patterns. John Hill, who studied under Macklin, described how 'It was his manner to check all the cant and cadence of tragedy; he would bid his pupil first speak the passage as he would in common life, if he had occasion to pronounce the same words; and then giving them more force, but preserving the same accent, to deliver them on the stage' (Hill, *The Actor*, p. 239).

it can be said, corresponds to the heyday of classical acting in Britain. The figure of Betterton is also significant in other ways, though, for while he exhibited a style that would come to be devalued, his reputation was none the less called upon in the campaign to raise the polite status of the theatres.

CLASSICAL ACTING AND ITS MID-CENTURY FATE: THOMAS
BETTERTON AND HIS POSTHUMOUS *LIFE*

Between the Restoration and his death in 1710, Betterton built a phenomenally successful career, during the last thirty years of which he was respected as the leading actor in the London theatre world.[18] Together with his regular stage colleague, Elizabeth Barry, Betterton set a standard for an acting style characterised by the restraint and modulation of its movement, and praised for its ability to express the passions. It can be said that Betterton performed with a patrician style which was lauded within a theatrical world still closely associated with the court and accustomed to aristocratic modes of address. Accounts suggest that Betterton's acting involved both the emotional involvement and the type of restrained gestures which Le Faucheur, following Cicero and Quintilian, recommends to the orator. Colley Cibber (1671–1757) admired Betterton's capacity to convey feeling, declaring that the actor who 'feels not himself the Passion he would raise, will talk to a sleeping Audience: But this was never the fault of *Betterton*'.[19] Other accounts give an impression of Betterton's bodily presence and of the types of gesture he employed. According to Antony Aston, Betterton was 'a superlative good Actor', despite labouring with an 'ill figure': '[he] had fat short Arms, which he rarely lifted higher than his Stomach. – His Left Hand frequently lodg'd in his Breast, between his Coat and Waist-coat, while, with his Right, he prepar'd his Speech. – His Actions were few, but just . . . [He] kept his Passion under, and shew'd it most.'[20] Bodily movement is limited, but, for Aston, the value of those

[18] See Highfill et al., *Biographical Dictionary of Actors*, vol. II, pp. 73–96. David Thomas states that the beginning of Betterton's pre-eminence occurred with 'the retirement of the leading actors of the pre-Commonwealth era in the early 1680s (notably Hart and Mohun), and with the uniting of the two acting companies in 1682' (David Thomas (ed.), *Restoration and Georgian England, 1660–1788*, Theatre in Europe: A Documentary History (Cambridge: Cambridge University Press, 1989), p. 143).

[19] Colley Cibber, *An Apology for the Life of Mr Colley Cibber* (1740), ed. B. R. S. Fone (Ann Arbor: University of Michigan Press, 1968), p. 62.

[20] Antony Aston, *A Brief Supplement to Colley Cibber, Esq; his Lives of the late Famous Actors and Actresses*, in Colley Cibber, *An Apology for the Life of Mr Colley Cibber*, ed. R. W. Lowe, 2 vols. (London, Nimmo, 1889), vol. II, pp. 299–301.

actions which are employed endows the visual event with an emotional force. It is a style whereby strength and dignity are conveyed partly by the body *not* moving – a display of the power of restraint. The restricted arm movement and the favouring of the right hand are clearly in line with Le Faucheur's recommendations to the orator, but Aston is not drawn to reject these gestures as artificial. As Betterton manually *prepares his speech*, he seems, like his successor James Quin, to be primarily concerned with producing a dignified rendering of the playwright's words, but while such an approach might later have been dismissed as 'oratorical' – a term which gained a pejorative tinge in theatrical criticism – it inspires only admiration from Aston.

With his sturdy body, Betterton achieved much of his dramatic impact through facial acting, and here again the type of restraint advocated by Le Faucheur can be observed. Cibber, describing Betterton's playing of Brutus, observed that 'in his Dispute with *Cassius*, his Spirit flew only to his Eye; his steady Look alone supply'd that Terror, which he disdain'd an Intemperance in his Voice should rise to'.[21] Cibber reinforces this impression of Betterton's manly, dignified visual presence, describing how in 'all his Soliloquies of moment, the strong Intelligence of his Attitude and Aspect, drew you into such an impatient Gaze, and eager Expectation, that you almost imbib'd the Sentiment with your Eye, before the Ear could reach it'.[22] Cibber applauds Betterton's careful modulation of his body's posture in readiness for the rendering of words, and while the description acknowledges the power of visual expression, Cibber here can only 'almost' catch the sentiment by visual means alone. Later actors attract description which is less tentative in its reading of visual performance, and, indeed, both criticism and performance reveal increased confidence in a varied application of visual expression. Betterton's restrained technique, though, was clearly regarded by many observers as a quite proper method for conveying the passions, and his success and public prominence ensured him a legacy that would help to sustain the presence of classical acting in the theatres – albeit a presence which would become increasingly beleaguered.

Betterton's death did not put an end to the significance of his acting style. Alongside the practice of actors such as Quin who were indebted to his example, his reputation was perpetuated and shaped by the publication of reminiscences, such as Aston's and Cibber's, as well as instructive works for the stage which invoked the name of the celebrated actor. A work I have mentioned before, *The Life of Mr. Thomas Betterton, The late Eminent*

---

[21] Cibber, *An Apology*, ed. Fone, p. 62.
[22] *Ibid.*, pp. 65–6.

Tragedian (1710), maintained a posthumous impact of Betterton upon the stage and is of particular interest in that, as it displays a veneration of the classical tradition, it also attempts to use the image of Betterton as a tool in the civilisation of the theatres. *The Life of Mr. Thomas Betterton* is a compilation of material relating to the theatre which was thrown together, in rapid response to Betterton's death, by the hack author and editor Charles Gildon (1665–1724). Under the guise of biography appears a collection of writings, among which is a lengthy consideration of, as the subtitle puts it, *The Action and Utterance of the Stage, Bar, and Pulpit*, and here it seems that Gildon grabbed at the most fitting existing work on the subject he had to hand, for the section is largely plagiarised from the English translation of Le Faucheur's *Traitté*. In fact, Gildon's work stages a meeting with the actor and puts Le Faucheur's prescriptions directly into Betterton's mouth, so that in this posthumous appearance Betterton's technique becomes completely grounded in the tradition of classical oratory.[23] Gildon's Betterton promotes gesture as a natural and universal language of the passions and recommends a judicious application of such a language for the affective appeal to the passions of the audience; at the same time, this language of gesture is modelled according to the demands of classical decorum. Readers of *The Life of Mr. Thomas Betterton* would have found, for example, Le Faucheur's warnings against licking or biting the lips, 'which are all ungenteel and unmannerly Actions' (p. 72), and against using only the left hand to gesture (p. 75). In places Gildon has adapted Le Faucheur's work to give it a specific applicability to the stage – in such cases, the advice encourages the actor to be, above all, stately, particularly when acting tragedy. Shrugging the shoulders is allowed, but Gildon's Betterton suggests that 'it seems more adapted to Comedy, than Tragedy, where all should be great and solemn, and with which the gravest of the Orators Actions will agree' (p. 73).

According to the demands of such somatic detailing, methods of training are suggested which depend upon the conscious manipulation of the

---

[23] Charles Gildon, *The Life of Mr. Thomas Betterton, The late Eminent Tragedian. Wherein The Action and Utterance of the Stage, Bar, and Pulpit, are distinctly consider'd. With The Judgement of the late Ingenious Monsieur de St. Evremond, upon the Italian and French Music and Opera's; in a Letter to the Duke of Buckingham. To which is added, The Amorous Widow, or the Wanton Wife. A Comedy. Written by Mr. Betterton* (London, 1710). Further references are given in the text. Through a comparison of passages from the sections on delivery with the translation of Le Faucheur's *Traitté*, the great extent of Gildon's borrowings from this source becomes obvious; Howell presents a selection of such comparisons in *British Logic and Rhetoric*, pp. 186–7. Howell notes the identification of the author from the letter of dedication to which, in some copies, his name is affixed.

body's parts and the refinement of movements through an external attention to the body – so while the manual promotes *feeling* as a basis for good
acting, it also promotes *looking* and correcting as a key component of the
craft. For the purposes of rehearsing movements, Gildon's Betterton
suggests that 'a Glass may prove very advantageous'; without this tool,
'some Friend, who is a perfect Master in all the Beauties of *Gesture* and
Motion' is recommended as an equally effective means of correction (p. 55).
As a visual source for models of eloquence, the manual recommends that
actors should study figures in history painting and in sculpture – significantly, sources for *static* postures rather than for sequences of movement
(pp. 63 and 139). *The Life of Mr. Thomas Betterton* itself serves as a similar
source of gestures, albeit using a literary rather than pictorial medium.
Such techniques might appear to be the basis of extreme mannerism, and it
is possible that the manual may have influenced performance techniques
between Betterton's death and Garrick's debut. Acting of that period –
particularly tragic acting – has long been characterised as manneristic for its
deployment of grand posturing. After 1710, as Thomas writes, 'tragic acting
styles became more mannered and externalised. [Robert] Wilks and Quin
were the most mannered, but even [Barton] Booth who attempted to
model his work on Betterton was not free from obvious mannerisms.'[24]
Barton Booth, it is worth noting, did imitate gestures from history painting
and from statuary; it is also worth noting that at least one observer, while
recognising the artificiality, declared that when Booth introduced such
devices they 'seemed but the Effect of Nature'.[25]

With its investment in classical eloquence, Gildon's work promotes a
language of the body which, my broad argument suggests, was ultimately
devalued as a vehicle of politeness. Like descriptions of Betterton himself,
The Life of Mr. Thomas Betterton shows a language of the passions filtered
through a patrician body image which is deployed so as to impress
audiences largely through somatic claims upon power. The Bettertonian
style is concerned with marking the singular, elevated status of the character: as declamatory speech asserts its abnormality and elevation above
conventional speech, so the Bettertonian/Gildonian body is manipulated
to assert the *distinction* of the performer – in terms of both difference and

---

[24] Thomas, *Restoration and Georgian England*, p. 127.
[25] This was Colley Cibber's son, Theophilus Cibber, who admired Booth's attitudes as 'all
picturesque', and pointed to Booth's 'good Taste for Statuary and Painting' (*The Lives and
Characters of the Most Eminent Actors and Actresses of Great Britain and Ireland* (London, 1753),
p. 51).

nobility. However, while Gildon sponsored a conservative somatic ideal, he intended that it should perform a modern social function, and his work can be seen to participate in the growth of politeness through its earnest attempts to transform the theatre into a moral institution. In this regard the name of Betterton again contributed authority to the project, for, unlike many of his contemporary colleagues, Betterton had been admired not only for his performances but also for the upstanding conduct of his private life. Invoking and dwelling upon this other aspect of Betterton's reputation, Gildon promotes dramatic entertainment as an occasion for moral instruction and religious edification. He has Betterton voice the view, for example, that 'the Moral Lessons, which the Stage presents, may make the greatest Impressions on the Minds of the Audience; because the Instruction is convey'd with Pleasure, and by the Ministration of the Passions' (pp. 18–19). The practice of Christian religion, he continues, is 'so forcibly recommended from the Stage by a purifying our Passions, and the Conveyance of Delight, [that] the Stage may properly be esteem'd the Handmaid of the Pulpit' (p. 19). By advertising such a view of drama's social function, Gildon was contributing to the elevation of the theatre's cultural position within its increasingly bourgeois social milieu, but the body image he projected into that modern context reached back to the court-centred theatres of the seventeenth century. His work is thus both progressive and conservative: in dashing off a work which would sell within the growing community of middle-class readers, Gildon appealed directly to modern, moral sensibilities, but he plagiarised an elocutionary theory which in time would be widely deemed inappropriate for generating 'natural symbols' of modern politeness.

Certainly classical acting retained a good deal of currency in the eighteenth century. Not only did classicism inform the so-called 'manneristic' actors of the 1720s and 1730s, but well into the mid and later century it continued to influence performers. Garrick's example did not oust traditional styles, although he is sometimes seen to have brought about a complete revolution in acting. In fact, well into his career Garrick was complaining about having to work with actors whose declamatory styles did not accord with his own.[26] As Arnold Hare has written, 'the Georgian

---

[26] See, for example, Garrick's comments in a letter of 18 October 1750 on working with Jane Cibber, who had been taught by her grandfather Colley Cibber: 'the Young Lady may have Genius for ought I know, but if she has, it is so eclips'd by the Manner of speaking ye Laureat has taught her, that I am affraid [*sic*] it will not do – We differ greatly in our Notions of Acting (in Tragedy I mean) & If he is right I am, & ever shall be in ye wrong road' (*The Letters of David Garrick*, ed. David M. Little and George M. Kahrl, 3 vols. (London: Oxford University Press, 1963), vol. I, p. 158).

theatre, despite the achievements of its leading actors, was more often than not characterised by a motley pattern of conflicting styles and conventions'.[27] And the classical style continued to be promoted through later acting manuals. Le Faucheur's doctrine is found again in *The History of the English Stage* (1741), a work actually attributed to Betterton on its title-page, but in fact by Edmund Curll (1675–1747). Curll, following Gildon's compositional methods, gleaned the instructions contained within Le Faucheur's *Traitté* directly from Gildon's *Life of Mr. Thomas Betterton*.[28] And later works, such as Roger Pickering's *Reflections upon Theatrical Expression in Tragedy* (1755) and Paul Hiffernan's *Dramatic genius* (1770), similarly uphold classical models as ideals of performance.[29]

The classical mode, however, was subject to questioning and reappraisal. During his first London season in 1741, Garrick audaciously and successfully mocked classical acting with satirical mimicry of its conventions.[30] But before Garrick's appearance upon the stage, a significant critique of classical acting had begun to be made public through the work of Aaron Hill. And Hill was determined that if acting was to be relevant to modern, polite society, then a radically different approach to performance would have to be developed.

THE CRAFT OF FEELING: AARON HILL'S ACTING THEORY

Aaron Hill began to expound his ideas concerning proper acting in *The Prompter*, a periodical committed to discussion of the contemporary theatre, which Hill produced jointly with William Popple (1701–64), a civil servant and aspiring author, from November 1734 to July 1736. *The Prompter* appeared twice weekly as a twopenny half-sheet, and it was printed by Samuel Richardson, with whom Hill had become well

---

[27] Thomas, *Restoration and Georgian England*, p. 349.

[28] The full title of Curll's work is *The History of the English Stage, from the Restauration to the Present Time. Including the Lives, Characters and Amours, of the most Eminent Actors and Actresses. With Instructions for Public Speaking; Wherein The Action and Utterance of the Bar, Stage and Pulpit are Distinctly considered. By Thomas Betterton* (London, 1741). While Gildon and Curll carried on the classical tradition, it is significant that the manner of their borrowing gave a greater priority to the use of gesture. Howell notes that 'Curll omitted almost everything that Gildon had said on utterance or voice; and this latter topic...had been made much less important by Gildon than it had been by Le Faucheur. But Curll gave most of Gildon's precepts on gesture' (*British Logic and Rhetoric*, p. 189).

[29] Joseph Roach points out that '[a]s late as 1815 Leigh Hunt was still grumbling about "declamation" and the "putting forth of the old oratorical right hand", well over a century after the physiology that supported this gesture had supposedly been rendered obsolete' (*The Player's Passion: Studies in the Science of Acting* (Newark: University of Delaware Press; London: Associated University Presses, 1985), p. 79).

[30] See Woods, *Garrick Claims the Stage*, p. 130.

acquainted by this time.[31] In all, 173 numbers were produced, with articles addressing broad social, economic, and ethical issues of the day, but with a particular focus upon events within the London theatre world. A fundamental aim for Hill and Popple was to raise the moral and cultural status of the theatres, and throughout the run of *The Prompter* theatrical performance is presented as an instrument which, when properly handled, is capable of generating social improvement. 'PUBLICK Spectacles', asserted an early number, 'are, by their very Essence, calculated to reform the Abuses that creep into Society', and implicated in this claim was a recognition that performances should 'move the Passions by such Images as imprint in the Mind *Terror* and *Compassion, Grief* and *Joy*'.[32] Later numbers drew verbatim upon the translation in 1734 of a work by Charles Porée, given the English title *An Oration, In Which an Enquiry is Made whether the Stage Is, or Can be Made a School for Forming the Mind to Virtue*, and Hill and Popple clearly supported Porée's view that the theatre could be made to serve a moral function although it was failing properly to do so at the time. The editors of a selected edition of *The Prompter* are right, then, to point out that the stage, 'to Hill and Popple, was primarily a moral institution, and the purpose of the theatre, like that of the pulpit, was to elevate the mind and spirit'.[33] Fundamental to the achievement of such ethereal ends, though, was the manipulation of the body.

Indeed, the theatre is presented in *The Prompter* as a '*Nursery* for both Mind, and Body' – a setting where models of polite eloquence should be set before the viewing public so as to inspire moral behaviour and to broadcast ideals of conduct.[34] 'The theatre', it is argued,

should be not only a *School*, wherein the *Passions* are corrected; and reduced, to the Measures of *Morality*. – It ought also to be the Place, whence *Examples* shou'd be copied, as to OUTWARD Graces, and *Deportment*: where the Delicacies of *Good-breeding* might be *learnt*, in their sublimest Purity; and the Elegancies of LANGUAGE, in its most refin'd, and absolute, Perfection.[35]

---

[31] T. C. Duncan Eaves and Ben D. Kimpel discuss the probability that Richardson printed *The Prompter* in *Samuel Richardson: A Biography* (Oxford: Clarendon Press, 1971), pp. 60–1. On the evidence of print ornaments, Keith Maslen confirms Richardson's role in *Samuel Richardson of London, Printer: A Study of his Printing based on Ornament Use and Business Accounts* (Dunedin: University of Otago, 2001), p. 30. See also Gerrard, *Aaron Hill*, p. 203.

[32] *The Prompter* 7 (4 December 1734).

[33] Aaron Hill and William Popple, *The Prompter: A Theatrical Paper (1734–1736)*, ed. William W. Appleton and Kalman A. Burnim (New York: Blom, 1966), p. ix. These editors point out the indebtedness of numbers 79 (12 August 1735) and 80 (15 August 1735) to Porée (pp. 88–92).

[34] *The Prompter* 113 (9 December 1735).

[35] *Ibid.*

In Hill's eyes, though, there were few actors on the contemporary stage who properly embodied 'good breeding' and who could thus perform this social function. Good breeding, for Hill, was certainly not represented by a declaiming, classical body, and in reaction against prevailing stage practice – the acting of Barton Booth and James Quin, for example – he championed alternative ideas of what proper acting entailed. He openly proclaimed himself a revolutionary, signing his early essays with a 'B' for 'Broomstick' to assert his desire to sweep old-fashioned methods from the stage, and his statements on performance urge explicitly that the craft of the actor be divorced from principles of classical oratory.[36] He complains of actors who, with Bettertonian gravity, apply strict rhetorical laws to their performance: 'As they *err*, in their Notions of *Voice*, They are equally mistaken when they discourse of, or consider the *Action*; For, instead of Examining *Nature*, they look into *Quintilian*: not reflecting that the Lessons, which *He* teaches his *Orator*, were directed to the BAR, not the STAGE.' It is absurd, Hill insists, for an actor, out of veneration of Quintilian, never to 'raise his HANDS, above the Height of his EYES'.[37] Hill is similarly intolerant of declamatory delivery, complaining of speeches that are '*All*, one, continued, undistinguish'd, *Rotation* of Cadence: *toned* away, like the *Cant* of a *Lesson*: with no *Endeavours*, no *Seemings*, toward . . . *Imitation of Nature*'.[38] Such modes of expression were, for Hill, inappropriate for addressing polite, bourgeois audiences – audiences which, in the mid 1730s, Hill and Popple were engaged in forging through their essays. Several *Prompter* essays urge for the improvement of audience behaviour, impressing upon theatregoers the need to sit in silence and concentrate upon the finer points of a performance in order to appreciate it. In one issue, Hill delightedly reports his sense that 'a *Refinement* in dramatic *Taste* [is] getting Ground, as it were, *insensibly*'. His evidence for this refinement is revealing: 'Due *Applauses*, are frequently given, to *soft*, and *delicate*, Touches of Nature, which wou'd, formerly, have pass'd, *unnoticed*.'[39] In such statements we witness the beginning of classical acting's loss of ground, as 'soft' and 'delicate' forms of expression – quite unlike the majestic, patrician forms of Bettertonian acting – begin to be granted cultural space.

---

[36] '*[T]he Great B, at the Bottom of my first Page is not placed there, to signify* Blockhead, *but* Broomstick' (*The Prompter* 2 (15 November 1734)).
[37] *The Prompter* 64 (20 June 1735).
[38] *The Prompter* 104 (7 November 1735).
[39] *The Prompter* 104 (7 November 1735).

As Hill rejects the forms of classical acting, so too he rejects the 'externalised' methods associated with it, and he puts forward his own theory of how the actor should summon the signs of the passions on stage. The actor, Hill maintains in *The Prompter*, should imaginatively feel the passion to be expressed and should allow the natural mechanism of the body to generate expressive movement. As Joseph Roach has demonstrated, his acting theory functions within a Cartesian paradigm of human physiology, where the body is understood to be a machine which can be animated by the will.[40] Hill's principal rules for acting are

> no more, than a connected Deduction of these plain, and natural *Consequences*.
> 1st. The *Imagination* assumes the *Idea*.
> 2ndly. Its *Marks*, and characteristical Impressions, appear, first, in the *Face*; because nearest to the *Seat* of the Imagination.
> 3rdly. Thence, impell'd by the *Will*, a commission'd Detachment of the *Animal Spirits* descending, into the dependant Organization of *Muscles*, and *Swelling*, and *adapting* them, in its Progress, bends, and stimulates, their Elastic Powers, into a *Position*, apt to *execute* the Purpose, (or *express* the Warmth of) the *Idea*.
> 4thly. Thus the *Look, Air, Voice*, and *Action*, proper to a Passion, preconceiv'd, in the *Imagination*, become *a mere, and mechanic*, necessity; without Perplexity, Study, or Difficulty.[41]

The process internalises the act of imitation so that the external sign is genuine. Specific definition of appropriate bodily movement, such as that found in Le Faucheur's work, invites an imitation of the external, where the will is directed to the signing parts of the body. Hill, on the other hand, recommends the reproduction of the stimulus itself which, through '*mechanic*, necessity', will cause the body's physical response. The actor is regarded as the operator of a machine which moves when impelled by the imagination, and so the actor's skill lies in the process of imagining:

> The whole, that is needful in order to impress any Passion on the *Look*, is, first, to conceive it, by a strong, and intent *Imagination*. – Let a Man, for Instance, *recollect some Idea of* Sorrow; his Eye will, in a Moment, catch the *Dimness* of *Melancholy*. his Muscles will *relax* into *Languor*; and his whole Frame of Body sympathetically *unbend* itself, into a *Remiss*, and *inanimate, Lassitude*. – In such a passive Position of *Features*, and *Nerves*, let him attempt to *speak* haughtily; and He will find it *impossible*... The Modification of his *Muscles* has affected the *Organs of Speech*; and, before He can express *Sounds* of Anger, in his *Voice*, He

---

[40] Roach, *Player's Passion*, pp. 78–82.
[41] *The Prompter* 118 (26 December 1735).

must, *by conceiving some Idea of Anger*, inflame his Eye into Earnestness, and *new knit*, and *brace up* his *Fibres*, into an *Impatience*, adapted to Violence; – and, *then*, not only the *Voice* will correspond with the *Visage*, but the *Step*, *Air*, and *Movement*, All, recovering from the LANGUID, and carrying Marks of the *Impetuous*, and the *Terrible*, flash a *moving* PROPRIETY, from the *Actor*, to the *Audience*, that, *communicating*, immediately, the Sensation it *expresses*, chains and rivets, our *Attention*, to the *Passions we are mov'd by*.[42]

For performance dependent upon such inevitable consequence, Hill does not here present explicit instruction regarding what type of gestures should be used to represent particular passions. In *The Prompter* he avoids prescriptive instruction because the physiological attitude that informs his theory of acting renders it redundant. In fact, he takes issue with other works which recommend particular techniques for developing passionate expression. He dismisses those who 'have form'd tedious, and laborious, Schemes, of adjusting their, *Gesture*, at *Looking-Glasses*', and is equally critical of the study of painting as a source from which to copy expression.[43] Gildon, it will be remembered, had recommended both of these techniques to the actor, but the internalised imitation demanded by Hill's theory cannot benefit from the external training of actual looking. What Hill does recommend is that the actor should cultivate the imagination and gain a thorough knowledge of the passions. Drawing upon Descartes's theory of the passions, he enumerates 'SIX *Dramatic Passions*, which are capable of being strongly *express'd*, by the LOOK'. The actor should become fully acquainted with 'JOY, SORROW, FEAR, SCORN, ANGER and AMAZEMENT'. Other 'auxiliary' passions, he maintains, are able to be expressed 'by a *Mixture*, of *Two*, or more, of the *Six Capital Dramatics*'. Jealousy, for example, 'requires a Combination of *Three* Passions, *Fear*, *Scorn*, and *Anger*'.[44]

The doctrine Hill laid out in his *Prompter* articles was expanded and revised in various versions – including the 1746 poem which so moved Richardson – and it was given its final expression in his 'Essay on the Art of Acting', published posthumously in *The Works of the Late Aaron Hill* (1753).[45] Throughout the development of his acting theory, Hill remains intolerant of declamatory styles, but comparing the later 'Essay' with the earlier articles indicates a significant shift in his methods of instruction – a shift which suggests that for an actor to appear 'soul-touched' and thus 'fire

---

[42] *The Prompter* 66 (27 June 1735).
[43] *The Prompter* 118 (26 December 1735).
[44] *The Prompter* 66 (27 June 1735).
[45] References to the essay are to vol. IV of *Works* and are given in the text.

a feeling Age', a good deal more bodily craftsmanship was required than Hill initially maintained.[46] In the 'Essay', Hill still insists that imaginative empathy with the character is the ideal method for generating expression, but it is accepted that this might prove difficult to achieve in performance. The four stages of gestural production are thus revised and no longer offer the actor a technique 'without Perplexity, Study, or Difficulty'. In fact, it is acknowledged that actors may not possess sufficient pliability of imagination, and the 'Essay' offers the actor a shortcut for generating gesture. The actor who is unable properly to imagine a feeling 'may help his defective idea, in a moment, by annexing, at once, the *look* to the *idea*, in the very instant, while he is bracing his nerves into springiness: for so, the image, the look, and the muscles, all concurring, *at once*, to the purpose, their effect will be the same, as if each had succeeded another, progressively' (p. 362). Rather cagily, perhaps, the passage promotes a technique which undermines the doctrine of acting controlled by the imagination. The principle of applying the '*look* to the *idea*' is slipped in under the cover of a description of nervous activity, and thus the methodological reversal which this represents is understated. But in fact, the revised method is demanding the external imitation of expressive signs, which is precisely the process criticised in *The Prompter*. Without drawing attention to this methodological shift, the 'Essay' ushers in its practical advice, whilst still declaring the ideal of acting to be purely imaginative.

According to the pragmatic needs of external imitation, the pedagogic method is also revised so as to present clearer instruction regarding the signs with which the passions manifest themselves. As a source for the actor's reference, the 'Essay' contains extensive descriptions of the body's activity when possessed by the principal passions (the number of which is here increased from six to ten). When a man is possessed by joy, for example,

his forehead appears open, and rais'd, his eye smiling, and sparkling, his neck will be stretch'd, and erect, without stiffness, as if it would add new height to his

---

[46] Discussions of Hill's writing on acting have tended to focus upon his early work: Roach, for example, bases his conclusions upon Hill's early writing, and a similar emphasis is given by David Thomas and Arnold Hare, who represent Hill's theory with extracts from *The Prompter* (Thomas, *Restoration and Georgian England*, pp. 170–3). Such an approach allows for a fair representation of Hill's depiction of 'the actor's art as a mechanical process of inwardly experiencing the passions at the will's command' (Roach, *Player's Passion*, p. 79), but it downplays Hill's development of the theory. I have discussed the shifts in Hill's acting theory in 'B for Broomstick? A Consideration of Aaron Hill's "Revolutionary" acting Theory', *Leading Notes: Journal of the National Early Music Association* 13 (Spring 1997), 19–23.

stature; his breast will be inflated, and majestically backen'd; his back-bone erect, and all the joints of his arm, wrist, fingers, hip, knee, and ancle, will be high-strung, and brac'd boldly. And *now*, if he attempts to speak *joy*, all the spirit of the passion will ascend in his accents, and the very tone of his voice will seem to out-rapture the meaning. (p. 361)

Hill describes what he sees as the natural signs of the passions. The imitative actor's task is to ensure that 'when natural impressions are imitated, exactly, by art, the effect of such art must seem natural' (p. 361). This, of course, is a requirement that Le Faucheur and his copyists also demanded, but while Hill's theory develops a methodological kinship with that of Le Faucheur, there remains a consistent antipathy towards rigid oratorical devices, which is shown by the type of bodily movement assigned to the passions. Hill's version of the natural does not have the decorous strictures of Le Faucheur's doctrine; Hill would by no means have the stage peopled by Bettertonian stoics, powerfully declaiming speeches which might *state* (but not *show*) the emotional upheaval of the character. The actor following Hill has more somatic freedom than one working within a system which allows, for example, the use of only the right hand. Astonishment, for Hill, acts upon the body by 'arresting the breath, eyes, gesture, and every power and faculty of the body, occasions an interruption of their several uses, that wou'd bring on an actual *cessation* – but, that the reason, struggling slowly to relieve the apprehension, gives a kind of hesitative articulation to the utterance, and gradual motion and recovery to the Look, the Limbs, and the Countenance' (p. 385). The passion expresses itself through the whole body, which remains free from the rules prescribed by the classical rhetoric Hill reacted against. Indeed, when he describes appropriate gestures, Hill is never as dogmatic as instructors of the classical school. In a summary of the passions' somatic signs, his descriptions are far from doctrinaire:

> JOY is expressed by muscles intense – and a smile in the eye.
> ANGER, by muscles intense – and a frown in the eye.
> PITY, by muscles intense – and a sadness in the eye.
> HATRED, by muscles intense – and aversion in the eye.
> WONDER, by muscles intense – and an awful alarm in the eye.
> LOVE, by muscles intense, – and a respectful attachment in the eye.
> GRIEF, by neither muscles, – nor eye intense but both languid.
> FEAR, by muscles and look both languid – with an alarm, in eye, and motion.
> SCORN, by muscles languid and neglected – with a smile in the eye, to express the *light*, or a frown in the eye, for the *serious* species.

JEALOUSY, by muscles intense, and the look pensive; or the look intense,
and muscles languid, interchangeably. (p. 401)

Ultimately, then, Hill's instruction is often indistinct in terms of specific
somatic detailing, and by being so it maintains its distinction from the
acting tradition in opposition to which it was conceived.

Precisely why Aaron Hill should have revised his acting theory is difficult
to determine, but that limitations should be perceived in his early theory is
understandable when it is considered that in the practice of so-called
'natural' acting, much more was demanded of the actor than a pure exercise
of deeply felt emotions. Garrick, whom Hill came greatly to admire, was
famously celebrated for his emotional 'transformations' into other characters, and in his own statements on performance he himself proclaimed
the importance of 'acting from his feelings'. In a letter of 1762, he explained
his method in a response to criticism against his use of broken, hesitant
delivery:

I have been frequently abus'd by ye Gentlemen of ye Pen for false Stops; & one in
particular wrote against me for stopping injudiciously in this line in Hamlet.

I think it was to See – my Mother's Wedding I certainly never *stop* there, (that is,
close ye sense) but I as certainly, *Suspend* my voice, by which Your Ear must know,
that the sense is suspended too – for Hamlet's Grief causes ye break & with a Sigh,
he finishes ye sentence – *my Mother's Wedding* – I really could not from my feelings
act it otherwise.[47]

It seems clear that Garrick invested his performances with his emotions,
but it is also clear that his acting was not straightforwardly an outpouring of
feeling. The emotional input was anchored to thorough technical prepara-
tion involving incredibly detailed textual analysis and a knowledgeable
application of very particular techniques of stagecraft. Garrick's own *An
Essay on Acting* (1744), in which an analysis of both tragic and comic acting
is framed within a satirical attack upon his own practice, exhibits the
careful study of character from which his performances derived. The
essay contains punctilious descriptions of how the body should appear at
crucial moments selected from both tragedy and comedy. He describes, for
example, the playing of Macbeth, and through a close examination of
Macbeth's vision of the dagger, he analyses the character's emotional
motivations and explains the necessary visual signs for the display of
these feelings. The line 'Come let me clutch thee', for Garrick, 'is not to
be done by one motion only, but by several successive catches at it, first

---

[47] 24 January 1762, *Letters of David Garrick*, vol. I, pp. 350–1.

with one hand and then with the other, preserving the same motion, at the same time, with his feet, like a man who out of his depth and half drowned in his struggles catches at air for substance'.[48] Such passages show Garrick's acute consciousness of the minutiae of gestural language, and they provide compelling testimony that the 'inspiration' involved in his acting was supported by rigorous craftsmanship and a deep knowledge of how certain effects might be achieved by the body on stage. Considering Garrick's commitment to craft, it becomes unsurprising that Hill should revise his theory during the course of its development and should come to acknowledge the importance to the actor of carefully and consciously rehearsed performance techniques. As an impassioned opponent of classical acting methods, Hill promoted a boldly new approach to performing the passions for the purposes of reforming the theatres and the society beyond them, but as this approach was reconsidered and revised he assimilated within his work a more developed awareness that the 'soul-touched' actor whose image would animate a 'feeling Age' must rely, to a large extent, upon a knowledge of craft. And by the mid century, Aaron Hill was not the only British acting theorist promoting this view.

'OF THE MEANS BY WHICH AN ACTOR MAY IMPROVE NATURAL SENSIBILITY': JOHN HILL'S *THE ACTOR* (1755)

In 1735, Aaron Hill noted the beginnings of a '*Refinement* in dramatic *Taste*'. By 1755, another Hill – one who, in common with his namesake, had a preoccupation with the theatre and with acting techniques – was able to write with confidence of 'the present good taste in the public'.[49] This later writer – Sir John Hill, MD (1716?–75) – was intervening in a significantly changed theatrical milieu when he turned his hand to performance theory. Not only were audiences appreciably more refined than when Aaron Hill began his campaigning in *The Prompter*, but, for the sentimentally inclined acting theorist, the stage presented admirable exponents of the modern craft. So whereas Aaron Hill was spurred largely by a resistance to declamatory styles, John Hill could ground his science of acting in reflections upon 'the excellence of the principal among the present performers' (p. 4). Indeed, the work of this later Hill suggests that, by the 1750s, the task for the modern acting theorist was not to

---

[48] David Garrick, *An Essay on Acting: In which will be consider'd the Mimical Behaviour of a certain Fashionable Faulty Actor* (London, 1744), p. 17.
[49] Hill, *The Actor*, p. 4. Subsequent quotations are from this edition, with references given in the text.

bring into being a new mode for expressing the passions, but rather to sustain and refine the mode that had already taken hold on the British stage. At the core of John Hill's writing on stagecraft is the contention that 'natural' acting must be *regulated*, and his work is thus significant as an articulation of the view that, if a body was to be recognised as both eloquent and polite, its performance had to be conducted within a framework of refined somatic aesthetics.

John Hill had trained as an actor under Charles Macklin – a good credential for a theorist of the modern craft – but he was also a physician, a herbalist, a celebrated botanist, and an immensely prolific writer of great range. He produced a large corpus of scientific writing, including works of popular medicine and the massive, twenty-six-volume *The Vegetable System* (1759–75). He also wrote several plays and a number of extended prose narratives, and, posing as the Honourable Juliana-Susannah Seymour, he authored works on conduct in marriage (1753) and on the education of children (1754).[50] His *The Actor: A Treatise on the Art of Playing* was initially adapted from a French treatise, Pierre Rémond de Sainte Albine's *Le Comédien* (1747), and was first published in 1750. He revised this treatise – to the extent that he was justified in calling it 'A New Work' – and this second version was published, with a title similar to the first, in 1755.[51]

In many ways, *The Actor* presents an already-established doctrine. Like other treatises, it recognises that there 'are peculiar gestures for every passion', and that 'these are not arbitrary, or what the player pleases; they are dictated by nature; they are common to all mankind, and therefore all men understand them' (p. 232). It presents the familiar advice to avoid affectation, because it is the actor's 'business to copy nature' (p. 80). It also subscribes to the technique of emotional identification for the purpose of affecting the audience, explaining how the 'player may have from nature a great deal of the pathetick, and may be able very happily to raise the passions of an audience by raising them first in himself; for this is the great art of doing it' (p. 33). By the 1750s, this type of instruction is, of course, familiar: it is a strand in the Le Faucheurian work of Gildon, and it

---

[50] G. S. Rousseau outlines Hill's biography and lists works known to be by Hill in 'John Hill, Universal Genius *Manqué*: Remarks on his Life and Times, with a Checklist of his Works', in J. A. Leo Lemay and G. S. Rousseau (eds.), *The Renaissance Man in the Eighteenth Century* (Los Angeles: University of California, 1978), pp. 45–129.

[51] The full title of the earlier version is: *The Actor: A Treatise on the Art of Playing. Interspersed with Theatrical Anecdotes, Critical Remarks on Plays, and Occasional Observations on Audiences* (London, 1750). Comparing both versions and the source text confirms Roach's view that 'with the second version of *The Actor*, Hill had in effect written an adaptation that could stand as an original work' (*Player's Passion*, p. 101).

forms the backbone of Aaron Hill's docine. Indeed, Aaron Hill is praised in *The Actor* as an author who should be 'studied as a classic' (p. 19). However, *The Actor* is not simply a reiterative work. It refines the established rules, and does so employing a terminology which derives from a new understanding of the physiology behind passionate expression. As Roach has shown, John Hill's work represents a shift away from Cartesian models of the body towards a new understanding of the body as an organism of nerves.[52] Accordingly, 'sensibility' is adopted as a term in *The Actor*, and indeed is the newly defined quality which the actor should possess. A premise of the treatise is that '[p]laying is a science, and is to be studied as a science' (p. 12), and its advice to the actor is presented in terms of the close analytical study of the nervous functions of the body. Hill's reformulation of what, in many ways, is a traditional doctrine thus provides a telling demonstration of the fact that shifts within theories of acting are contingent upon shifting physiological paradigms, but, in relation to the representation of politeness, what is most significant about Hill's work is his recurrent emphasis upon the need to regulate the body's expressive apparatus. 'Understanding will make a player perceive properly', Hill explains, 'and sensibility will make him do it feelingly; but all this may be done in reading the passage; it is this fire and spirit that produce the living character, and he who has judgment to regulate this, can never have too much of it' (p. 119). And so throughout the treatise, it is not just the possession of necessary qualities but the *control* of them which is impressed upon the actor. Hill is concerned to show, as two of his chapter headings put it, '*the means by which an actor may improve natural sensibility*' (p. 78) and '*the due regulation and proper use of Sensibility*' (p. 84). He argues, for example, that a 'hundred people know how to indulge their natural faculties, for one who has the art to check them; but on such a regulation depends all the glory of the compleat performer' (p. 17). For Hill an ungoverned outpouring of sensibility does not make for eloquent stage performance: 'It would be easy to produce instances, among the present players, of those who have so much sensibility, that they will cry when they should be angry. The business is therefore, not how much of this quality they have, but how it is regulated' (p. 34).

---

[52] Roach, *Player's Passion*, pp. 99–103. Hill's use of 'sensibility', Roach writes, 'brought theatrical theory in line with current science, in which vitalistic theories of bodily organization, assuming the innate capacity of matter to respond variously to stimuli, were complicating the mechanistic' (p. 100).

Sensibility is essential to proper dramatic expression, for Hill, but in order for it to be truly affecting, it must be managed and refined within an aesthetic code. And in this respect, it is perhaps not surprising to discover that *The Actor* was used as a source by Diderot in *The Paradox of the Actor* (1770–84), where it is famously argued that sensibility is an *undesirable* quality in an actor, for it tends to disturb the necessary craft of imitating nature.[53] 'Great poets, great actors, and perhaps all the great imitators of nature', Diderot insists, 'gifted as they are with a fine imagination, a delicate touch and sure judgement, are the least emotional of beings.'[54] Diderot goes on to argue that 'Extremes of feeling make for indifferent actors; an average amount of feeling gives you the great mass of bad actors; a complete absence of feeling is what is needed for a great actor' – and he controversially claims that Garrick's greatness depended upon such emotional vacuity.[55] Hill does not go so far as Diderot, but importantly, the roots of Diderot's argument are in evidence in *The Actor*. Hill maintains the value of sensibility in good acting, but he argues for a strict control of this emotional foundation, and in this way Hill's treatise attempts to manipulate and refine the public body in order to satisfy and sustain the growing refinement of audiences.

A striking example of this codification of somatic eloquence is found in the honing of lachrymosity. The actor is told that sometimes 'one tear will affect an audience, where they would have despised a flood of them. The single drop of sorrow, the involuntary tribute of humanity, may be great and graceful, while the profusion of tears would be unworthy and contemptible' (p. 27). A refined, single tear has long been recognised as a central trope in sentimental expression – numerous examples of the device are collected in a 1963 essay on 'The Single Tear: A Stereotype of Literary Sensibility' by Alfred G. Engstrom.[56] John Hill's work reveals that expressions of this type were not just a matter for literary fiction where authors could provide readers with close-ups of such gesture in action. Assuming attentive, sharp-eyed audiences – or with the aim of embracing spectators within a community where attentiveness to small gestures is a necessary component of cultural appreciation – Hill elevates such delicate conventions and promotes their appropriateness upon the stage.

---

[53] Jacques Chouillet has shown Hill's treatise to have been a source for Diderot in 'Une source anglaise du *Paradoxe sur le comédien*', *Dix-huitième siècle* 2 (1970), 209–26.
[54] Diderot, *Selected Writings*, p. 106.
[55] *Ibid.*, p. 108.
[56] *Philological Quarterly* 42 (1963), 106–9.

We might regard this aesthetic in terms of the same fear of excessive gesture which inspired the reactions against Methodist enthusiasm and Orator Henley's more manic performances. For a polite society, emotional display is ratified as constitutive of proper behaviour, but only with qualifications which circumscribe that display. It is, in fact, allowed in *The Actor* that moments of being genuinely 'overcome' with passion will be an affecting device, and, as in other treatises, it is the word that crumbles with the surge of passion:

tho' it is very happy for the player to possess this quality of sensibility, it is necessary for him to have that command of himself, that he can keep it from interrupting his utterance, or taking away the articulation of his voice: but there are passages in which it may be allowed even this effect; and instead of a blemish it will communicate the greatest beauty. (p. 56)

However, Hill is careful to state that such faltering speech should be only rarely used:

Strokes of this kind in playing are like figures in oratory, a few of them enliven, elevate, and give an unconquerable power to a discourse; but to be eternally introducing them, robs them of all their merit and force: for the one, as well as the other, by this frequency, will be found to be the result of art and consideration, not of nature and sensibility. (p. 57)

Hill, then, puts forward his own paradox: if an actor floods the stage with genuine sensibility, it will appear to the audience as artificial, but if signs of sensibility are *introduced* with tact and subtlety, they will be found powerfully affective. The sentimental body emerges paradoxically from Hill's account as a 'natural construction' with an innate propriety – precisely the sort of 'natural symbol' Mary Douglas describes. Sensibility is presented in *The Actor* as an innate bodily quality, but Hill aestheticises it so that what we find in Hill's work, in fact, is the promotion of a new model of somatic decorum. If Charles Gildon's performance theory represents the dominance of 'classical decorum' upon the stage, and Aaron Hill's work reflects and contributes to its erosion, the work of John Hill shows the solidification of an innovative model of 'sentimental decorum' – a rhetoric of sensibility. This rhetoric is as much a cultural construction as the classical form it came to prevail over, but it is a construction which emerged through dialogue with *contemporary* cultural upheavals – including the transformation of the theatre's social function. Thus, increasingly unlike the declamatory acting which Richard Cumberland could only denounce as the remnant of 'a tasteless age', this innovative somatic decorum could appeal symbolically to the values and attitudes of a large proportion of contemporary theatregoers – spectators whose own refinement could be assayed through their appreciation of sentimental acting. But it was perhaps not only literal *spectators* for whom the polite bodies emerging from eighteenth-century acting discourse performed a function.

Regarding the dispersal of polite body images through acting theory, it is worth, in conclusion, commenting briefly on the type of genre that is constituted by *The Actor* and by other works of acting theory of whatever school. Hill's *The Actor* presents a carefully conceived and detailed science of acting, but it should be stressed that it is not written exclusively for specialists or for those working within the business of the theatre. Indeed, like most of the works on acting I have considered, *The Actor* is aimed at a broad market of literary consumers with interests in the theatre. As the subtitle to the 1750 version announces, Hill's discourse on acting is *Interspersed with Theatrical Anecdotes, Critical Remarks on Plays, and Occasional Observations on Audiences* – it is, in other words, conceived in part as a work of instructive entertainment in itself. Indeed, as I noted in the Introduction, acting theory often appeared under popular guises, and it emerged to become a fashionable, if relatively small, genre in its own right. When the four posthumous volumes of Aaron Hill's works were published, the only work to be specifically named in the overall title was his 'Essay on the Art of Acting' – by 1753, a work of acting theory was seen to be a positive selling point.

Recognising that acting theory became a popular genre is significant because it has implications for how we should regard the cultural reach or impact of such works. In drawing certain parallels between emergent sentimental acting theory and mid-century stage practice, I have suggested that acting theory is implicated in the emergence of innovative body images that were dispersed from the stage itself. In this regard, acting theory supports the emblematic exhibition of civilised virtues through the actual bodies of actors in front of large groups of spectators – it serves a functional role in the enterprise of public performance. I have aimed not to oversimplify the relation between theory and practice, and would not suggest that there was any straightforward relation of influence between the two, but I have none the less taken the view that published theories were of some relevance to what was performed on eighteenth-century stages.

As a popular genre, though, we might also recognise in acting theory a cultural importance that did not involve the actual public performances of actors. We might see acting theory also as a *literary* genre which offered satisfactions of a more private kind to readers. Recalling Samuel

Richardson as he trembled his way through *The Art of Acting*, we could certainly be tempted to see in acting theory a power which is independent of the official purpose of training actors. Richardson's reading, in fact, illustrates how a sympathetic exchange between bodies could be mediated through printed words; the passions, the incident suggests, could be efficiently encoded and decoded by means of verbal representation. It is unlikely that many readers of acting theory felt quite the degree of emotional upheaval that struck Richardson – if they did, they left few records of their experiences. But the popular status of acting theory is none the less of interest, for it does suggest that readerly satisfactions of some kind were being discovered through the literary consumption of fictional bodies. As the next chapter looms, it may come as no surprise when I suggest that there are analogies between this type of reading and the reading of sentimental fiction. By 1746, when Richardson read and printed *The Art of Acting*, sentimental fiction had, following the impact of *Pamela* (1740) and its aftermath, attained an immensely popular status, and a notable part of its appeal lay in extenuated representations of the passions' expression. Indeed, it might be claimed that sentimental fiction – of which Richardson was a master creator – had contributed to the popular appeal of literary representations of the passions, and hence may have enlivened the mid-century market for acting theory. But sentimental fiction's role in elocutionary discourse was more than merely supportive of those texts which explicitly taught somatic practice. Sentimental fiction, like eighteenth-century works on oratory and acting, was itself implicated in the creation of eloquent bodies, and, as we shall see, it provided its readers with ample opportunities to perform politeness.

CHAPTER 5

Polite reading:
sentimental fiction and the performance of response

I remember so well its [*The Man of Feeling*'s] first publication, my
mother and sisters crying over it, dwelling upon it with rapture! And
when I read it, as I was a girl of fourteen not yet versed in sentiment,
I had a secret dread I should not cry enough to gain the credit of
proper sensibility.

Lady Louisa Stuart (1826)[1]

READING AS PERFORMANCE

In what ways were sentimental novels implicated within elocutionary
discourse? Why is a popular form of narrative fiction – a genre which
dominated British prose fiction for the four decades or so after 1740 –
worthy of attention in a study of the textual functions served by the body in
eighteenth-century polite culture? A short answer to these questions might
run along these lines: in the didactic, morally concerned novels of
Richardson and his literary followers can be witnessed the construction
of a sentimental somatic eloquence which is analogous to the 'body
projects' of elocutionists; such novels were not only sites for the literary
staging of sentimental somatic eloquence but sought actively to produce
such eloquence among the reading public; it is apparent, furthermore, that
there grew up around sentimental novels a culture in which bodily
responses were widely lauded as signs of moral status. The reading of
sentimental fiction, then, became an important mechanism by which
polite expression could be exercised. Sentimental fiction provided
the eighteenth century's growing number of readers not only with entertainment but also with opportunities to perform polite literary responses

[1] Lady Louisa Stuart to Walter Scott (4 September 1826) in *The Private Letter-Books of Sir Walter Scott*, ed. Wilfred Partington (London: Hodder and Stoughton, 1930), p. 273.

(and/or to report and advertise such responses), thereby asserting polite identities.

To anyone versed in the extensive critical debate surrounding senti-mentalism, elements of that short narrative may seem familiar. As I noted in the Introduction, the body's central role within fiction's language of sentiment is already widely recognised. John Mullan and others have shown how Richardson's novels and those that followed in Richardson's wake are, on a fundamental level, exhaustive dramatisations of contem-porary thinking about the body's capacity to express character. Such novels present virtuous heroines and heroes whose bodies articulate a sincere language of the passions, and they place these men and women 'of feeling' within a competing world of self-interested hypocrites and tricksters – figures whose bodies conventionally conceal real character beneath a deluding mask of sociability.

A further characteristic of the sentimental genre which is also recognised is its tendency to encourage emotional responses in readers and to prescribe the manner in which such responses should be made manifest. The 'mark of sentimental literature', Janet Todd has written, is the 'arousal of pathos through conventional situations, stock familial characters and rhetorical devices', and it 'demands an emotional, even physical response'. Such literature 'is exemplary of emotion, teaching its consumers to produce a response equivalent to the one presented in its episodes. It is a kind of pedagogy of seeing and of the physical reaction that this seeing should produce'.[2] If these points, then, already constitute a critical consensus, what new insights can be discovered by placing sentimental fiction and its reading in the light of elocutionary discourse?

Firstly, examining the mediation of the body through fiction will allow us to explore further the generic variety of the texts which comprise what I have been calling elocutionary discourse; in novels and novel reading we find another area of activity wherein the body was implicated as a negoti-able text, and thus we see further the multiplicity of cultural tools and techniques by which polite somatic ideals were dispersed in eighteenth-century Britain. But with regard to the history of the novel, what the consideration of sentimental fiction as a component of elocutionary dis-course can achieve is to bring into relief the theatrical, rhetorical, and even coercive character of the somatic language that emerged from such fiction and permeated its early consumption. The elocutionary focus can allow us

---

[2] Todd, *Sensibility*, pp. 2 and 4.

to see the theatricality of representations and reading habits which recent literary critics and historians have tended to examine in relation to contemporary theories of physiology.[3]

Sentimentalism's investment in contemporary medical theory and fiction's deployment of illness as an eloquent tool has been admirably demonstrated by several critics, notably G. S. Rousseau and Mullan. For Mullan, the sentimental hero or heroine is like a refined patient nobly suffering through nervous indispositions, the feminised symptoms of which are emblematic of moral sensitivity. Certainly illness and signs of physical weakness are essential to the vocabulary of sentimentalism, but what is typically understated or ignored is the manner in which illness and weakness are mediated through conventions and frameworks which have as much in common with the stage as with the sickbed. The ailing patient certainly provides an appealing analogy for sentimentalism's men and women of feeling, but an equally compelling analogy – or a complementary one – is also found in the figure of the contemporary actor or orator. The heroic bodies of sentimental fiction are typically endowed by their creating authors with those same tools of suasion which we have seen in mid-century oratory and stagecraft, and a key trope of the genre is found in the positioning of these bodies before fictional witnesses upon whom the effects of sentimental eloquence is dramatised. This *staging* of somatic eloquence, it can be said, is the basis of such fiction's importance within eighteenth-century body politics – it was the means of constructing the gaze of readers, which, together with related strategies exerted *around* the fiction (in prefaces, reviews, and so on), underlay the valorisation of a suasive bodily language within certain eighteenth-century reading circles. It is in this way that fictional bodies of sentiment contributed to the shaping of eighteenth-century expressions of 'polite reading'.

The above-quoted recollection of literary consumption by Lady Louisa Stuart (1757–1851) provides a good account of the conception of polite reading, the emergence of which I aim to illuminate here. Writing in 1826 to her friend Sir Walter Scott, she is recalling the conditions in which she first read that most successful and maudlin of sentimental novels, Henry

---

[3] A study which does explore the theatricality of sentimentalism is Robert Markley's 'Sentimentality as Performance: Shaftesbury, Sterne, and the Theatrics of Virtue', in Felicity Nussbaum and Laura Brown (eds.), *The New 18th Century: Theory, Politics, English Literature* (New York: Routledge, 1987), pp. 210–30. Markley does not pursue the potential of the body to perform – he focuses rather upon benevolent acts of charity as a means of asserting a sentimental character – but his approach to the 'theatrics of virtue' and the potentially coercive ends to which a performable spectacle of benevolence might be applied has none the less been helpful in shaping my own account.

Mackenzie's *The Man of Feeling* (1771), and more than fifty years after the event, she has gained a critical distance from her experience. Interestingly, what she does *not* relate here is memories of reading itself; her actual engagement with Mackenzie's work is overshadowed in her memory by the powerful visual image of a familial drama: her 'mother and sisters crying' over the work, 'dwelling upon it with rapture', and her own fears that she might 'not cry enough to gain the credit of proper sensibility'. Among the lachrymose women of her family, Louisa Stuart is involved in a social consumption of literature pervaded by an overt emotionalism by which Mackenzie's novel is made to elicit tears – response is determined as much by the reader's relationship with local society as by an engagement with the text. Through a form of consensus announced in their shared bodily responses, the readers arrive at a settled interpretation of the text: its meanings are serious, and of an import which demands crying.

The Stuart family can be said to comprise here a microcosmic embodiment of what Stanley Fish calls an 'interpretive community'. Such communities, Fish writes, 'are made up of those who share interpretive strategies not for reading (in the conventional sense) but for writing texts, for constituting their properties and assigning their intentions... these strategies exist prior to the act of reading and therefore determine the shape of what is read rather than, as is usually assumed, the other way around'.[4] Fish's useful account depicts texts becoming meaningful structures only at the point of interpretation and only according to predetermined strategies of interpretation. Any consensus regarding interpretation must be arrived at, in such an understanding, through 'the fragile but real consolidation' that such groups, with their common practices, make possible.[5] Louisa Stuart, in fact, describes both an interpretive community, made up of her mother and sisters, and the process of such a community's expansion as she herself is brought into its fold, and in this community both literary appreciation and an individual's virtue are measured and assayed in terms of *visible sensibility*. Looking back upon her teenage self, she depicts sensibility not as any innate quality but as a form of behaviour to be learnt or to be etched upon a *tabula rasa*, and, in her youthful inchoation – she is 'not yet versed in sentiment' – she finds her training in the image of her mother and sisters. Evidently there were forceful pressures upon her to conform to the familial display which could create in her 'a secret dread' that she might fail properly to perform in the

[4] Fish, *Is There a Text in This Class?*, p. 171.
[5] *Ibid.*, p. 172.

exchange of gesture – a dry eye here could function as a brand of insensibility. She recognises the role that is inscribed for her, and does her utmost to perform its characteristics.

Louisa Stuart is subject to a coercive somatic image of polite reading – an image which has a basis *within* sentimental fiction, but which also transcends fiction itself to be reproduced and promoted through other channels of discourse (such as the bodies of the Stuart family). How such an image became empowered as a structuring device of a mid-eighteenth-century interpretive community can be illuminated by exploring 'theatrical' aspects of sentimental literary culture – including fictional strategies for representing bodies and for steering the manner of their perception – from roughly 1740, the year of Richardson's novelistic debut, to the 1770s. These years saw the popularisation of new tendencies in the representation of the body – tendencies which pervade works by, amongst others, Richardson, Sarah Fielding (1710–68), Henry Brooke, Frances Sheridan (1724–66), and Mackenzie. For illustration in what follows, I draw upon works by each of these authors, highlighting fictional tropes and techniques which, through repetition, evolved into conventions (and which are thus one of the reasons why these works can be recognised collectively as a genre). I refer most of all to Richardson's *Pamela* (1740). This is to provide a focal point, but the choice of that particular work is also due to *Pamela's* exceptional significance as a 'watershed' novel – one which, together with the controversies and debates it inspired, not only directed the course of much novelistic literary production in the decades that followed it, but also generated or crystallised many of the key issues concerning fictional bodies and the manners in which they might be approached and appropriated by readers. Stimulating a vogue of sentimental fiction (several authors of which, such as Sarah Fielding and Frances Sheridan, were directly assisted or sponsored by Richardson), *Pamela* provides a starting point for explicating the ways in which, for several decades at least, the performance of pre-legitimated literary responses became implicated within polite reading.

In proposing the significance of the 'performing body' within not only works of fiction but also the activity of reading, it will be clear that I am putting forward a view of early novel reading contrary to that of many critics such as Peter Brooks, who, following Ian Watt, argues that '[t]he rise of the novel is closely tied to the rise of the idea of privacy. The condition of privacy characterizes the reading and writing of novels.'[6] 'Performing'

---

[6] Peter Brooks, *Body Work: Objects of Desire in Modern Narrative* (Cambridge, MA and London: Harvard University Press, 1993), p. 29.

responses to novels, writing about one's responses, reading communally, bringing the effects of novels into conversation, approaching fiction with assumptions regarding its didactic potential – all such practices, which in the mid eighteenth century were associated with polite reading, have the effect of 'socialising' the novel, transforming the individual's private experience of narrative into some form of social currency. And the performing body, I want to suggest, was an instrumental component of that currency.

THEATRICAL VIRTUE IN RICHARDSONIAN FICTION

In the history of literary bodies, Samuel Richardson clearly stands at an important turning point. In a wide-ranging survey of *Body Language in Literature* (1993; trans. 1997), Barbara Korte identifies the mid eighteenth century as the historical moment at which fiction in English begins to grapple seriously, and without resort to stock conventions of the romance genre, with representing the body as an eloquent object. 'It is with Richardson', Korte writes, 'that a novel tradition begins to emerge in which the expressive potential of body language can be exploited to the full.'[7] Richardson, Korte suggests, rejected an established set of literary conventions for representing the body, but in considering the devices that Richardson did employ, it is worth noting Korte's more general claim that 'the depiction of body language in the English novel has been affected by historical developments in non-verbal behaviour itself, by theoretical writings on NVC [non-verbal communication], as well as by the representation of NVC in other forms of art'.[8] Richardson's fiction may have steered a shift away from romance conventions of representing the body, but what must be stressed is that it was not a shift towards 'the body' in a less mediated sense, but rather towards an alternative cultural system of representation.

The manner in which Richardson emblematises virtue through the somatic expressions of idealised characters readily demonstrates that his work shares common ground with the projects of contemporary elocutionists and acting theorists. Indeed, there are moments when his fiction becomes self-conscious about the body language it valorises, and his characters voice statements that would not be out of place in an acting manual or a guide for orators. For example, in Richardson's final novel,

[7] Barbara Korte, *Body Language in Literature* (Toronto: University of Toronto Press, 1997), p. 184.
[8] *Ibid.*, p. 16.

Sir Charles Grandison, Harriet Byron asks: 'Do not love, hatred, anger, malice, *all* the passions, in short, good or bad, shew themselves by like effects in the faces, hearts, and actions of the people of every country? . . . And is not the language of nature one language throughout the world, tho' there are different modes of speech to express it by?' (I, p. 185). Faced with such passages, it becomes tempting – and not altogether speculative – to locate in Richardson's fiction an influence from his friend Aaron Hill or from other agents which may have informed the author's sense of how the passions are rendered visible. And when it is observed that his fiction is full of characters dropping on their knees, flinging themselves at the feet of others, raising up their hands and eyes, shedding delicate tears – full, in short, of 'theatrical' gestures which appear repeatedly in standard phrases – it can again become tempting to look outside the fiction for something to explain its character-istics. In an essay on 'Theatrical Convention in Richardson' (1963), Leo Hughes points out the often 'stagy' manner in which Richardson's char-acters perform and are costumed, and he suggests very plausible sources for these devices in the stage directions and illustrations of plays familiar to Richardson through his printing business and through his acquaintance with Hill and Colley Cibber. Richardson's awareness of theatrical conven-tions, Hughes suggests, contributed an aspect of 'the method by which his imagination and observation operated'.[9] But Richardson's investment in the 'theatrical' also runs deeper than that.

The consequential inference to be drawn from the points of contact between Richardson's fiction and contemporary drama here is the recog-nition that Richardson and reformers such as Hill were addressing themselves to a similar cultural project, whereby a persuasive language of the body is modelled as part of an effort to moralise the reading or theatregoing public. Clearly the transition of a body construct between different cultural sites is

---

[9] Leo Hughes, 'Theatrical Convention in Richardson: Some Observations on a Novelist's Technique', in C. Camden (ed.), *Restoration and Eighteenth-Century Literature: Essays in Honor of Alan Dugald McKillop* (Chicago: University of Chicago Press, 1963), p. 239. Hughes's essay honours a critic who himself had examined the relations between Richardson's fiction and drama: Alan Dugald McKillop discusses *Clarissa*'s indebtedness – in terms of its leading characters and overall plot – to dramatic sources in *Samuel Richardson: Printer and Novelist* (Chapel Hill: University of North Carolina Press, 1936), pp. 138–54. In *Samuel Richardson & the Dramatic Novel* (Lexington: University of Kentucky Press, 1968), Ira Konigsberg expands McKillop's search for Richardson's dramatic sources and includes some discussion of Richardson's 'scenic achievement' (p. 102), with a view to showing his importance as an initiator of 'the English character novel' (p. 123). For Mark Kinkead-Weekes, the 'dramatic' quality of Richardson's fiction resides primarily in the articulation of characters through their own voices, rather than through the mediating presence of an overriding author/narrator figure (*Samuel Richardson: Dramatic Novelist* (Ithaca, NY: Cornell University Press, 1973)).

by no means straightforward – not least when different modes of representation are involved – but sentimental fiction none the less reveals a
preoccupation with the somatic display of the passions which is analogous
to the promotion of sentimentalised eloquence on the eighteenth-century
stage and on other platforms of live performance. Richardson and his
literary descendants typically inscribed the bodies of their idealised characters with sentimental signs of virtue, and they developed literary strategies
to encourage the dispersal of such signs among their communities of readers.
These novelists, in fact, generated a literary language of the passions, which
ultimately became recognisable as a new set of formulaic tropes. The amateur
poet Mary Alcock (1742?–98) presented a wry view of stock literary conventions in 'A Receipt for Writing a Novel', which whimsically comments upon
the typicality of devices used by the sentimentally inclined writer:

> Hysteric fits at least a score,
> Or, if you find occasion, more;
> But fainting fits you need not measure,
> The fair ones have them at their pleasure;
> Of sighs and groans take no account,
> But throw them in to vast amount;
> A frantic fever you may add,
> Most authors make their lovers mad.[10]

Alcock's facetious advice to the would-be novelist insists upon a construction of a fictional body which finds its own version of heroism in suffering, and which expresses its qualities through its physical responses to distress.
The formula satirised in her poem demands the attribution to virtuous
characters of an exaggerated array of legible symptoms – a language of
gesture by which virtue achieves a speechless eloquence. And the description is by no means an inaccurate reflection of the actual techniques
practised by many authors from Richardson onwards.

In the enormously influential *Pamela* and those fictions written, to a
greater or lesser extent, in *Pamela*'s image, the vital role of the body
immediately becomes apparent. As Richardson's worthy Pamela resists
the vigorous attempts at seduction by her predatory master, Mr B., readers
witness a mode of intense feeling made manifest primarily through the
heroine's body. 'O how my Eyes overflow!', Pamela writes in the first letter

---

[10] Mary Alcock, *Poems* (London, 1799), p. 90. The date of 'A Receipt for Writing a Novel' is not
apparent from *Poems*, which is a posthumous collection compiled from Alcock's papers by her
niece. Alcock's broad critique targets the conventions of sentimental literature, but its attention to
conventions of gothic fiction suggest a relatively late-century composition.

of this epistolary narrative, and such self-conscious physical awareness continues throughout the account, in which Pamela's body is not only the prime stake of the drama – the object of Mr B.'s desire and of Pamela's protective energies – but is furthermore implicated as the vehicle of the heroine's virtue and the gauge of her emotional condition.[11] Sensibility in Richardson's fiction is, as Mullan observes, 'not so much spoken as displayed. Its instrument is a massively sensitized, feminine body; its vocabulary is that of gestures and palpitations, sighs and tears . . . it is everything that punctures or interrupts speech'.[12] This natural language, Richardson's fictions contend, is the signifier of virtue, and in each of his novels the righteousness of 'simple', candid expression is upheld, even when, as in *Clarissa* (1747–8), it is implicated in the tragic downfall of the heroine.[13]

Natural eloquence, for Richardson, is particularly an attribute of proper femininity; it is the visible mark of the virtuous, sober, and dutiful disposition that his didactic novels and other writings promote as proper to womanhood.[14] In *Pamela* the gushing somatic eloquence of the heroine is contrasted with the behaviour of modish women whose sophistication

---

[11] Samuel Richardson, *Pamela; or, Virtue Rewarded,* ed. Peter Sabor (Harmondsworth: Penguin, 1980; repr. 1988), p. 43. Sabor's edition is based on *Pamela*'s 1801 text, which incorporated several stages of revision by Richardson. A comparison of this text with the first edition suggests that the description of the body was one of Richardson's foci as he revised: in the first edition, for example, the quoted remark reads 'O how my Eyes run!'; Richardson's replacement of 'run' with 'overflow' is in keeping with the general tendency of the revisions, which, in response to criticism of *Pamela*'s 'low' style, elevate Pamela's language. Among other revisions were new passages (including the next I quote), which probe the issue of the body's eloquence. The recent edition by Thomas Keymer and Alice Wakely (Oxford: Oxford University Press, 2001) is based on *Pamela*'s first edition, and Keymer's introduction includes discussion of Richardson's 'elevating' revisions (pp. xxviii–xxxiv). Unless stated otherwise, subsequent quotations are from Sabor's edition, with references provided in the text.

[12] Mullan, *Sentiment and Sociability,* p. 61.

[13] In contrast to the wish-fulfilling narrative of *Pamela*, where sentiment transforms vice, *Clarissa*, as Mullan writes, 'envisages a heartfelt language cast off from the moorings of social habit' (*Sentiment and Sociability*, p. 63). Mullan's overall argument emphasises the general tendency of sensibility to find its location in retreat from a hostile and duplicitous world.

[14] For insights into Richardson's views on the behaviour that is proper to women and into the gender-forming intentions of his fiction, see his letter to Lady Dorothy Bradshaigh (17 August 1752): 'But when, in this country, the sex is so generally running into licentiousness; when home is found to be the place that is most irksome to them; when Ranelaghs, Vauxhalls, Marybones, assemblies, routs, drums, hurricanes, and a rabble of such-like amusements, carry them out of all domestic duty and usefulness into infinite riot and expense; day and night inverted; and that sex, in which virtue, modesty, sobriety, ought to be characteristically found, in order to save a corrupted world, were those qualities and graces to be lost in the generality of the other; – then would I beg leave to remind the wild pigeons of the sex, that they are not the doves they were designed to be; and that such cannot claim the privileges allowed to English wives, with any justice' (*Correspondence of Samuel Richardson,* ed. Barbauld, vol. VI, p. 211).

has masked the body's language. When, for example, Pamela has been confronted with some of Mr B.'s fashionable friends – a dissolute crowd to which she is exhibited as a marvellous curio – she writes of the women:

> one of the chief beauties of the sex seems banished from the faces of ladies, in these days: for they not only don't know how to blush themselves, but they laugh at any innocent young creature that does, as rustic and half-bred; and (as I have more than once heard them) toss their jests about, and their *double meanings*, as they own them, as freely as the gentlemen. But whatever reputation these freedoms may give to their *wit*, I think they do but little credit to their *hearts*. (p. 84)

Quite how these frivolous, witty women have surrendered their ability to blush is not made clear. Indeed, their remarkable transcendence of an unconscious physiological process is revealing of the way in which Richardson exploits the body as an ideologically loaded motif. He treats the body's relationship with nature – its intimacy or its alienation – as a trope by which to adjudicate between versions of femininity. As Sheridan contrasted the natural hues of British ladies with the powder and paint of the French, so Richardson ventriloquises through Pamela a similar opposition in order to advance a view of proper womanhood; but where Sheridan drew his division along lines of nation, Richardson's comparison spans a gulf of class. These upper-class women who cannot blush have transgressed into a masculine sphere of wit (a sphere which Richardson is careful to condemn as corrupting to *both* sexes). They have strayed into a dubious social arena where the valued language is *verbal* and where 'double meanings' are actively celebrated. Alienated from the unpretentious, blushing eloquence shown by Pamela, a witty woman, the novel implies, is a denaturalised and debauched creature. From the sophisticate's point of view, Pamela's own expressiveness is 'rustic and half-bred', but in this novel – which uneasily critiques the behaviour and values of the upper classes before promoting Pamela, through marriage, to their ranks – being 'half-bred' implies remaining in touch with the virtues of 'natural' womanhood.

Such representations forge an association between the simple eloquence of the body and proper femininity, but emotional expression is by no means upheld as the preserve of females or of female characters in such fiction. As male orators and actors were urged to recognise emotional display as entirely appropriate to masculinity, so too a version of the language exhibited by Pamela became the attribute of many male heroes in fiction. '[I]t is a touching thing to see a man cry' (p. 153), remarks Pamela, whose reward in the novel is contingent upon her transformation of male behaviour – that of Mr B., whose relinquishing of rakish ways and embrace of modern virtue is emblematic of Richardson's didactic project as a whole.[15] Richardson created his supreme emblem of masculine emotional susceptibility in his sentimental superman, Sir Charles Grandison, a hero who, the novel's preface declares, acts 'uniformly well thro' a Variety of trying Scenes, because all his Actions are regulated by one steady Principle: A Man of Religion and Virtue; of Liveliness and Spirit; accomplished and agreeable; happy in himself, and a Blessing to others' (I, p. 4). Through Grandison, Richardson asserts the compatibility of emotionalism and worldly effectiveness: Grandison can be visibly moved – although not, it should be noted, to the effusive degree of Pamela or Clarissa – and his emotions do nothing to destabilise his influential position within public life. Other male heroes from the period – the weeping 'men of feeling' who are feminised to a degree of powerlessness unknown to Grandison – expose the more problematic status of sentimentality within a thrusting world of competitive commerce. The eponymous hero of Sarah Fielding's *The Adventures of David Simple* (1744 and 1753) and Harley in Mackenzie's *The Man of Feeling* are ultimately destroyed by their acute sensibility, which leaves them vulnerable to the challenges of a typically unsentimental, commercial world. The virtue that such novels propose is not practicable – unlike *Sir Charles Grandison*, *The Man of Feeling* is, as Mullan puts it, 'a type of writing which does not so much recommend correct conduct to its readers as assume virtue in their capacity to understand the sentimental text'.[16] These weaker figures are vulnerable and threatened in worldly terms, but are none the less celebrated for their ideals and emotions within the relationship created between reader and text. And as with Pamela, the primary space for the inscription of their virtue – impracticable as it is – is the flesh. *David Simple*'s hero is 'simple' in the sense of 'artless' – he is 'very bad at acting any Part that was not quite sincere', and is ever ready to shed tears at the sight or report of suffering.[17] Indeed, Fielding's narrator explains that David, on hearing one tale of distress, is not 'able to stifle his Sighs and Tears' precisely because 'he did not think it beneath a Man to cry from Tenderness' (p. 57) – the novel becomes quite explicit in its promotion of visible emotionalism as an attribute of male manners.

[15] Barker-Benfield argues that Richardson 'made softened manhood a central goal of his participation in the reformation of manners' (*Culture of Sensibility*, p. 141).
[16] Mullan, *Sentiment and Sociability*, p. 119.
[17] Sarah Fielding, *The Adventures of David Simple*, ed. Linda Bree (London: Penguin, 2002), p. 40. Subsequent references are given in the text.

Mackenzie's Harley is likewise valorised for his emotionalism and is always ready to respond to distress with 'the tribute of some tears'.[18]

In relation to both male and female characters, then, sentimental fiction insists upon an association between visible emotionalism and modern virtue, but the actual *eloquence* of bodies represented in fiction – the basis of their emotive hold over readers, and thus the basis of their social potential – hangs not only upon their embodiment of eighteenth-century thinking about the passions' visibility, but also upon the mechanics of the scenes in which they are depicted. Where the social effect of fiction is concerned, it is not sufficient to examine only the *type* of body language depicted; we must attend also to what that language *does* in the fiction and the way in which it is mediated for readers. And in sentimental fiction the body is conventionally rendered eloquent by being *seen to be* eloquent in the presence of a fictional witness. It is largely this key narrative strategy that lends sentimental fiction its 'theatrical' character – expressive bodies are rarely depicted in solitary isolation, but rather appear before a viewing figure (or several) whose own responses provide a testimony of the virtue on display. John Cleese has remarked of visual comedy that a man falling over is not funny, but a man *being seen* falling over has comic potential – an astute observation which is pertinent also to sentimental scenes. An incorporated viewing figure 'triangulates' a scene for the actual viewer or reader, directing the gaze, emphasising that the viewed object is engaging or of interest *by virtue of* its visual appearance or movements, and often modelling an appropriate response to the acting figure – an effect which Jean-Jacques Mayoux, commenting on sentimental *tableaux* in Sterne's fiction, has called 'reciprocal witnessing'.[19] The staging of *witnessed* eloquent gesture has the effect of constructing the gaze of the reader; it is an effect which might be resisted, but if embraced, it is a means of interpellation – a means of hailing readers and inviting them to occupy positions created within the fiction where spectatorial and ideological perspectives are integrated. It is a means of directing a mode of reading.

Numerous scenes from *Pamela* could be cited where the narrator-heroine records both her passions on display in the presence of a viewing party and the effects of her display upon that party. In fact, characters in the novel openly acknowledge and indulge in the visual attractions of Pamela's

---

[18] Henry Mackenzie, *The Man of Feeling*, ed. Brian Vickers (Oxford: Oxford University Press, 1987), p. 34. Subsequent references are given in the text.
[19] Jean-Jacques Mayoux, 'Laurence Sterne', in John Traugott (ed.), *Laurence Sterne: A Collection of Critical Essays* (Englewood Cliffs, NJ: Prentice-Hall, 1968), p. 112.

emotional displays, and Richardson even has them engineer scenes where her turmoil can be viewed. One extenuated scene, in which Pamela is reunited with her father, is quite literally staged for the entertainment of Mr B.'s friends and neighbours, whose desire to watch Pamela in action becomes the device (a creakingly artificial one, it might be complained) by which Richardson emphasises Pamela's appeal as *spectacle* to readers. Writing of the event to her mother, Pamela records how she is kept ignorant of the arrival of her father (who is anxious to learn the state of his daughter's virtue – in the Richardsonian context, her virginity), while Mr B., now on the path of reform, manages the visual drama of the reunion amidst the card-tables, telling Pamela that she is to meet the clergyman, Mr Williams:

My master . . . went to the company, and said, 'I have been agreeably surprised. Here is honest Mr Andrews come, full of grief, to see his daughter; for he fears she is seduced; and tells me, worthy man, that, poor as he is, he will not own her, if she be not virtuous.'

'O', said they all, with one voice almost, 'Dear sir! shall we not see the good old man you have so much praised for his plain good sense and honest heart; and for his love to his daughter, as well as his daughter for her duty to him?' 'I intend', said my master, 'to surprize her. She shall not know her father is come till she sees him.' 'Dear, dear Mr B.' said Miss Darnford (and they all joined in the same request) 'let us be present at their first interview!' But was this not very cruel, my dear mother? For well might they think I should not support myself under such an agreeable surprize.

He said, kindly, 'I have but one fear; that the dear girl may be too much affected' . . .

He then took my father by the hand, and led him in, against his will, to the company . . .

They would have had him sit down by them, but he chose to sit in the corner of the room, behind the door; so that he could not be seen as one came in; because the door opened against him, as I may say. The ladies all sat down. My master sent for me. And down I came.

Miss Darnford, in order to engage me from looking at my father, as I put to the door after me, welcomed me down. I saw not, therefore, my father presently: and his heart was so full that he could not speak to me: but he got up and sat down three or four times successively, in silence, and was quite unable to come to me. The ladies all had their eyes upon him; but I would not look that way, supposing Mr Williams was there: and they made me sit down between Lady Darnford and Mrs Jones; and asked me what we should play at. I referred myself to their choice, and wondered to see them smile, and look now upon me, and then to that part of the room; but still, as Mr Williams had not been presented to me, I looked not that way, though my face was to the door, and the table before me.

'Did you send your letter to the post-house, my good girl', said my master, 'for your father?' 'To be sure, sir', answered I; 'I did not forget that. Mr Thomas carried it.' 'What', said he, 'I wonder, will the good old couple say to it?' 'O sir', replied I, 'the news of your great goodness will be a cordial to their worthy hearts!'

At that, my father, not able to contain himself, nor yet to stir from the place, gushed out into a flood of tears, and cried out, 'O my child!'

I knew the voice, and lifting my eyes, and seeing my father, gave a spring, overturned the table, without regard to the company, and threw myself at his feet. 'O my father! my father!' said I, 'can it be! Is it you? Yes, it is! it is! O bless your happy – ' daughter! I would have said, and down I sunk.

My master was concerned. 'I feared', said he, 'that the surprize would be too much for her spirits.' All the ladies ran to me, and made me drink a glass of water; and recovering, I found myself in the arms of my dearest father. (pp. 327–9)

The passage depicts a dense, complex web of seeing and looking, with the drama balancing upon the knowledge attached to each gaze. As narrator, Pamela is in a rather curious position here, having to supply background information so as to establish the dramatic irony of a scene which depends upon her obliviousness to her father's presence: as retrospective narrator she must be knowing, but as chief actor in the scene – the shaken casualty of surprise – she must be ignorant. The first-person epistolary form is conventionally regarded as a means by which Richardson opened up the inner consciousnesses of his narrators, fostering intimate processes of identification between reader and narrator. The narration here, however, partly *distances* readers from Pamela (as actor) and supplies them with the same privileged knowledge that allows Mr B.'s company to enjoy the staged spectacle. Readers are placed upon the same plane of knowledge as the guests, who with one voice crave, first and foremost, to *see* the reunion, and who then sit themselves in the theatre of the drawing room awaiting the entrance of the main actor. Readers are invited to occupy a vantage point which in fact gives little insight into Pamela's inner experience of the event, but which provides a dramatic perspective upon how that experience is manifested visually. The depicted event is really an elaborate practical joke, but one which serves the ends of a voyeuristic emotional indulgence in which readers are encouraged to share. But in Richardson's fictional world, experiencing the display of highly charged passions is not purely indulgent; rather it is an agent of moral reform, and throughout *Pamela* the heroine's 'performances' are endowed with the capacity to *transform* those who witness them. In this scene, it is not merely incidental that the card-table is overthrown at the moment of reunion: representative of the frivolous pleasures to which Mr B. and his company have been devoted, the card-table is toppled here as a new object of attention gains precedence. Pamela's virginity can be said to be the nucleus of the scene. The father's realisation that Pamela remains chaste triggers the reunion, which in turn brings on

Pamela's eloquent faint, and as the ladies are moved to rush round with water, the proselytising power of the sight of virtue is vividly dramatised: Pamela's responsive audience has become a crowd of good Samaritans.

Pamela's eloquent body is, of course, not always the focus of quite such *public* scrutiny, but in more intimate scenes Richardson none the less has his heroine record in meticulous detail the actions of her body and, importantly for a reading experience, its persuasive power over its witnesses. When Mr B., finally reformed, promises to provide a living for Pamela's parents, Richardson has her record her reaction thus:

> 'I have not words, sir', said I, (my eyes, I am sure, glistening with grateful joy) 'to express sufficiently my gratitude. Teach me, dear sir', and I pressed his hand to my lips, 'teach me some other language, if there be any, that abounds with more grateful terms, that I may not thus be choaked with meanings, for which I can find no utterance.'
>
> 'My charmer!' says he, 'your heart speaks at your eyes in a language that words *indeed* cannot utter. You most abound, when you seem most to want!' (pp. 390–1)[20]

The ironies of a character loquaciously declaring an inability to speak are very obvious; it suffices here to say that the passage is clearly one which allows the reading, grabbed by opponents of the novel (of which more later), of Pamela as an artful hypocrite, able consciously to manipulate those around her by means of persuasive performance. Her parenthetical remark may be read as a retrospective narrative interpretation of the event, but, together with the contradiction between her act of speaking and the subject of her speech, it also suggests her self-consciousness, allowing her character to be read as that of a scheming politician. But if we follow the more straightforward, 'author-approved' view of Pamela as sincere and undesigning, the passage can be seen to dramatise ideal sentimental eloquence in action. The expressive use of the body then becomes a totally unconscious event – one which cannot be taught and learnt – and indeed, is in action while its performer remains oblivious to its occurrence. Pamela's case, read with its sincerity assumed, represents a textbook enactment of the unconscious somatic language lauded by elocutionary writers such as Sheridan and Aaron Hill: the physical sign springs from feeling unbidden, as her eyes, those idolised organs of eloquence, are seen to articulate her gratitude perfectly. And Richardson ensures that the eloquence of the 'charmer' does not go unnoticed. Mr B.'s role in the scene is not only

---

[20] This is another passage that Richardson significantly refined as he revised *Pamela* (for the first edition text, see *Pamela*, ed. Keymer and Wakely, p. 365).

important in terms of what happens; his presence also mediates Pamela's physical eloquence for readers. Mr B. *observes* Pamela and provides a commentary on her eloquent expression; Richardson builds into the scene a viewer whose gaze encourages Pamela to be conceived of in physical terms by readers and whose comments provide confirmation of her eloquence. Richardson's technique may be 'theatrical' because he appropriated gestures from contemporary drama, but it is also 'theatrical' in the way in which scenes are staged with eloquent bodies placed on show before spectators.

Incorporated observation is so central to the effects of sentimental fiction that witnessing is arguably one of the chief functions served by that institution of the genre: the 'man of feeling'. This character type, from Fielding's David Simple to Harry Moreland in Henry Brooke's *The Fool of Quality* (1764–70) and Harley in *The Man of Feeling*, not only suffers eloquent distresses himself, but is also a constant witness and mediator of the distresses of others. Indeed, Sterne's semi-wry version of the type, Yorick in *A Sentimental Journey* (1768), is essentially a tourist of the emotions, making, as he puts it, 'a quiet journey of the heart in pursuit of NATURE, and those affections which rise out of her'.[21] In Sterne's episodic fiction, Yorick's function is largely that of a mobile viewpoint – he is an observer, an alert and responsive tourist who focuses his gaze upon affecting scenes and filters them through his idiosyncratic narration. Yorick's actual involvement in the moving scenes he discovers *en route* through France often extends no further than a point where he has prompted an affecting performance, which he can then witness, feel, and record.

The more straightforward men of feeling created by Fielding, Brooke, and Mackenzie become embroiled in plots less fleeting than those incidents that occupy Yorick, but these characters are also, in part, sentimental tourists, whose sensitive dispositions are confirmed by their responses to witnessed distress. Their narratives develop along semi-picaresque lines. David Simple, Harley, and Harry Moreland all travel, and their stories involve numerous encounters between the man of feeling as observer and virtue in distress. The premise of *David Simple* is David's eccentric resolution to 'travel through the whole World, rather than not

[21] Laurence Sterne, *A Sentimental Journey through France and Italy and Continuation of the Bramine's Journal: The Text and Notes*, The Florida Edition of the Works of Laurence Sterne, vol. 6, ed. Melvyn New and W. G. Day (Gainesville: University Press of Florida, 2002), p. III. Subsequent references are given in the text.

meet with a real Friend' (p. 23). David narrows the whole world down to London, but the device none the less sets him on the path of a voyaging voyeur, who assays potential friends through his faith in the visibility of virtue. His quest demands his delving into an array of friendly human exteriors, to locate those individuals whose inner characters are consonant with their social display. He is a 'Hero, on whose Tenderness the least Appearance of Grief in others made an immediate Impression' (p. 90), and his sensitive character becomes the lens through which readers encounter the numerous *appearances* of grief that Fielding places before him. The third-person narration of *David Simple* is *focalised* through David, and his responses to distress – speechlessness, tears, sighs – are positioned as model responses to readers. For example, the poverty of two young worthies in *David Simple* – Camilla and her ailing brother Valentine, who are suffering under a malevolent landlady – is introduced to the novel only *as it appears* to David: he enters 'a Garret, where he saw a most moving Scene' (p. 115), and David's perspective governs the description of distress that follows. David 'stood like one struck dumb; he stared at the Man on the Bed, – viewed the young Woman; – then turned his Eyes on the Landlady' (p. 115). His response to his careful looking comes in the form of tears and inarticulacy, which in turn lead to charity towards Camilla and Valentine and the condemnation of the landlady – again, displayed emotion becomes integrated with moral action. Standing at the novel's moral centre, David at one point presents his own strong views on literature: 'the only Way of writing well was to draw all the Characters from Nature, and to affect the Passions in such a manner, as that the *Distresses* of the Good should move Compassion, and the Amiableness of their Actions incite Men to imitate them; and the *Vices* of the Bad stir up Indignation and Rage' (p. 78). His behaviour within the fictional world that contains him is, in many ways, that of a model reader of moral literature.

Men of feeling occupy countless scenes which dramatise eloquent characters *having an effect* over other characters. Fiction's language of the passions serves a diagnostic function – signalling turbulence beneath the skin – but its socialising potential derives from its presentation as a *persuasive* force, an eloquent medium of sympathy. Such fiction dramatises the *contagion* of the passions – the force that elocutionists and acting theorists aimed to harness for persuasive ends in the pulpit and on the stage. Brooke's *The Fool of Quality* is awash with contagious passions as delicate characters witness each other's emotion and consequently become overwhelmed themselves. Brooke, one of the leading Irish playwrights of the mid century, was a 'lifelong friend' of Thomas Sheridan, and in *The Fool of Quality* he advances a view of the body's eloquence which would readily have been endorsed by his friend.[22] One of Brooke's characters explains how 'the soul is the man ... and the body is but as a sign, to give notice to others, that such a man dwells within', and this theory, which itself might have come from the pen of Sheridan, is put into repeated practice throughout the novel.[23] Brooke's characters are leaky vessels, which, motivated by nervous activity, become easily filled with pathos and brim over with contagious tears. When, for example, the young Harry Moreland, the benevolent and open-hearted 'fool' of the title, meets his guardian Fenton in a state of tears, 'the muscles of his infant-aspect began to relax, and he wept and sobbed as fast as his companion' (I, p. 50). Harry's body is ever susceptible to a sympathetic mirroring of virtuous examples, as later when Fenton is speaking and 'the muscles of Harry's expressive countenance, like an equally-tuned instrument, uttered unisons to every word he heard' (I, p. 181). The eloquence of Fenton is assured by the response he elicits from Harry, and readers are presented with a *tableau* scene of emotive gesture and are urged to share in its sentiment. When Fenton is crying yet again, Harry 'plentifully vented the contagious shower' (III, p. 12); and Harry later asks him 'How comes it, dada, that crying should be so catching?' (III, p. 105). Brooke, in fact, self-consciously images the tearful sentimentalist as a type of emotive public speaker: an early scene presents Harry delivering a moving speech which is concluded as his emotions overcome him: 'Here orator Harry ceased to speak, except by his tears, which he could no longer restrain, and which proceeded to plead most emphatically for him' (I, p. 165). Certainly 'orator Harry' is no more than an epithet, but it is a revealing one betraying the typical manner in which sentimental characters are imagined as eloquent beings performing persuasively in front of witnesses.

The theatricalism that surrounds such scenes of eloquent lachrymosity also shapes sentimental fiction's many representations of nervous illness. With its narratives of illness – the lingering death of Clarissa being perhaps the supreme example – the sentimental novel has, as I have noted, been seen as a significant mediator of contemporary medical thought, by which novelists capitalised upon lively public interests in the body, its disorders,

---

[22] Sheldon, *Thomas Sheridan of Smock-Alley*, p. 138. Sheldon also points out that Brooke was the 'favourite pupil' of Sheridan's father and that Sheridan produced his plays (p. 9).

[23] Henry Brooke, *The Fool of Quality; or, The History of Henry Earl of Moreland*, 5 vols. (London, 1792), vol. II, p. 164. Subsequent references are given in the text.

and their treatment. As G. S. Rousseau pointed out in 'Nerves, Spirits and Fibres', and as Mullan has argued more thoroughly, there exist close correlations between the construction of the body in the imaginative literature of sensibility and that found in eighteenth-century medical discourse, itself a subject which was undergoing rapid popularisation to become a topic of fashionable discussion.[24] But fiction's language of sensibility is not derived from contemporary models of nervous illness without interference from other cultural pressures. Mullan proposes that sensibility retreats from a recognition of social impossibility into a *metaphor* of illness,[25] and this metaphorical status is crucial for understanding sensibility's gestural language, for sentimental novels tend not to depict illness in any realist sense, but rather construct a version of physical weakness which is codified for the purposes of eloquent effect. In Richardson's fiction and that which follows it, the decline of characters into illness can follow a pattern of diagnostic medical reporting, but emotionally persuasive symptoms are typically foregrounded ahead of the type of material of a realist medical account. For one thing, the sick of sensibility are conventionally the most sanitary of patients; the gross physical evacuations, such as are described by medical writers like George Cheyne, are typically excluded from these polite fictions.[26] Indeed, it can be said that sentimental fiction presents a *polite performance* of illness.

Fictional accounts of illness are not always completely sanitised. Richardson, friend and patient of Cheyne, on occasion represents some of those aspects of illness and its treatment which are conventionally seen as offensive. This is not, however, for any purpose of achieving a realist account; rather symptoms are deployed in the process of characterisation.

---

[24] See also: Ann Jessie Van Sant, *Eighteenth-Century Sensibility and the Novel: The Senses in Social Context* (Cambridge: Cambridge University Press, 1993).

[25] Mullan, *Sentiment and Sociability*, p. 240.

[26] That bodily discharges form an essential part of the diagnosis of nervous disease is evident from any number of medical tracts. A passage from perhaps the most popular, Cheyne's *The English Malady* (1733), reveals the type of detail that is 'written out' of illness in novels: 'Those who are subject to Evacuations of any Kind, in any Degree greater than what is natural and common to sound Constitutions; or those, who by Accident, a Fever, or any acute Distemper whatsoever, have suffer'd long under any preternatural Evacuation, are already, or soon will, become subject to a loose, relax'd, or weak State of Fibres and Nerves: Those who frequently run into Purging and Costiveness alternately, or into Floods of pale Water, or into profuse Sweatings, upon little or no Exercise, into a constant Spitting or Salivation at the Mouth, or too plentiful Discharges from the Nose and Eyes: Those who have lost much Blood, or frequently fall into *Hæmorrhages*: Those who have labour'd long under an obstinate *Diarrhæa*, or Looseness: Or those of the Sex who have purify'd long in greater Quantities, or oftener than is usual or natural: All these originally are, or commonly become of weak and relax'd Nerves, and suffer under them' (3rd edn (London, 1734), pp. 102–3).

In *Clarissa*, Richardson undertakes a selective distribution of symptoms between characters of contrasting moral integrities, so as to depict emblematically the type of association which finds cleanliness to be the neighbour of godliness. For example, Mrs Sinclair, the fleshy brothel-keeper and gaoleress of Clarissa, dies with a reluctance and messy violence seen to be appropriate to her life of vice. The scene of her death is recounted in a letter by Belford – here again there is a body performing before a witness. Repulsed by the malodorousness of the room in which, surrounded by prostitutes, she lies dying, Belford describes with disgust the pangs of the roaring and bellowing woman before him, as her corpulent body performs a repertoire of indecorous twitchings, and her corrupt physicians debate the benefits of amputating her disease-ridden leg.[27] This foul demise provides a vivid contrast to the refined death of Clarrisa herself – a protracted decline showcasing a purified selection of the symptoms of which a body might genuinely be capable. Clarissa's death cannot satisfactorily be attributed to any recognisable illness – if she dies of anything it is of sensibility itself, and, in her remarkably stain-resistant white dress, her death is a calm and tidy business. As a Christian writer, Richardson produces in his heroine's death a type of religious fable, and Clarissa's exemplary decline involves her becoming progressively paler and thinner, but her saintly body produces few of the sickening qualities of earthly illness. '[W]hat a gradual and happy death God Almighty (blessed be His Name!) affords me!', Clarissa remarks of her own deterioration; 'by little and little, in such a gradual sensible death as I am blessed with, God dies away in us, as I may say, all human satisfactions, in order to subdue his poor creatures to Himself'. For readers, the eloquent potential of such illness – and of Clarissa's humble acceptance of it – is underlined by her regularly being surrounded by moved spectators. Belford describes 'how affected' he and other onlookers become in response to Clarissa's 'moving account of progressive weakness. We heard it with wet eyes; for what with the women's example, and what with her moving eloquence, I could no more help it than they.'[28]

In *Sir Charles Grandison*, Harriet Byron suffers in a manner comparable with that of Clarissa. When Harriet is unwell, Charlotte Grandison finds her to be 'the most charming sick woman that ever lived', with an illness which appears only in 'her faded cheeks, her pale lips, and her changed

---

[27] Samuel Richardson, *Clarissa; or, The History of a Young Lady*, ed. Angus Ross (Harmondsworth: Penguin, 1985), pp. 1388–94.

[28] *Ibid.*, pp. 1336–7.

complexion' (II, p. 659). Again we have both a performer and a witness: a patient with symptoms so delicate that they can charm and move, and an observer whose presence and commentary confirm the eloquent effect. The most sustained narrative of illness in *Sir Charles Grandison* is that concerning Clementina, the beautiful Italian devotee of Sir Charles, who is prevented from marriage to him by her Catholicism, and who consequently suffers a condition which degenerates into madness. Through Clementina, Richardson presents an extensive investigation into deranged sensibility, charting in detail the causes of its onset and the attempts to find a cure. Clementina's illness involves her in fits and sweats, and her treatment includes blistering and the application of leeches, but, in textual terms, the emotional eloquence of her body is located primarily in her behaviour surrounding her suffering. We might isolate one highly charged scene in which Clementina's family and Sir Charles are in favour of her being bled; although she is initially reluctant, she agrees to the operation, believing, with the generosity typical of sensibility, that it will comfort those around her. Sir Charles describes Clementina's address to him:

For *your* sake, Chevalier? – Well, will it do you good to see me bleed?
    I withdrew to the window. I could not stand this question; put with an air of tenderness for me, and in an accent *equally* tender.
    The irresistible Lady (O what eloquence in her disorder!) followed me; and laying her hand on my arm, looking earnestly after my averted face, as if she would not suffer me to hide it from her – Will it, will it, comfort *you* to see me bleed? – Come then, *be* comforted; I *will* bleed: But you shall not leave me. (II, p. 193)

All here recognise the power of witnessed illness. The eloquence acknowledged by Sir Charles indeed seems to be too much for him here, and he must actually *avert* his gaze, and it is through the performance of treatment – *seeing* her bleed – that Clementina proposes to give him restorative comfort. She consciously allows herself to be transformed into a viewable object for the emotional cure of others. In fact, as far as Sir Charles (and consequently the text he, as epistolary narrator, produces) is concerned, her eloquence does not occur in her bleeding, which receives only scant description – 'The puncture being made, and she bleeding freely' (II, p. 194). For Sir Charles, and for a reading experience, it is the business surrounding the moment – Clementina's hesitant speeches and her dramatic looks – which carries the emotional import. Indeed, Clementina, unable to reciprocate weeping, says before the imminent operation: 'as I cannot give you tears for tears, from my eyes, Shall not my arm weep!' (II, p. 193). She becomes a type of devotional object, and the language of Catholic miracles seems to be called upon to present her as a version of the bleeding virgin. But to bestow persuasive meaning upon the operation, it is transformed, through metaphor, into the familiar eloquent device of tearfulness. It is as though illness has no intrinsic emotional linguistic power, but functions as a focus and *raison d'être* for this more conventional language of pathos. For a patient suffering derangement, it is certainly an impressive performance.

But then the deranged of sentimental fiction are conventionally good performers. When Mackenzie's Harley goes on a tour of Bedlam, London's hospital for the insane, he witnesses almost a cabaret of psychosis. Mackenzie sets up his Bedlam scene in a way which pointedly erodes the boundary between illness and interesting spectacle (something at which the proprietors of the actual Hospital of St Mary of Bethlehem were apparently themselves adept). 'Of those things called Sights, in London', the episode begins, 'which every stranger is supposed desirous to see, Bedlam is one', and Harley takes the tour there after attending 'several other shows' (p. 29). Inside the hospital, a 'keeper' presents a succession of inmates, and, as a skilled compère, he provides dramatic introductions to the living exhibits. As the tour develops, the passage generates an aesthetic taxonomy of the mad, privileging a particular type of eloquent derangement, which can nourish the polite gaze of sensibility. The tourists hurry away from those 'in the most horrid state of incurable madness', whose chains, cries, and imprecations form 'a scene inexpressibly shocking' (p. 30). They choose rather to indulge in – and thus invite readers of *The Man of Feeling* to indulge in – an altogether more affecting, more *polite* spectacle. The episode's principal lunatic – the star of Bedlam – is, unsurprisingly for the genre, a young, distressed, female virgin: 'Separate from the rest stood one, whose appearance had something of superior dignity. Her face, though pale and wasted, was less squalid than those of the others, and showed a dejection of that decent kind, which moves our pity unmixed with horror: upon her, therefore, the eyes of all were immediately turned' (pp. 32–3). The episode perhaps illustrates how, in T. S. Eliot's phrase, 'Human kind cannot bear too much reality': only so much squalor is engaging; if dejection should be put on show, at least let it be decent dejection. It marks the same distinction that we have seen in the work of those writers on enthusiasm who applaud displays of the passions but seek also to delimit just how much passion should decently be exposed. Like those writers, Mackenzie circumscribes a zone in which the body's performance is both eloquent and polite, and he constructs such perform-ance as the emblem of virtue. The distressed young lady, the keeper informs the tourists, is the victim of lost love and a cruel father, but throughout her trials she has, like Pamela, Clarissa, and other sentimental heroines before her, retained her virtue. And it is a virtue she proceeds to assert through performance before Harley and his fellow tourists. Following the keeper's introduction, she produces on cue a series of distracted reflections upon her dead intended, 'poor Billy!'; she assures the crowd that she prays; and she draws their tears with a little song, leaving 'except the keeper's . . . not an unmoistened eye around' (p. 34). The display ends with an invitation to Harley to test the goodness of her heart: '"my heart is harmless: my poor heart! it will burst some day; feel how it beats". – She press'd his hand to her bosom, then holding her head in the attitude of listening – "Hark! one, two, three! be quiet, thou little trembler; my Billy's is cold!"' (p. 35). With this concluding diagnosis of her goodness – an intimate test, the potential eroticism of which is apparently not noted by the almost negatively priapic Harley – Mackenzie draws the familiar sentimental association between physiology and virtue. But this patient's condition and the eloquent power of her virtue can none the less only be partially deciphered through reference to contemporary physiological thought. She is, as she remarks, 'a strange girl', but it would be hard to find a counterpart for her strangeness within contemporary medical discourse. Her decent, virtuous oddities are deployed above all as a beseeching performance of polite madness played out in front of a tearful audience, which focalises the representation for readers.

As Harley repays this spectacle not only with his tears but also with 'a couple of guineas' (p. 35), some readers may find in the scene an irony working at the expense of Harley and his sentimentalism. With *The Man of Feeling* published in 1771, the scene might be read as a subtle exposé of an established sentimental industry in which shrewd entrepreneurs cynically exploit the charitable impulses of naïve sentimental dupes (in fact, the young lady's behaviour could then become a *performance* in its truest sense). Such a reading is perhaps available, but it demands resisting the gaze which *The Man of Feeling* attempts to construct here for its readers; indeed, it involves reversing that gaze, so that instead of sharing and indulging Harley's perspective on the world – experiencing vicariously via Harley the affective attractions of the Bedlamite – the focus rests upon Harley. Clearly, Harley *is* the focal point for much of the novel: for example, at his own death – another conspicuously polite business – he is promoted to principal performer, and other characters take on the role of witness. But on his travels, in episodes such as the Bedlam scene, he is, so far as the experience of a compliant reader is concerned, serving an important functional purpose – focalising or reflecting polite spectacles through his presence as observer. It is a function which is embedded in numerous examples of the genre, and for a significant number of years during the mid eighteenth century it appears that there existed a sufficient community of compliant readers – those within Louisa Stuart's family, for example – for that function to be widely accepted and indulged.[29]

Considering such tendencies within the sentimental genre, it is perhaps possible to refine the conventions outlined in Mary Alcock's *Receipt for Writing a Novel.* Albeit whimsical and satirical, the poem contains astute observation of novelistic convention, and a refined recipe for sentimental fiction should certainly retain the principal ingredients that Alcock suggests should be supplied by the body: the hysterical fits, the fainting, the sighs, the groans, fevers, and madness. But we should improve the recipe by specifying that, where virtuous characters are concerned, only a particular grade of highly refined, polite illness should be included. And importantly we should add to the formula those strategies by which sentimental novelists conventionally attempted to construct the gaze of readers – to direct the manner in which the sentimental text should be read and to shape the type of responses it should generate. It is in this aspect of sentimental fiction, I believe, that we discover the novel's most vital role within eighteenth-century body politics. It is here that we see the novel not so much implicated within a project of somatic representation as involved in shaping the superstructure of polite culture through somatic definition – aspiring to inscribe the bodies of readers as natural symbols of politeness.

But to what extent could sentimental fiction really interpellate readers by urging them to occupy a particular perspective upon representations of virtue? Was the representation of virtue through the body a sufficiently unambiguous enterprise to create a stable interpretive community of 'polite readers'? And why indeed should fiction of this type be marked by

---

[29] The correspondence of Richardson is laden with the accounts of readers, such as Colley Cibber and Lady Dorothy Bradshaigh, who delighted in displaying before the author the effects that his novels had had upon their bodies. The poet and memoirist Lætitia Pilkington relished writing to Richardson to convey the distress she saw Cibber suffering when he heard that Clarissa's story would end with her rape and death. Cibber raved, she reported; she 'never saw passion higher wrought than his' (29 June 1745, *Correspondence of Samuel Richardson*, ed. Barbauld, vol. II, p. 128). Cibber's distress was the delight of Pilkington, who records her arousal at the sight of such virtue on display: 'I can scarcely, Sir, express the pleasure I received from the dear gentleman's warmth, nay heat, on this occasion; as it shewed me at once both the virtue of his own heart, and the power of the writer, who could so melt, engage, and fire it' (vol. II, pp. 129–30). Dorothy Bradshaigh told Richardson that she had 'shed a pint of tears' over *Clarissa*, and she insisted that 'Had you seen me, I surely should have moved your pity' (6 January 1749), vol. IV, p. 240). Such readers dramatise the effects of fiction upon their bodies, and their reports of these effects mingle flattery of the author with a pleasure in their own sensitive receptivity. Whether such statements can be taken to reveal how Richardson's fiction was read is, of course, debatable; a more certain conclusion is that these readers employed an image of the body moved by reading as a trope in polite social exchange.

a desire – or perhaps an anxiety – to prescribe a manner for its own consumption? To begin to address particularly this last question, it is necessary to consider the contemporary cultural position of fiction itself.

THEATRICAL READING AND THE DANGERS OF FICTION

The literary form that we have come to call 'the novel' was by no means an unproblematic platform from which to disperse the tenets and expressive modes of politeness. Indeed, it can be said that one reason why demonstrating a worthy response to fiction became important to polite (or would-be polite) readers was that fiction, for much of the eighteenth century, was widely regarded as morally dubious and its consumption was regularly condemned as anything from an idle waste of time to a deranged and corrupting indulgence in fantasy. Cheryl Turner has shown how, increasingly during the eighteenth century, 'parts of the literature market were linked with the growth of a leisure industry, enriching the pursuit of pleasure which was gaining credence as a legitimate human ambition'.[30] The elevation of pleasure-giving literature – particularly novelistic literature – did not, however, occur without an intense struggle over the potential values or dangers that might arise from its reading. Considering the current 'high' status of the novel, it is easy now to overlook the fears that once surrounded the consumption of novels, but it is essential to recall these fears in order to grasp why asserting or advertising 'proper' literary responses should become a form of polite exchange among consumers of fiction.

The discourse of attack and defence that surrounded eighteenth-century novels has been addressed in several studies and has been given its fullest recent treatment in William B. Warner's *Licensing Entertainment: The Elevation of Novel Reading in Britain, 1684–1750* (1998). Warner's study reconsiders the eighteenth-century 'rise of the novel' not as a collective effort to institute a new form of literature, but rather as a project to reform reading practices, and as such it provides a constructive context within which to regard assertively polite reading. Eighteenth-century anti-novel discourse is preoccupied with the fear that, as Warner puts it, 'the novel reader will become absorbed in unconscious mimicry' of the entertaining scenarios proffered in the fiction.[31] This fear motivates, for example, the

---

[30] Cheryl Turner, *Living by the Pen: Women Writers in the Eighteenth Century* (London: Routledge, 1992; repr. 1994), p. 13.
[31] William B. Warner, *Licensing Entertainment: The Elevation of Novel Reading in Britain, 1684–1750* (Berkeley and Los Angeles: University of California Press, 1998), p. 143.

strict cautions administered in *The Whole Duty of Woman, Or an infallible Guide to the Fair Sex* (1737), which warns against the reading of 'romances, which seems now to be thought the peculiar and only becoming Study of young Ladies . . . Those amorous Passions, which it is their Design to paint to the utmost Life, are apt to insinuate themselves into their unwary Readers, and by an unhappy Inversion a Copy shall produce an Original.'[32] Typically deploying a stereotype of an unbalanced female reader, anti-novel discourse projects readers as potential automata – as quixotes who can become possessed, transformed, and unhinged by exposure to the written word.[33] And when, in the early century, the fiction on the market was dominated by piquant and scandalous tales of love – the 'amatory fiction' produced by such popular writers as Aphra Behn, Eliza Haywood, and Delarivière Manley – the response of moralists seeking to promote chaste, dutiful virtue was to attempt to proscribe novelistic writing.[34]

By examining Richardson's reading of Aaron Hill's *The Art of Acting*, I have already shown an example of the way in which a literary text might produce a transformation of its reader. A temporary quixote, Richardson himself becomes a type of automaton as his body becomes possessed by the power of Hill's words. Recognition of this potential in literary representation was, in fact, crucial to what Warner identifies as an innovative strand of anti-novel discourse by which, from the 1720s, the printed word's capacity to transform readers was harnessed to a new cause: the promotion of virtue. Warner describes a new type of 'anti-novel' enterprise, which is located *within* the fictions of morally concerned writers such as Daniel Defoe, Penelope Aubin, and Richardson. These writers, Warner argues, approach the reform of novel reading not by attempting to proscribe the activity outright, but rather by writing novels *differently*. Specifically, they write *didactically*, aiming to transform their readers by positing exemplary models of modern virtue and politeness. So, as Warner points out, 'both the danger of novel reading and its teaching opportunity . . . arise from the same idea: that a reader/consumer can be made to conform to the object'.[35] The body, it is worth stressing again at this point, was an important device

---

[32] *Ibid.*, p. 183.

[33] Warner follows Cheryl Turner in maintaining that eighteenth-century novels appealed to a wide spectrum of readers of both sexes, and so presents the topos of the unhinged woman reader 'not as a representation of what was, but as a discursive formation' which enabled the separation of 'good' and 'bad' reading (*Licensing Entertainment*, p. 141).

[34] I take the term 'amatory fiction' from Ros Ballaster's now classic study of the form, *Seductive Forms: Women's Amatory Fiction from 1684 to 1740* (Oxford: Clarendon Press, 1992).

[35] Warner, *Licensing Entertainment*, p. 143.

within sentimental writers' efforts to make readers conform. Equally, though, it was the body, with its tendency to be aroused 'improperly', which implanted insecurities in the venture.

Richardson's endeavours to moralise the novel of amorous intrigue and the widespread but precarious success of this project with the sensationally popular *Pamela* are, of course, well known. As a story of attempted seduction, *Pamela* – an offshoot from a scheme to write a conduct manual – had generic investments in the scandalous fiction of Behn, Haywood, and Manley, which Richardson knew from his work as a printer. But by framing and larding a plot of sexual intrigue with the tropes and moral thrust of conduct literature, Richardson transformed a titillating literary type into something far more respectable.[36] Looking back upon the composition of *Pamela*, Richardson outlined to Aaron Hill his hopes that he might 'introduce a new species of writing, that might possibly turn young people into a course of reading different from the pomp and parade of romance-writing, and dismissing the improbable and marvelous, with which novels generally abound, might tend to promote the cause of religion and virtue'.[37] And certainly this plan met with considerable success. Loudly declaring a useful, moral function, *Pamela*, and subsequently *Clarissa* and *Sir Charles Grandison*, undoubtedly helped to overturn much of the critique which traditionally would settle upon fiction – or at least, these works contributed to the creation, within a multifaceted literary marketplace, of an innovative type of fiction which was distinguished by its capacity to be seen as reputable. Part of *Pamela*'s novelty lay in the public respectability of its consumption; reading Richardson's works – unlike, say, the scandalous early works of Eliza Haywood – became rapidly and widely accepted as a polite activity.[38] But those involved with novels none the less had to tread carefully in order to maintain a proper public image of the form.

---

[36] John Richetti discusses the generic developments brought about by Richardson in *The English Novel in History: 1700–1780* (London and New York: Routledge, 1999) – see particularly the chapter 'From Passion to Suffering: Richardson and the Transformation of Amatory Fiction' (pp. 84–120). Margaret Anne Doody discusses such generic hybridity in Richardson's fiction in *A Natural Passion: A Study of the Novels of Samuel Richardson* (Oxford: Clarendon Press, 1974), pp. 14–35.

[37] *Selected Letters of Samuel Richardson*, ed. Carroll, p. 41.

[38] In his early study of the growth of epistolary fiction, R. A. Day identified polite acceptability as a key component of the novelty of Richardson's work – *Pamela* was 'something new in fiction, a novel which one need not be ashamed of reading' (*Told in Letters: Epistolary Fiction before Richardson* (Ann Arbor: University of Michigan Press, 1966), p. 208).

Pamela, as has been seen, attempts both to represent wordless passions in action and to encourage corresponding sensations in its readers (or, at least, the attentive readers it specifically invites). Richardson's pseudo-editor, who introduces Pamela's letters, promotes the book's ability 'to raise a distress from *natural* causes, and excite a compassion from *just* ones'. Pamela's story 'shall engage the passions of every sensible reader', which the pseudo-editor guarantees by appealing 'from his *own* passions, (which have been uncommonly *moved* in perusing it) to the passions of *every one* who shall read with attention' (p. 31). The reader's lesson in virtue would be administered via an easily consumed but emotionally challenging fictional journey. But *Pamela* was open to readings against the grain of the interpretive model which Richardson impressed upon readers as the proper way to approach the story. As I suggested in relation to *The Man of Feeling*, readers of fiction may resist following a proffered interpretive pathway, and such hermeneutic openness was clearly a problem for novelists such as Richardson whose didactic projects – and the attendant respectability and marketability of their works – depended upon readers arriving at particular, predetermined responses to the events depicted in the fiction. As is familiar to any student who has been led along the much-trodden path from *Pamela* to Henry Fielding's parodic *Shamela* (1741), Richardson's novel could be radically 'misread' so as to uncover a story that could contribute little to the moral edification of readers. *Shamela* – just one of many works that engaged in the intense cut and thrust debate of what Warner calls 'The *Pamela* Media Event' – treats Richardson's text by grasping potential semantic slippages in Pamela's account.[39] Its strategy, as one critic describes it, is 'to commandeer the ambiguities and uncertainties of the original narrative, and to make them cohere around a single ridiculously travestied reading of that text'.[40] So in Fielding's version, there is a reversal of the vulnerable Pamela resisting the threat of Mr B., and Pamela reappears, this time supposedly revealing a genuine image, as a crafty, manipulative prostitute achieving her own material rewards through the cunning duping of a naïve 'Mr Booby'. *Shamela* is not really concerned to declare that this version *is* what really happened, but rather that *Pamela*'s narrative is open to challenge and to readings contrary to that which it

---

[39] This is the title of Chapter 5 of Warner's *Licensing Entertainment* (pp. 176–230). Texts contributing to this event have recently been collected in *The* Pamela *Controversy: Criticism and Adaptations of Samuel Richardson's* Pamela, *1740–1750*, ed. Thomas Keymer and Peter Sabor, 6 vols. (London: Pickering & Chatto, 2001).

[40] Ian Bell, *Henry Fielding: Authorship and Authority* (London: Longman, 1994), p. 66.

urges its readers to follow. *Shamela* suggests that Pamela's story of '*Virtue Rewarded*' *might* be read as a tale of rampant female desire and financial plotting, and so demonstrates that such fiction could carry the same type of inflammatory dangers as were seen in the amatory fiction it supposedly transformed.

With regard to eighteenth-century reading practices, the overall 'event' of *Pamela* is significant in that it advanced the respectability of reading fiction – further ushering the consumption of novels into the realms of 'polite reading' – but it also demonstrated that that respectability was tenuous and open to challenge. The *Pamela* controversy exposed and brought to public attention the unstable status of moral fiction; it exposed the limitations and pitfalls inherent in the attempt to apply fiction to didactic ends, when that didacticism is contingent upon a pattern of interpretation that cannot be assumed to be adopted by actual readers. And this unstable status can, I believe, partly explain why in the mid eighteenth century the 'polite reader' of fiction emerged as a popular and powerful image, not only appealed to within novels themselves, as we have seen, but also fostered more widely – and more explicitly – within the culture surrounding novels. Reading fiction was not suddenly and unproblematically 'moralised' in the mid eighteenth century. It remained an activity which, in order for its polite footing to be maintained, had to be conducted with careful and continual monitoring, and with public assertions of its usefulness.

An image of the reader as a conspicuously polite being could, then, perform a two-layered function: it could assert the virtue of the reader whilst at the same time parrying potential charges that the reading of fiction was anything other than useful. And such an image of reading gained significant mid-century currency. The construction of the polite reader *within* sentimental novels may have been an insecure and problematic venture, but that construction was significantly bolstered and empowered by vigorous activities in the culture surrounding those novels. Efforts to define a proper, polite mode of fictional consumption emerged which were more direct than those literary techniques of staging the eloquent body which, I have argued, strive to construct the gaze (and the sensibility behind the gaze) of the reader. But in those more direct efforts, the eloquent body remains an important text for negotiation and a key emblem of politeness.

An early attempt to display the usefulness of reading sentimental fiction is found, in fact, in a series of letters from Aaron Hill to Richardson, written over the course of some weeks shortly after *Pamela*'s anonymous publication on 6 November 1740.[41] Richardson had sent a copy of *Pamela* to Hill, initially without declaring his authorship, and Hill responded to Richardson with several letters enthusiastically reporting the waves of emotion that Pamela's moving story had caused to sweep over his house-hold.[42] In the first letter, Hill confesses to a total captivation by *Pamela*: 'I have done nothing but read it to others, and hear others again read it, to me', he told Richardson. '[I]f I lay the Book down', he continued with prolix effusion, 'it comes after me. – When it has dwelt all Day long upon the Ear, It takes Possession, all Night, of the Fancy. – It has Witchcraft in every Page of it: but it is the Witchcraft of Passion and Meaning.'[43] These eulogistic letters linger over the emotive effects of the novel and are confident in guaranteeing the didactic value of such writing – and significantly, Hill gauges this value by observing the power of the text to control readers' bodies. In Hill's household, *Pamela* was not a pleasure to be privately indulged but was a centrepiece of communal leisure – in a letter of 29 December, Hill reported to Richardson:

We have a lively little Boy in the Family, about seven Years old . . . ever since my first reading of Pamela, he puts in for a Right to be *one* of her Hearers; and, having got half her Sayings by heart, talks in no other Language but hers . . . The first Discovery we made of this Power [of *Pamela*] over so unripe and unfix'd an Attention, was, one Evening, when I was reading her Reflections at the *Pond* to some Company. The little rampant Intruder, being kept out by the Extent of the Circle, had crept under my Chair, and was sitting before me, on the Carpet, with his Head almost touching the Book, and his Face bowing down toward the Fire. – He had sat for some time in this Posture, with a Stillness, that made us conclude him asleep: when, on a sudden, we heard a Succession of heart-heaving Sobs; which while he strove to conceal from our Notice, his little Sides swell'd, as if they would burst, with the throbbing Restraint of his Sorrow. I turn'd his innocent Face, to look toward me; but his Eyes were quite lost, in his *Tears*: which running down from his Cheeks in free Currents, had form'd two sincere little Fountains, on that Part of the Carpet he hung over. All the Ladies in Company were ready to devour him with Kisses: and he has, since, become doubly a Favourite – and is perhaps the youngest of *Pamela's Converts.*[44]

---

[41] As will be seen, the letters were used by Richardson as the basis of his preface to *Pamela's* second edition in 1741; I quote from the letters as they appear in the preface which Keymer and Wakely append to their edition of *Pamela*.

[42] Richardson announced his authorship in a letter of 22 December 1740, although, as Christine Gerrard suggests, 'Hill probably guessed almost immediately that Richardson was *Pamela's* author' (*Aaron Hill*, p. 205).

[43] 17 December 1740, *Pamela*, ed. Keymer and Wakely, p. 506.

[44] 29 December 1740, *Pamela*, ed. Keymer and Wakely, p. 515.

Given what we have seen of Hill's attitude to the expression of the passions on stage, it is perhaps unsurprising that in relaying *Pamela*'s reception he should deploy the body as the final and decisive arbiter of literary value. In describing the responses of the boy, Hill dramatises a scene of literary consumption which might be seen as a paradigm for polite mid-century reading: not so much a paradigm for what the inevitably diverse activity of reading actually *was*, but a model of an influential *idea of polite reading* – a mythic image of the proper consumption of fiction, which may have grown out of and impacted upon actual reading habits, but which should none the less be recognised as in part a discursive formation. It is a formation which is aspired to within novels themselves, but which is reinforced in representations like that in Hill's letter. There are three aspects of the scene which are of particular significance here: firstly, reading is presented as a socially engaged activity; secondly, proper responses are marked upon the body and are acknowledged by being seen; and thirdly, reading is presented as a process through which one can be transformed and improved. For the company described, 'reading' in fact means listening to Hill read. Fiction reaches these 'readers' through the mediating presence of an upright patriarch, who controls both the choice of literary work and the manner in which it is used. Reading, here, is no closeted indulgence in fantasy – no dangerously isolated quixotic pursuit – but is a communal gathering around a pious text which contains, Hill assured the upright patriarch who wrote it, 'all the *Soul* of Religion, Good-breeding, Discretion, Good-nature, Wit, Fancy, Fine Thought, and Morality'.[45] Indeed, centred round such a work, the scene is not unlike a religious service, and it is worth remembering that Richardson self-consciously intended that his fiction should serve a religious purpose. Religion, he told Dorothy Bradshaigh in 1748, 'never was at so low an ebb as at present. And if my work must be supposed of the novel kind, I was willing to try if a religious novel would do good.'[46]

For Hill, the ultimate assurance that *Pamela* 'did good' within his household comes in the form of the boy's tears: his 'heart-heaving Sobs', the 'two sincere little Fountains'. By implication ingenuous, the child's tears naturalise and validate the power of *Pamela*, and his response to the text stimulates a type of innocent orgy of celebration from the assembled company. The boy's response is given collective approval, and Hill himself presents the reaction as a model of good reading as he associates the boy's

---

[45] 17 December 1740, *Pamela*, ed. Keymer and Wakely, p. 506.
[46] 6 October 1748, *Correspondence of Samuel Richardson*, ed. Barbauld, vol. IV, p. 187.

emotional relationship with *Pamela* to a more general conversion in his behaviour; he has, for example, been transformed into an earnest pupil, becoming 'fond of his Book; which (before) he cou'd never be brought to attend to'.[47] In fact, this scene of reading closely mirrors those scenes *within* the novel which dramatise responses to the heroine herself: Pamela and *Pamela* are shown equally to have the power to move, transform, and moralise those who enter their presence and come under their spell. And like Pamela's eloquent performances, the boy's reading is rendered 'dramatic' – not because we might suspect that his reactions are false, but because Hill 'theatricalises' the event through his account, which builds an anecdote into an advertisement for proper reading. Hill creates a miniature moral drama in which *Pamela*'s didactic power is felt, witnessed, and celebrated; the propriety of emotional response is ratified and, in the process, suspicions that this pious form of fiction might be dangerous to young and/or female minds are rejected.

Hill's letters, in fact, were incorporated by Richardson in the prefatory material appended to *Pamela*'s second edition, which appeared, three months after the first, on 14 February 1741. As Hill's home was seemingly transformed to become an annex of Pamela's idealising world, so too the texts describing that transformation became an extension of the text of *Pamela*. Brought together in the preface, the letters thus played a role in the 'event' of *Pamela*, becoming part of Richardson's attempt to control the reception of his work by dictating the manner in which readers should respond. The letters provide an explicit dramatisation of the effects which the main text of *Pamela* urges upon readers, and by including them in the preface, Richardson was, as it were, showing readers explicitly what they should do with *Pamela*, since it was becoming evident that this could not be unambiguously articulated by the text itself.

Hill's contributions to Richardson's preface are usually found to be of interest because when published, like the main text of *Pamela*, they came under the fire of Henry Fielding: prefacing *Shamela* is a letter from one 'Parson Tickletext', a caricature clearly modelled partly upon Hill. As Fielding teased out potential ambiguities in Richardson's body-filled text in order to locate pornography where Richardson intended sentiment, so he sought to parody Hill as a reader whose interests in *Pamela* (and in Pamela) were as much erotic as they were sentimental. Hill's possession by the work – its tendency to affect him physically and to prompt his

[47] 29 December 1740, *Pamela*, ed. Keymer and Wakely, p. 515.

nocturnal disturbance – is parodically transformed by Fielding into a type of onanistic arousal: 'Oh! I feel an Emotion even while I am relating this: Methinks I see *Pamela* at this Instant, with all the Pride of Ornament cast off.'[48] Fielding does not have to manipulate Hill's words much here, and the ease of his critique illuminates the fact that the languages of sex and sentiment can readily collapse into one.[49] As James Grantham Turner points out, both celebrators and critics of *Pamela* engage in fundamentally the same reading practice and often use the same terms to describe their experiences. Pamela is found, for example, to be 'touching' in ways both sexual and sentimental, because 'we must imagine her embodied and located; the sentimental or internal-emphatic reception therefore relies on the scenic or external-spectatorial imagination that the novel's critics use against it'.[50]

It is certainly important to recognise that Hill's letters, like the novel they discuss, lay open to knowing 'misinterpretation', and that, more broadly, Richardson's attempts to control the reading of his work often merely proliferated further interpretations which ran contrary to his plans. As Warner writes, 'Richardson's carefully orchestrated promotional campaign is striking . . . for its success in anticipating future misreadings of *Pamela*, and for its failure to protect the novel from these misreadings.'[51] But the enduring attractions of 'cultural contest' should not foreclose an attention to effects of Hill's letters which may have been more in line with his and Richardson's ambitions for literary culture. The letters, I would suggest, were not only fuel for satire but participated, along with other stimuli, in the mid-century emergence of powerful ideals of polite reading and in the solidification of a polite interpretive community which was coherent enough to be recognised as a community until at least the 1770s. It has been complained by one critic that the 'introductory material in *Pamela* is, so far as critical theory is concerned, slight and incoherent', and certainly the preface does not provide a coherent theory of the novel.[52] But it does present an expression (or dramatisation) of a theory of how

---

[48] Fielding, *Joseph Andrews with Shamela*, p. 277.
[49] Hill's formulation is: 'When modest Beauty seeks to hide itself by casting off the *Pride* of *Ornament*, it but displays itself without a *Covering*' (*Pamela*, ed. Keymer and Wakely, p. 508).
[50] James Grantham Turner, 'Novel Panic: Picture and Performance in the Reception of Richardson's *Pamela*', *Representations* 48 (Fall 1994), 73. Turner's use of 'performance' refers to the stage adaptations of *Pamela*.
[51] Warner, *Licensing Entertainment*, pp. 208–9.
[52] R. S. Brissenden in his introduction to Samuel Richardson, *Clarissa: Preface, Hints of Prefaces, and Postscript*, Augustan Reprint Society No. 103 (Los Angeles: William Andrews Clark Memorial Library, 1964), p. i.

fiction should be read – a theory which was apparently subscribed to by many mid-eighteenth-century novelists, critics, and readers with interests in fostering polite culture, and which enlisted the performing body as a device for asserting the virtues of reading fiction.

The sentimental genre is shot through and surrounded by a discourse of literary instruction – a coercive running commentary explaining or dramatising a manner in which polite reading should be practised and displayed. Prefaces, as Richardson recognised when mounting his defence of *Pamela*, were valuable textual spaces which could be exploited for the inscription of a feeling, morally alert reader, and he continued to use these introductory occasions to assert the effects upon the passions which he intended his fictions should induce. The 'Author's Preface' to *Clarissa* presents a detailed guide to the text's didactic usefulness and promotes the propriety of an emotional response to excitingly tense, epistolary writing. The letters that comprise *Clarissa* 'are written while the hearts of the writers must be supposed to be wholly engaged in their subjects', which immediacy in their production produces 'instantaneous descriptions and reflections, which may be brought home to the breast of the youthful reader'.[53] Similar attempts to steer the reading process – or to validate the narrative by advertising its usefulness – are found in the prefaces of numerous novels following Richardson, and they regularly deploy the image of an emotionally moved body as an icon of proper reading.

An emotional, physical response to literature is validated, for example, in dramatic form in 'The Editor's Introduction' to *The Memoirs of Miss Sidney Bidulph* (1761), an epistolary novel by Frances Sheridan, wife of the elocutionist. Dedicated to Richardson, this novel, like *Pamela's* expanded preface, describes in its pseudo-editorial material a scene of communal reading. It involves the 'editor' and his friend as readers, and an audience comprising an elderly lady 'of an excellent taste' – one who 'loved reading' – and 'a neighbouring lady (a sensible woman) who had drank tea with us'. Their chosen text is *Douglas*, a sentimental tragedy by John Home, which had been performed and published in 1757. The two readers could almost have been modelled by Thomas Sheridan – they read the play 'alternately, to relieve each other, that we might not injure the performance by a wearied or flat delivery' – and they prompt from the ladies a model response which is displayed through the body: 'both gave that true testimony of nature to its merit – tears'.[54] Prefacing *Sidney Bidulph*, a novel

---

[53] Richardson, *Clarissa*, ed. Ross, p. 35.
[54] Sheridan, *Sidney Bidulph*, p. 5.

which shares the tragedy and pathos of *Douglas*, the ladies' response positions such a mode of consumption as appropriate to the coming narrative. Set in a polite world of tea-drinking and literary discussion, the scene vividly dramatises both 'how to read' and the capacity of properly used literature in the business of exhibiting virtue.

Even more insistent as a literary pedagogue was Sarah Fielding. In *David Simple* we have already seen Fielding's strategies for shaping a mode of moral reading; it was a project that she maintained through her later literary career, and like Richardson – who enthusiastically supported her work – Fielding used prefaces to delineate both how her fiction should be consumed and, more generally, how polite reading should be conducted. For example, Fielding's *The History of The Countess of Dellwyn* (1759), the publication of which was assisted by Richardson, contains a long preface, which presents reflections upon ways of writing before then becoming explicit in declaring that ways of reading are equally important factors in the literary contract between an author and the reading public. 'I have somewhere read an Observation', she writes, 'That many Persons have endeavoured to teach Men to write; but none have taught them to read; as if Reading consisted only in distinguishing the Letters and Words from each other', and she proceeds with a didactic presentation dramatising modes of reading.[55] The preface pretends to reproduce a manuscript essay by an 'old Gentleman . . . a curious Observer of Nature' (p. xxxiv), who has made a study of different individuals' characters in relation to their habits of reading, particularly their various responses to Virgil's *Aeneid.* The old essayist is really a proto-reader-response critic with didactic ends – a combination of Stanley Fish and Harold Bloom, perhaps – and he articulates a view of literature in society which acknowledges that reading is a multifaceted pursuit and that different readers will interpret and use literary works in different ways, but which advertises an emotional responsiveness to moral representations as the proper, polite mode of literary consumption. And as in *David Simple*, polite reading is modelled here in terms of somatic display. The old gentleman, observing readers of Virgil, describes, for example, a father with a worthy son who discovers a counterpart of his own good fortune in Aeneas' father: 'Tears of Pleasure started from his Eyes, and his whole Countenance glowed with generous Warmth . . . his old Eyes sent forth Floods of Tears on every Story' (p. xxxvi). With similar physical eloquence, a 'fond Mother' reading an echo of herself in a distressed

---

[55] Sarah Fielding, *The History of the Countess of Dellwyn*, 2 vols. (London, 1759), vol. 1, pp. xxxiii–xxxiv. Subsequent references are to vol. 1 and are given in the text.

parent 'will shudder with Apprehensions . . . and feel by Sympathy every Pang which she knows must overwhelm her with Sorrow' (p. xxxviii). The old man's conclusion is that individuals – of whatever moral stamp – will reveal themselves when reading: 'The truly softened Heart hath a Tear ready for every human Misfortune which is represented to his Imagination by Reading; and the truly hardened Heart supplies no Moisture which can flow from the Eyes, but when poor Self alone is disappointed of any favourite Pursuit; and then indeed Sorrow is poured forth' (p. xl). This preface, though, is not only *describing* types of reader; it is also promoting the 'softened Heart', and demonstrating the language by which, through the act of reading, it can be asserted. Positioned before Fielding's sentimental narrative, the preface, in fact, is providing both a lesson in reading and a coercive justification of the genre about to be read. If such writing produces no tears, it suggests, the fault lies not in the novel but in the hardened heart of the reader; if a reader cannot respond with visible sympathy, that reader has no claim upon modern, polite virtue. Indeed, the preface dwells upon these hardened readers – malevolent types, who read satire only to enjoy its power to wound – and Fielding's old gentleman declares: 'with no such Man would my Soul wish to hold *Acquaintance*: I say not, *Friendship*; because it would be the highest Absurdity to suppose such a one in the least degree capable of being animated with the generous Warmth which that Appellation requires' (p. xlii). Fielding's lesson in reading holds open a door to a sentimental interpretive community; those who decline to enter, it suggests, must live with their vice, friendless in the moral barrenness outside.[56]

Fielding was not only interested in moulding the readers of her own fiction. In her *Remarks on Clarissa* (1749) she also participated in directing a way in which Richardson's fiction should be read.[57] *Remarks on Clarissa* is an early example of a literary guidebook and certainly one of the first to be addressed to the interpretation of a novel. Part eulogy (one which offers unstinting praise but also justifies aspects of *Clarissa* that had been

---

[56] A comparable passage, where Fielding directly distinguishes between good and bad readers of her fiction, appears in her 1753 continuation of *David Simple*, 'Volume the Last'. Her narrator interrupts an account of David's happy community, asserting: 'Those . . . of my Readers, who have a Relish for the same kind of Conversation, will, I doubt not, make use of their own Imaginations, in drawing the Picture to the life: but to those, who mistake *bon-mots*, *insulting* Raillery, malicious Ridicule, and murtherous Slander for the *Attic* Salt of Society, I write not. Indeed, to such I *cannot* write' (*David Simple*, p. 293).

[57] In fact, she also participated in directing the way his fiction was rewritten. Peter Sabor discusses how 'Sarah Fielding's pamphlet played a significant role in shaping Richardson's revisions and additions to *Clarissa*' in his introduction to *Remarks on Clarissa*, Augustan Reprint Society Nos. 231–2 (Los Angeles: William Andrews Clark Memorial Library, 1985), p. vi.

criticised), *Remarks on Clarissa* is in large part a manual instructing readers
how to respond to and how to learn from Richardson's text. Like an early
York Notes but with a moralising edge, it describes an accessible agenda for
textual interpretation, and in line with the emerging discourse of polite
reading, the textual commentary is dramatised in welcoming scenes of
domestic society as a series of polite conversations and letters between
imagined readers. In its depicted debate between characters of varying
sensibilities, generalised observations and described responses to key points
in the text are judged so as ultimately to present an exemplary reading of
the novel. It stages three scenes of conversation. In the first, a Mr Clark
justifies *Clarissa*'s length and the minuteness of its descriptions, while
Mr Dellincourt objects to certain orthographic and neologistic liberties
taken by Richardson, but these objections are answered by Miss Gibson,
who emerges as one of Fielding's model readers. The next scene describes
tearful responses to *Clarissa*, as Miss Gibson seamlessly develops her
account of literary 'Scenes of well-wrought Distress' into a discussion of
Garrick performing King Lear, at which, she had thought, 'even Butchers
must have wept'.[58] Elsewhere reactions to specific passages of *Clarissa* are
described. Appearing in a letter to a sensitive male reader, Miss Gibson's
account of her response to Clarissa's protracted death displays the now
familiar association between bodily response and moral improvement:

Surely the Tears we shed for *Clarissa* in her last Hours, must be Tears of tender Joy!
Whilst we seem to live, and daily converse with her through her last Stage, our
Hearts are at once rejoiced and amended, are both soften'd and elevated, till our
Sensations grow too strong for any Vent, but that of Tears; nor am I ashamed to
confess, that Tears without Number have I shed . . . nor can I hardly refrain from
crying out, 'Farewell, my dear *Clarissa*! may every Friend I love in this World
imitate you in their Lives, and thus joyfully quit all the Cares and Troubles that
disturb this mortal Being!'[59]

In this paradigmatic response the emotional capacities of the body trigger
an acceptance of the novel's ideology in the world in which it is consumed.
Remarks on Clarissa mediates this consumption, and depicts a proper social
function of *Clarissa* as an agent of the world's moral improvement. In
Fielding's dramatisation, sentimental fiction is absorbed into neither a
world of solitary readers nor a group of professional critics, but rather
enters a domestic literary culture of serious conversation and moral reflection. *Remarks on Clarissa* itself seeks to enter that same world, and to

---

[58] *Ibid.*, p. 31.
[59] *Ibid.*, pp. 55–6.

manage it from within by stabilising a challenging text which immediately became a central pillar of that culture.

The preface to *The Countess of Dellwyn* and *Remarks on Clarissa* are representative of a strand of mid-eighteenth-century literary instruction, the coercive body-centred rhetoric of which can begin to explain why Louisa Stuart, reading *The Man of Feeling* in 1771, should feel 'a secret dread' that she 'should not cry enough to gain the credit of proper sensibility'. This powerful rhetoric underpins the community around sentimental fiction; it binds and indeed creates that community, deploying the body, with its capacity to perform politeness, as a token of exchange – a means of displaying fellowship and ideological consensus in relation to a work of fiction. In fact, if her mother and sisters had not filled her with sufficient angst, Louisa Stuart could have found further torment by reading assessments of *The Man of Feeling* in the reviewing magazines – another channel through which lessons in reading were conveyed. Literary reviewing as a practice was growing and being shaped in the decades of sentimental fiction's prime, and during these years novel reviews could function, like the works they addressed, as platforms for promoting an image of the proper reader.[60] 'By those who have feeling hearts, and a true relish for simplicity in writing, many pages in this miscellaneous volume will be read with satisfaction', the *Critical Review* declared of *The Man of Feeling*.[61] Pity those who are unsatisfied by the work, the reviewer suggests, for they know not how to feel. The critic in the *Monthly Review* was more direct still, insisting that 'the Reader, who weeps not over some of the scenes it [*The Man of Feeling*] describes, has no sensibility of mind'.[62] By 1771, sentimentalism's 'natural' language of the passions had become an almost unashamedly manipulative cultural tool.

But such a mode of reading and the fragile interpretive community it consolidated could not ultimately endure. The community described by Louisa Stuart had dissolved by 1826 when she told Walter Scott of her first reactions to *The Man of Feeling*. Rereading Mackenzie's novel half a century on, amidst a new community of readers, she finds that the work has almost become a satire of what it was when first published. 'I am afraid', she told Scott, 'I perceived a sad change in it, or myself – which was

---

[60] On the increasing cultural significance of literary reviewing, particularly after the founding of the *Monthly Review* in 1749, see Frank Donoghue, *The Fame Machine: Book Reviewing and Eighteenth-Century Literary Careers* (Stanford: Stanford University Press, 1996), pp. 16–55.

[61] *Critical Review* 31 (June 1771), 482.

[62] *Monthly Review* 44 (May 1771), 418.

worse; and the effect altogether failed. Nobody cried, and at some of the passages, the touches that I used to think so exquisite – Oh Dear! They laughed.'[63] In fact, the interpretive community she once belonged to had already splintered years earlier. An article in a 1796 issue of the *Monthly Magazine* can only describe sentimental reading practices in the past tense, as it recalls 'a time when sensibility was taken under the patronage of that powerful arbiter of manners – fashion. Then, height of breeding was measured by delicacy of feeling, and no fine lady, or gentleman, was ashamed to be seen sighing over a pathetic story, or weeping at a deep-wrought tragedy.' The article is addressing the question 'Ought Sensibility to be cherished, or repressed?', and the author is obliged to note that the 'current of taste and opinion seems at present, to tend towards the negative side of this question'.[64] By the end of the eighteenth century, as Barker-Benfield and others have shown, there had developed a widespread opposition to the culture of sensibility – it was an assault which operated on a number of political, social, and moral fronts, and which integrated a forceful critique of sentimentalism's feminised expressions of virtue.[65] And significantly where the body in fiction and the reading body are concerned, what underlies much late-century opposition to sentimentalism is recognition that the exaggerated language of gesture is a performance. Distanced from the powerful cultural forces that, for many in the mid century, had naturalised an image of the sentimental body, later commentators clearly recognise the workings of culture behind that image and see the tool-marks of construction upon it. And with this recognition, they draw attention to the emotional body's alienation from the virtue of which it had been an instrument. The writer in the *Monthly Magazine* sees the power of fashion to mould the body; in a similar vein, Louisa Stuart concludes her thoughts on *The Man of Feeling* by reflecting upon how literary responses are inevitably subject to the 'alterations of taste produced by time'.[66] For Mary Alcock, writing her 'Receipt for Writing a Novel', the sentimental body has become a cluster of formulaic, risible conventions, while among other sceptical commentators was the poet Hannah More, who, in *Sensibility: A Poetic Epistle* (1782), wrote of sentimentalism's 'tender tones' and 'fond tears', regretting that 'these fair marks,

---

[63] *Private Letter-Books of Sir Walter Scott*, p. 273.
[64] *Monthly Magazine* 9 (October 1796), 706.
[65] See particularly Barker-Benfield's chapter on 'Wollstonecraft and the Crisis over Sensibility in the 1790s' (*Culture of Sensibility*, pp. 351–95).
[66] *Private Letter-Books of Sir Walter Scott*, p. 273.

reluctant I relate, / These lovely symbols may be counterfeit.'[67] Such commentaries identify the sentimental body as the vehicle of a *performable language*, and with that identification they puncture the image's claim upon naturalness and shatter its potential as a 'natural symbol' of politeness. These critics register an evolution of the body's language from manner to mannerism; what had emerged as an instrument of civility has developed into a hollow indulgence – a language cast off from the virtue to which writers such as Richardson had attempted to harness it.

This recognition was newly widespread towards the end of the century, but it was not new. As I have suggested, from their early appearances in (and around) Richardson's fiction, bodies of sentiment were subject to scrutiny, interrogation, and scepticism. Could the reading body – that organic vessel filled with unpredictable urges – really be tethered to the strict moral code proffered by sentimental authors? Could the erotic potential that Henry Fielding immediately saw leaking from the sentimental body really be kept at bay by a bombardment of persuasive rhetoric? Does emotionalism have a proper role within civic practice, or is it a self-congratulatory expression of socially impotent virtue? The fragility of the sentimental interpretive community, together with its fragmentation towards the end of the century, suggests that such questions could never be fully resolved.

[67] Hannah More, *Poems* (London, 1816), p. 181.

Epilogue

POLITENESS, PERFORMANCE, AND APOSIOPESISES

Ye who govern this mighty world and its mighty concerns with the *engines* of eloquence, – who heat it, and cool it, and melt it, and mollify it, — and then harden it again to *your purpose* —

Ye who wind and turn the passions with this great windlass, – and, having done it, lead the owners of them, whither ye think meet –

Ye, lastly, who drive — and why not, Ye also who are driven, like turkeys to market, with a stick and a red clout – meditate–meditate, I beseech you, upon *Trim's* hat.[1]

Thus readers of Laurence Sterne's *The Life and Opinions of Tristram Shandy, Gentleman* (1759–67) are urged to contemplate the central prop of a most eloquent performance. Before an audience of his fellow servants in the kitchen of Shandy Hall, Corporal Trim has made expressive use of his hat while reflecting upon the news that Tristram Shandy's brother is dead: 'Are we not here now, continued the corporal, (striking the end of his stick perpendicularly upon the floor, so as to give an idea of health and stability) – and are we not – (dropping his hat upon the ground) gone! in a moment!' (p. 431). It is an eloquent gesture, the power of which is confirmed by the responses of its witnesses: '*Susannah* burst into a flood of tears ... *Jonathan, Obadiah*, the cook-maid, all melted ... The whole kitchen crouded about the corporal' (p. 431). As narrator of the event, Tristram meditates for several pages upon the manner of the hat's release: 'The descent of the hat was as if a heavy lump of clay had been kneaded into the crown of it ... Had he flung it, or thrown it, or cast it, or skimmed it, or squirted, or let it slip or fall in any possible direction under heaven ... it had fail'd, and the effect upon the heart had been lost' (pp. 432–3). But the effect of

---

[1] Sterne, *Tristram Shandy*, vol. I, p. 433. Further references are given in the text (without volume number since page numbers follow a single sequence).

the gesture has not failed – indeed, Tristram insists that 'Nothing could have expressed the sentiment of mortality, of which it was the type and fore-runner, like it' (p. 432). Wryly – but not necessarily ironically – the passage suggests that such gestures are a driving force within 'this mighty world and its mighty concerns'.

This narrative business surrounding Trim's hat forms just one of numerous meditations upon 'the *engines* of eloquence' produced by Laurence Sterne, the long-serving Yorkshire parson who in middle age transformed himself into the celebrity author of *Tristram Shandy*, seven volumes of sermons (1760–9), and *A Sentimental Journey through France and Italy* (1768). In fact, when Sterne was finding his way as an author it appears that he was planning to write an extended bawdy satire upon the whole art of sermonising – his 'Rabelaisian Fragment' (1759) presents the opening two chapters of such a work – and, while Sterne altered course as a writer before that project was complete, he never altogether abandoned the matters of eloquence he had begun to explore in that early literary effort.[2] Sterne's fiction is laden with eloquent bodies and with reflections upon the manner of their eloquence, and for that reason it presents us with a knowing interrogation of the elocutionary discourse I have been examining in this book.[3] Furthermore, the way in which that interrogation evolved throughout Sterne's literary career – from the 'Rabelaisian Fragment' to *A Sentimental Journey* – provides a revealing demonstration of what had to happen to both a body and a body-fixated author if they were to become at all acceptable within contemporary polite culture. Sterne partially accommodated his writing to polite tastes – a process which involved tailoring his representations of the body along recognisably sentimental lines. But in Sterne's fiction, unlike in that of most of his contemporaries, a rhetoric of

---

[2] I am using the title given to the fragment by Melvyn New in his enlightening edition of the text in 'Sterne's Rabelaisian Fragment: A Text from the Holograph Manuscript', *PMLA* 87 (1972), 1083–92. This incomplete work is traditionally called 'A Fragment in the Manner of Rabelais' after its publication – in a radically sanitised form – under that title in *Letters of the Late Rev. Mr. Laurence Sterne. To his most intimate Friends... published by his Daughter, Mrs. Medalle*, 3 vols. (London, 1775). The date of the work's composition is not certain, but I am accepting New's convincing location of it in early 1759 and his view of the fragment as Sterne's 'first attempt at what ultimately became *Tristram Shandy*' (p. 1085). Later quotations are from New's unsanitised edition of the text.

[3] Like previous writers on Sterne, I am indebted in my terminology here to Coleridge, who hit upon one of the most apt terms for describing Sterne's fiction when he wrote of its 'sort of *knowingness*' – the phrase appears in notes for an 1818 lecture on 'Wit and Humour' reproduced in *Sterne: The Critical Heritage*, ed. Alan B. Howes (London and Boston: Routledge and Kegan Paul, 1974), p. 354.

sensibility comes integrated with a self-conscious analysis of its own forms and techniques, alongside a playful articulation of those aspects of bodily experience which politeness conventionally represses. Sterne's career in fiction thus provides an ideal vehicle for a concluding consideration of issues and ironies which are inherent within the refinement of 'natural', somatic behaviour that eighteenth-century projectors of polite eloquence aspired to achieve.

Sterne's explorations of bodily eloquence in his fiction doubtless had some basis in his own experience of public performance as a clergyman. Sterne fulfilled this role, it appears, in a manner which, for the most part, would have been approved of and admired by elocutionists of the senti-mental school. Records of Sterne in the pulpit are scant, but they none the less provide good hints of his style of eloquence, and they suggest that he possessed considerable expertise in eliciting emotional responses from his congregations – as a preacher, he was evidently a skilled deployer of pathos when the occasion demanded it. Richard Greenwood, a servant of Sterne's, recorded how 'he never preached at Sutton [Sterne's first Yorkshire parish] but half the congregation were in tears',[4] and his preaching was respected sufficiently to earn him, in 1747, the honour of delivering a charity sermon in York, at which, Arthur Cash records, he used his affecting powers to inspire a notably bountiful collection.[5] Further suggesting the emotional-ism of his preaching is a comment from Sterne himself, which appears in a letter responding to an invitation in 1761 to deliver another charity sermon at the Foundling Hospital in London. '[P]reaching (you must know)', Sterne told his correspondent, 'is a theological flap upon the heart.'[6]

Another glimpse of Sterne as a preacher is provided by John Wilkes, the political radical and refugee with whom Sterne became acquainted in Paris. In 1764, Sterne was invited by Lord Hertford, the English ambassador to France, to deliver a sermon on the occasion of the opening of the new embassy in the Hôtel de Brancas in Paris. Sterne was then passing a sociable and supposedly curative time in France, and despite a weakness of voice caused by his chronic lung disease, he agreed to preach the sermon. Wilkes,

---

[4] In Arthur H. Cash, *Laurence Sterne: The Early and Middle Years* (London: Methuen, 1975; repr. London and New York: Routledge, 1992), p. 127. Cash also provides an account of Sterne's preaching in 'Voices Sonorous and Cracked: Sterne's Pulpit Oratory', in Larry S. Champion (ed.), *Quick Springs of Sense: Studies in the Eighteenth Century* (Athens: University of Georgia Press, 1974), pp. 197–209.

[5] Cash, *Early and Middle Years*, pp. 215–16.

[6] To George Whatley (25 March 1761), *Letters of Laurence Sterne*, ed. Lewis Perry Curtis (Oxford: Clarendon Press, 1935), p. 134.

encouraging a friend to attend, wrote of Sterne: 'Tho' you may not catch every word of Tristram, his *action* will divert you, and you know that *action* is the first, second, third, &c parts of a great orator.'[7] Wilkes portrays Sterne as an effective preacher with the ability to engage an audience, not through verbal dexterity (indeed, the letter predicts Sterne's inaudibility), but through the eloquent movement of his body. An experienced orator himself, Wilkes presents public speaking as primarily a somatic skill, and in tune with the reordering of the Ciceronian parts of oratory, which we have seen in the work of contemporary elocutionists, he prioritises the art of action, and advertises Sterne as a gifted exponent of this art. With this bodily eloquence and his playing to the emotions of his congregations, Sterne would seem, in terms of the priorities of mid-century elocutionists, to have been something of a model sentimental preacher.

Sterne's pulpit performances were, though, marked by an element of personal idiosyncrasy and by energies which, subtly but significantly, disturb an image of Sterne as a model preacher of this kind. The published versions of the sermons – together with their reception – suggest that, while Sterne occupied a basically conventional theological position within eighteenth-century latitudinarianism, his techniques of composition offered significant originality and eccentricity. Of the published sermons, one early critic complained that Sterne had 'adulterated the word of God with a vicious mixture of foreign or unnatural ornaments. Loose sparkles of wit, luxuriant descriptions, smart antitheses, pointed sentiments, epigrammatical turns or expressions, are frequently to be met with.' Sterne, for this critic, suffered from an 'insatiable *lust* of being *witty*'.[8] And Sterne's wit led to occasional displays of unseemly comedy in the pulpit, which, by audiences expecting a polite performance, were not always well received. Opening the sermon at the Hôtel de Brancas, Sterne caused a minor scandal with an ill-judged and lewd embellishment of his chosen biblical text, and there were other occasions when Sterne was, as Cash puts it, unable 'to suppress his sense of comedy'.[9] Sterne might well have agreed with a diagnosis that saw in him insatiable urges – writing of the incident in Paris, he told a correspondent how 'that unlucky kind of fit seized me,

---

[7] Details concerning the sermon are given in Arthur H. Cash, *Laurence Sterne: The Later Years* (London: Methuen, 1986; repr. London and New York: Routledge, 1992), pp. 184–7; Wilkes's letter (to the journalist Jean-Baptiste-Antoine Suard) is quoted by Cash (p. 185).

[8] Thomas Weales, *The Christian Orator Delineated* (London, 1778), pp. 110 and 114. For a fuller discussion of Weales's responses to Sterne, see my 'Thomas Weales's *The Christian Orator Delineated* (1778) and the Early Reception of Sterne's Sermons', *The Shandean* 13 (2002), 87–97.

[9] Cash, 'Voices Sonorous and Cracked', p. 201.

which you know I can never resist, and a very unlucky text did come into my head'.[10]

There is no evidence to suggest that such unlucky fits were frequent, and during the course of Sterne's long church career, actual transgressions of conventional pulpit politeness were probably few. Sterne was certainly no preaching 'zany' in the manner of, say, John Henley, although his use of 'Yorick' as the name for his fictional alter-ego easily encouraged a view that he was some kind of jester in the pulpit. In fact, Sterne's presentation of himself as Mr Yorick – the name under which he notoriously offered his own sermons to the public – has doubtless contributed to his having sometimes been presented as more playful and 'Shandean' a sermonist than a reading of the published sermons suggests he was.[11] As Melvyn New insists, Sterne probably behaved, for the most part, as a fairly ordinary, conscientious, eloquent, and effective Anglican clergyman – not like Yorick in *Tristram Shandy*, who, following his namesake in *Hamlet*, would be forever 'scattering his wit and his humour, – his gibes and his jests about him' (p. 29). But given Sterne's occasional breaches of decorum, and the very fact that he chose to identify himself with a character renowned for his infinite jest, there none the less emerges from the figure of Sterne in the pulpit a subtle tension between the polite, sentimental eloquence of the body and the knowing, ironic play of the mind. And in significant ways such tensions came to shape the representation of bodies in Sterne's fiction.

Those tensions are arguably *not* present, or at least not prominent, in Sterne's aborted 'Rabelaisian Fragment', a piece of writing which – unsurprisingly, given its debts to the bawdy writings of François Rabelais (1483?–1553) – shows little accommodation to polite literary tastes. The fragment opens with one Longinus Rabelaicus proposing a grand elocutionary project to a group of clergy:

Would it not be a glorious Thing, If any Man of Genius and Capacity amongst us for such a Work, was fully bent within Himself to sit down immediately and compose a thorough-stitch'd System of the KERUKOPÆDIA, daintily setting

---

[10] To William Combe? (July? 1764), *Letters of Laurence Sterne*, p. 219.

[11] An *a priori* view of Sterne as a jesting preacher is the starting point for Byron Petrakis's 'Jester in the Pulpit: Sterne and Pulpit Eloquence', *Philological Quarterly* 51 (1972), 430–7. Petrakis shows Sterne's preaching to be 'dramatic' and emotive, but he actually presents very little evidence suggesting that 'Sterne chose to "play the fool" in the pulpit' (p. 431). For a study which sees not Sterne but Tristram Shandy as an orator in the mould of preachers such as Henley, see Richard A. Davies, 'Tristram Shandy: Eccentric Public Orator', *English Studies in Canada* 5:2 (1979), 154–66.

forth . . . all that is needful to be known and understood of . . . the Art of making all kinds of your theological, hebdomadical, rostrummical, humdrummical what d'ye call 'ems. (p. 1088)

With this *tour de force* of Rabelaisian mock-learning is introduced the topic under scrutiny in the work: the art of the sermon – 'the Art of making 'em . . . [and] of preaching 'em' (p. 1088). What the fragment might have grown into cannot be determined for sure, but Sterne appears here to have been embarking upon a satirical examination of the type of project that contemporaries such as Thomas Sheridan, James Fordyce, John Mason, and John Ward were undertaking seriously. In the same year as the public were being offered Ward's Royal Society lectures as *A System of Oratory*, Sterne was developing a literary enterprise which would wittily probe efforts to produce 'thorough-stitch'd' systems of oratory. And the 'Rabelaisian Fragment' shows furthermore that, while elocutionists were concerned with harnessing the polite potential of the body, Sterne was interested in exploring the baser aspects of embodiment – those aspects which resist or break through the disciplining tendencies of politeness – and in comically exploiting the gulf between real bodies and the idea of the refined, circumscribed body that was elevated within polite cultural discourse.

The 'Rabelaisian Fragment' shows Sterne indulging in scatological language and humour with an openness rarely seen in his later, better-known writings. A telling example of this comes in an account of a preacher called Homenas, who, it is reported, '*has broke his Neck, and fractured his Skull and beshit himself into the Bargain, by a fall from the Pulpit two Stories high*. Alass poor *Homenas*! – *Homenas* has done his Business!' (p. 1089). This fall of Homenas in many ways encapsulates the ribald deflation of polite eloquence undertaken in the 'Rabelaisian Fragment' – it is an emblematic traversal of the gap between the elevated image of socialised man and the creature which that image partly veils. Homenas is literally lowered from his exalted social position in the pulpit, and whatever polite symbolic power he might have possessed there is swiftly dispatched through his incontinent descent. Where elocutionists sought to fill the pulpits of Britain with eloquent symbols of politeness, Sterne's 'Rabelaisian Fragment' stresses the physiological origins of those symbols. Sterne creates comedy, in fact, by overturning the 'rule of distance from physiological origin' which, as we saw in the discussion of Le Faucheur, typically under-lies constructions of public somatic dignity. Sentimental elocutionists loosened the classical formulation of that rule, but none the less sustained

it within modernised notions of decorum. Sterne provides a rude reminder
that a distance from physiology can be performed but can never be anything more than a performance.

For an aspiring author such as Sterne, however, such rumbunctious
deconstructions of politeness were problematic, for they clearly do not
make for polite reading. A work such as the 'Rabelaisian Fragment' might
well have been enjoyed by some of Sterne's more riotous friends – those,
for example, who gathered as the 'Demoniacs' and exercised a shared
interest in bawdy literature – but it was not viable as a commercial work
within the modern literary marketplace, wherein, as I hope the previous
chapter has shown, respectable fiction, when it portrayed the body, typically did so politely.[12] Sterne, as his biographers have stressed, was ambitious to thrive within that marketplace, and his eventual success as an
author, as Ian Campbell Ross puts it, lay 'in the skill with which – in
collaboration with his booksellers – he reached out to . . . those prosperous
middle-class readers who increasingly made up the great bulk of the reading public'.[13] An important step in Sterne's ultimate ability to appeal to
that readership lay in his modification of the manner in which he wrote
about the body – indeed, a significant stylistic idiom of Sterne's fiction
arises from the tension between the realities of embodiment and the polite
or playfully pseudo-polite literary language which Sterne came to employ
for their mediation.

There are, in fact, passages in the manuscript of the 'Rabelaisian
Fragment' which suggest, as New points out, that at this point in his
literary career 'Sterne was aware of changing tastes and changing standards
of decorum' (p. 1085). At one stage in the composition, Sterne had set up a
bawdy pun by having Homenas plagiarise from a sermon by Dr. John
Rogers: '*Homenas* who had to preach next Sunday . . . was all this while
Rogering it as hard as He could drive' (p. 1084). But Sterne revised the
passage and removed the jest, and he changed all other references to
'Rogers', bringing in 'Clarke' as an innocuously named replacement
(pp. 1084–5). In this revision, we see Sterne choosing to sacrifice an opportunity for 'low' somatic humour – he by no means makes the 'Rabelaisian
Fragment' 'polite' by doing so, but the revision perhaps reflects a recognition on the part of Sterne that, if he was to succeed commercially as an

---

[12] On the club of Demoniacs, see Cash, *Early and Middle Years*, pp. 185–95.
[13] Ian Campbell Ross, *Laurence Sterne: A Life* (Oxford: Oxford University Press, 2001), p. 11.

author, he would have to find alternative, subtler ways in which to write about the body and its activities.[14]

Sterne's commercial breakthrough came with the first, two-volume instalment of *Tristram Shandy*, published towards the end of 1759 (the four further instalments would follow in 1761, 1762, 1765, and 1767). Like the 'Rabelaisian Fragment', these two volumes display a fascination with the body and with the arts that seek to discipline it, but they also show a change in Sterne's way of writing about these matters. Here, in fact, Sterne has made the difference between polite and impolite ways of writing about the body one of his themes, as Tristram – the fictional autobiographer whose life is ever exceeding his capacity to write his life story – probes these narrative alternatives self-consciously. During a discussion of why Tristram's mother might prefer a female midwife to a male one, for example, Tristram's Uncle Toby remarks that she may 'not care to let a man come so near her****' (p. 115) – the sentence concludes with one of the suggestive ellipses which became a notorious feature of Sterne's fiction. Tristram sees in this remark 'one of the neatest examples of that ornamental figure in oratory, which Rhetoricians stile the *Aposiopesis*...Make this dash, —— 'tis an Aposiopesis. – Take the dash away, and write Backside, – 'tis Bawdy' (pp. 115–16). With Tristram's intervention, Sterne playfully shifts the focus from Mrs Shandy's lower body to an analysis of the aposiopesis – a rhetorical device whereby, as the *OED* puts it, 'the speaker comes to a sudden halt, as if unable or unwilling to proceed'. Replacing direct bawdry with a pseudo-scholarly analysis of what constitutes the bawdy does not, of course, make this passage 'polite', and the comedy of such moments in *Tristram Shandy* clearly resides in the creation of a narrative pose of innocence or disinterested intellectual scrutiny through which bawdry is invoked as readers are nudged into producing their own bawdy interpretations of what is not explicitly bawdy. And yet by thus making bawdiness *indirect* the passage does, in a way, take a rhetorical step into the realms of polite literature – and this is a step which Sterne reinforces in *Tristram Shandy* by tempering some of his more straightforwardly vulgar vocabulary, particularly that pertaining to the body. For example, where the narrator of the 'Rabelaisian Fragment' remarks 'I know no more of Greek & Latin

---

[14] In 'Translating Rabelais: Sterne, Motteux, and the Culture of Politeness', *Translation and Literature* 10:2 (2001), 174–99, Shaun Regan gives an insightful account of the status of Rabelais in mid-eighteenth-century Britain, of Sterne's assimilation of Rabelaisianism, and his taking 'measures to accommodate his writing to new tastes by genteelizing his play of wit' (p. 175).

than my Arse' (p. 1088), Tristram, with his 'Backside', adopts a tamer lexical register, and this is consistent throughout the work.[15] *Tristram Shandy* makes a play of the aposiopesis and it leads readers to fill in the textual ellipses that aposiopetic stops create, but by invoking rather than printing the vulgar, and by appreciably relinquishing vocabulary with 'single-*entendre*' impropriety (words offering no polite *option*) in favour of euphemisms or *double-entendres*, it makes an ironic yet none the less actual claim upon a level of politeness above the coarser Rabelaisian mode in which it has its origins. By incorporating concessions to politeness – albeit that they are mostly ironic – *Tristram Shandy* acquires a shade of the polite discourse which it ironises. And a similar type of polite 'elevation' is apparent in the direction Sterne's satire of elocutionary matters takes in *Tristram Shandy*.

Sterne does not abandon the Rabelaisian clerics of the fragment, but they wait until the second instalment of *Tristram Shandy* for their main reappearance.[16] In the first instalment, meanwhile, the ironic probing of elocutionary discourse is adapted so as to cluster around the figure of Corporal Trim, a character who, Tristram recalls, 'loved to hear himself read almost as well as talk' (p. 138). Long before readers encounter Trim dropping his hat (in volume V), Trim's eloquence has been at the centre of one of *Tristram Shandy*'s best-known scenes, in which Sterne introduces a sermon of his own and has it read by Trim to an audience of Tristram's father Walter Shandy, his Uncle Toby, and Dr Slop, the 'man-midwife' (p. 119). Introducing Trim's performance, Tristram finds that he 'must first give . . . a description of his attitude':

He stood before them with his body swayed, and bent forwards just so far, as to make an angle of 85 degrees and a half upon the plain of the horizon; — which sound orators, to whom I address this, know very well, to be the true persuasive angle of incidence; – in any other angle you may talk and preach; – 'tis certain, – and it is done every day; – but with what effect, – I leave the world to judge!

The necessity of this precise angle of 85 degrees and a half to a mathematical exactness, – does it not shew us, by the way, – how the arts and sciences mutually befriend each other?

---

[15] Tristram uses 'backside' earlier in a line which clearly and cleanly echoes that in the 'Rabelaisian Fragment': 'My mother . . . knew no more than her backside what my father meant' (p. 4). Revealingly, in the 1775 edition of the 'Fragment in the Manner of *Rabelais*', the line is emended to 'I know no more of Latin than my horse' (*Letters of the Late Rev. Mr. Laurence Sterne*, vol. III, p. 167).

[16] See particularly pp. 375–93.

How the duce Corporal *Trim*, who knew not so much as an acute angle from an obtuse one, came to hit it so exactly; – or whether it was chance or nature, or good sense or imitation, *&c.* shall be commented upon in that part of this cyclopædia of arts and sciences, where the instrumental parts of the eloquence of the senate, the pulpit, the bar, the coffee-house, the bed-chamber, and fire-side, fall under consideration.

He stood, – for I repeat it, to take the picture of him in at one view, with his body sway'd, and somewhat bent forwards, – his right leg firm under him, sustaining seven-eighths of his whole weight, – the foot of his left leg, the defect of which was no disadvantage to his attitude, advanced a little, – not laterally, nor forwards, but in a line betwixt them; – his knee bent, but that not violently, – but so as to fall within the limits of the line of beauty; – and I add, the line of science too; – for consider, it had one eighth part of his body to bear up; – so that in this case position of the leg is determined, – because the foot could be no further advanced, or the knee more bent, than what would allow him, mechanically, to receive an eighth part of his whole weight under it, – and to carry it too.

☞ This I recommend to painters; – need I add, – to orators? – I think not; for, unless they practise it, – they must fall upon their noses.

So much for Corporal *Trim*'s body and legs. – He held the sermon loosely, – not carelessly, in his left hand, raised something above his stomach, and detach'd a little from his breast; – his right arm falling negligently by his side, as nature and the laws of gravity order'd it, – but with the palm of it open and turned towards his audience, ready to aid the sentiment, in case it stood in need. (pp. 140–2)

Through Tristram, Sterne offers a massively exaggerated, parodic version of the type of analysis that contemporary elocutionists were applying to somatic expression. The disciplining tendencies of elocutionary discourse are held up to ridicule through Tristram's noting an absurd degree of 'mathematical exactness' in Trim's posture, while the dignity of this branch of learning is punctured as Tristram looks beyond the usual fora of 'the senate, the pulpit, [and] the bar' so as to assume the importance of an art of eloquence within humbler and more mundane locations. And the passage is, of course, playing with the whole idea of the aestheticisation of a natural object, with its pseudo-scientific then bathetic reminder that, amidst the flights of eloquent refinement, the orator must never overlook the fact that the body is subject to the force of gravity – that, ultimately, there are certain inviolable natural rules that frame and dictate the body's behaviour.

The art of oratory is not the only source for this passage of pseudo-theorisation, and the field of the graphic arts – specifically Hogarth's *The Analysis of Beauty* (1753) – provides Tristram with another theoretical tool, as he calls upon the renowned 'line of beauty' in order to convey and explain Trim's attitude. But the passage, while it does not obviously relate to any particular work of the elocutionary movement, is predominantly a parody of contemporary writing on elocutionary reform.[17] Influential accounts of the description of Trim, and of Sterne's 'pictorial passages' more generally, have, in fact, tended to subordinate such engagement with contemporary elocutionary projects in a drive to show Sterne's indebtedness to theories of painting. R. S. Brissenden, for example, places the reading of the sermon in terms of 'the field of painting', and suggests that 'In his description of Trim, Sterne seems to have drawn mainly on Leonardo's *Treatise* [*A Treatise of Painting* (1721)], though he obviously had Hogarth's *Analysis of Beauty* . . . very much in mind also.'[18] The reference to Hogarth is indeed obvious; that the passage is indebted to Leonardo's *Treatise* is less so, and Sterne could have garnered the idea of a figure's 'attitude' as easily from an elocutionary work as from Leonardo's *Treatise*, as Brissenden proposes. Similarly, in William V. Holtz's extended study of Sterne's 'pictorialism', the field of painting is seen to generate the dominant eighteenth-century discourse of visual expression. Holtz, indeed, makes an assumption that elocutionary works more or less all derive from theories of painting. He suggests, for example, that Charles Le Brun's writing on painting the passions 'found its way . . . into a series of actors' handbooks', and he cites *The History of the English Stage* by 'Thomas Betterton' as an example.[19] Holtz thus overlooks the fact that, as we have seen, *The History of the English Stage*, besides not being by the long-dead Betterton, in fact derives its material on performing the passions from the English translation of Le Faucheur's work on oratory via Charles Gildon's *The Life of Mr. Thomas Betterton*. The Florida edition's expansive notes on *Tristram Shandy* annotate the description of Trim by referring readers to Brissenden and Holtz, but the editors make the welcome additional point that 'One might also approach Trim's posture through various eighteenth-century manuals of pulpit oratory', citing Wesley's *Directions concerning Pronunciation and Gesture* (itself derived from Le Faucheur) as 'one of the most interesting' examples.[20] *Tristram Shandy*

---

[17] In this sense the passage is an example of *Tristram Shandy*'s 'aleatory intertextuality' – a nonspecific allusive mode, which, as Thomas Keymer puts it, gestures 'towards a plurality of potential intertexts through its play on terms, tropes, or conventions that all of them hold in common', but which specifies 'no single' intertext (*Sterne, the Moderns, and the Novel* (Oxford: Oxford University Press, 2002), p. 16).

[18] R. F. Brissenden, 'Sterne and Painting', in John Butt (ed.), *Of Books and Humankind: Essays and Poems Presented to Bonamy Dobrée* (London: Routledge and Kegan Paul, 1964), pp. 99–100.

[19] William V. Holtz, *Image and Immortality: A Study of* Tristram Shandy (Providence: Brown University Press, 1970), p. 12.

[20] Melvyn New with Richard A. Davies and W. G. Day, *The Life and Opinions of Tristram Shandy, Gentleman: The Notes*, The Florida Edition of the Works of Laurence Sterne, vol. 3 (Gainesville, FL: University Presses of Florida, 1984), p. 167.

obviously *does* engage with theories of painting on many occasions, but its pictorialism also involves the art of oratory, in which Sterne had long-term serious and satiric interests, and it is pertinent to be alert to this other area of contemporary theory, not least when the character being described is on the brink of delivering a sermon. The description of Trim is addressed to 'sound orators', and it introduces, it transpires, a basically sound piece of oratory.

In *Tristram Shandy*, Sterne is still concerned with the body's baser 'physiological origins' – as the many plays upon aposiopesises and ellipses make clear – but unlike in the 'Rabelaisian Fragment', an ironic approach to the art of oratory is not the immediate occasion for their exposure. Trim suffers no fall like that of Homenas. Following the description of Trim's posture is reproduced the whole of Sterne's sermon on the 'The Abuses of Conscience' (first preached at York Minster in 1750, this was one of two of Sterne's sermons that had been published prior to *Tristram Shandy*), and throughout the scene some of the wryness of its introduction remains as Trim's reading is comically interrupted by his own and his audience's reactions to what is preached. Since these reactions are often in conflict with the sermon and each other – particularly where Dr Slop's Catholicism causes disagreement – the scene in part provides a droll display of a sermon *failing* to hold sway over a congregation. But at the same time, Trim can be seen to deliver something of a 'flap upon the heart', and there are moments where Trim's eloquence functions as a model of sentimental oratory as he binds his audience with contagious passions. In Trim, Sterne presents an exaggerated depiction of an orator who attains eloquence by genuinely feeling the passions appropriate to the subject matter being presented. As an essentially naïve reader, Trim comes to believe that passages in the sermon are describing the suffering of his own brother at the hands of the Inquisition, and while the misconception provides the grounds of comedy, it is also the basis of Trim's hold over his audience: 'Oh! 'tis my brother, cried poor *Trim* in a most passionate exclamation, dropping the sermon upon the ground, and clapping his hands together — I fear 'tis poor *Tom*. My father's and my uncle *Toby*'s hearts yearn'd with sympathy for the poor fellow's distress, — even *Slop* himself acknowledged pity for him' (p. 162). The exemplary quality of Trim's eloquence is discussed at the sermon's conclusion:

Thou hast read the sermon extremely well, *Trim*, quoth my father . . . I should have read it ten times better, Sir, answered *Trim*, but that my heart was so full. – That was the very reason, *Trim*, replied my father, which has made thee read the sermon as well as thou hast done; and if the clergy of our church, continued my father, addressing himself to Dr. *Slop*, would take part in what they deliver, as deeply as this poor fellow has done, – as their compositions are fine, (I deny it, quoth Dr. *Slop*) I maintain it, that the eloquence of our pulpits, with such subjects to inflame it, – would be a model for the whole world. (pp. 164–5)

The sermon reading ends as it began, then, with an allusion to contemporary elocutionary writing, and it seems here that Sterne may have had a particular elocutionist in mind, for Walter Shandy, with his vision of improved oratory spawning global admiration of things British, iterates the exact claims of Thomas Sheridan, who, by the time of *Tristram Shandy*, had become well established as a self-appointed doyen of elocutionary reform. But the scene has also done more than parody the projects of elocutionists such as Sheridan. From its parodic beginnings, the depiction of Trim reading the sermon develops into one of the first of Sterne's many versions of the archetypal vignette of sentimental fiction, whereby a feeling character is depicted performing their emotions before a responsive audience. Where men and women of feeling in Richardsonian fiction are, as has been seen, regularly depicted as orator-like figures, Sterne comes to replicate this staple of mid-century fiction through a wry representation of oratory itself. When Trim has recounted the sorry tale of his brother, readers are told that the 'tears trickled down *Trim's* cheeks faster than he could well wipe them away: – A dead silence in the room ensued for some minutes. — Certain proof of pity!' (p. 144). There is little to distinguish these phrases from those that make up the appeals to the passions in classic sentimental fiction. The immediate wry context in which the phrases appear might render them awkward to read without an unsettling sense of *Tristram Shandy's* tangible satiric energies, but the intimacy of oratory and sentimental fiction is none the less shown by the fact of a depiction of oratory in action generating the classic scene structure and phraseology of sentimental fiction. The representation of Trim's eloquence reveals Sterne's capacity as a writer to pull off in his fiction the type of affective eloquence he achieved in the pulpit; at the same time, the broader framework of bawdry in *Tristram Shandy* – despite its mediation through playfully polite codes – shows Sterne's unwillingness to reduce the bodies in his fiction to the type of circumscribed polite objects around which sentimental eloquence was more conventionally constructed.

With its sentimental moments thus mixed with moderated but enduring Rabelaisianism, *Tristram Shandy* appeared to some early readers to offer jewels buried in mud: moral and affecting passages surrounded by lewdness, but not totally compromised or contaminated by it. Horace Walpole was generally unimpressed by the work, but noted that the 'best thing in it is a sermon – oddly coupled with a good deal of bawdy, and both the composition of a clergyman'.[21] The sermon is similarly presented as a moral oasis amidst 'gross and vulgar tales, as no decent mind can endure without extreme disgust' in a letter to a bishop from Samuel Richardson. The words are not directly those of Richardson, who claims to have had his daughter transcribe in the letter 'the sentiments of a young lady, as written to another lady . . . on the publication of the two first volumes'. The young lady expresses just the type of disgust and moral outrage that would please Richardson, but she admits that in *Tristram Shandy* 'there is subject for mirth, and some affecting strokes; Yorick, Uncle Toby, and Trim are admirably characterised, and very interesting, and an excellent sermon of a peculiar kind, on conscience, is introduced'.[22] Such an evaluation bifurcates *Tristram Shandy*: some passages are affecting, polite, and praiseworthy; others are disgusting, impolite, and reprehensible – what is significant is that the latter are not taken to devalue the former. The parson, the lady suggests, has produced a curate's egg, and by not identifying a holistic mode in the work – by not seeing the sentiment as in any way trumped by the bawdry – she actually allows Sterne the virtues of a modern polite author, albeit that they come hand in hand with 'gross' low humour.

In the later instalments of *Tristram Shandy*, Sterne continued to supply irreverent bawdiness, but he also amplified the work's affective appeal with further sentimental scenes: the continuation of the story of Trim's brother, the story of the illness and death of Le Fever, Tristram's encounter with the movingly mad Maria of Moulins, and many other more fleeting moments of sentimental exchange. Sterne also continued to reflect wittily upon the manner in which bodies affect other bodies, and he widened his parodic attention to somatic aesthetics so as to address theories of acting alongside those of oratory and painting.[23] The social elevation that came with *Tristram Shandy*'s first instalment had given Sterne privileged access to the London theatre world and to its celebrities including David Garrick, and such new openings and experiences as the early volumes afforded clearly provided Sterne with material for the volumes that followed. As *Tristram Shandy* grew, though, it was primarily its displays of sentiment – apparently extractable from their potentially complicating contexts – that attracted the public approval of readers and reviewers. When volumes V

---

[21] Letter to Henry Zouch (7 March 1761) in Howes, *Sterne: The Critical Heritage*, p. 55.
[22] To Bishop Mark Hildesley (January/February? 1761), *Selected Letters of Samuel Richardson*, pp. 341–2.
[23] See, for example, p. 213.

and VI were published, a reviewer in the *Monthly Review* was pleased to find them 'not so much interlarded with obscenity as the former', and, after quoting the whole of the Le Fever episode, he put forward the view that Sterne's 'excellence lay not so much in the humorous as in the pathetic; and in this opinion we have been confirmed by the above story of Le Fever. We appeal to the Heart of every reader whether our judgement is not right?'[24] Ralph Griffiths (1720–1803), the founder of the *Monthly Review*, looked back upon and reinforced this judgement when he reviewed volumes VII and VIII in 1765. Addressing his views directly to Sterne, Griffiths anticipated that the public 'will have *had enough*' of *Tristram Shandy*'s indelicate comedy by the end of the eighth volume, and he suggested

Suppose you were to strike out a new plan? Give us none but amiable or worthy, or exemplary characters . . . Paint Nature in her loveliest dress – her native simplicity. Draw natural scenes, and interesting situations – In fine, Mr. Shandy, do, for surely you can, excite our passions to *laudable* purposes – awake our affections, engage our hearts – arouze, transport, refine, improve us. Let morality, let the cultivation of virtue be your aim – let wit, humour, elegance and pathos be the means; and the grateful applause of mankind will be your reward.[25]

With this public entreaty, Griffiths sought to transform Sterne into a polite author – or at least he encouraged Sterne to renounce his Rabelaisian tendencies and to fulfil the polite potential he had already displayed, so as to become a fully fledged polite author. Earlier in the review, Griffiths had noted Sterne's ability sometimes to exceed the delicate literary heights of even Richardson, and here he urges Sterne to cultivate that side of his talent and to exercise a little self-censorship so that the public might be allowed to appreciate his polite virtues without having to overcome the 'obstacles' of Shandean comedy.

Whether influenced by the review or not, Sterne did pursue his future writing in the directions extolled by Griffiths – somewhat. In the final volume of *Tristram Shandy*, he was tapping his sentimental vein with the depiction of Maria of Moulins – an affecting abandoned virgin who would become a hugely popular icon of sentimental culture. And in relating Yorick's travels in his final work, *A Sentimental Journey through France and Italy*, Sterne engineered numerous scenes which can be taken to invite the type of emotional, moral responses which Griffiths's review suggests readers were seeking to have exercised through their encounters with

---

[24] *Monthly Review* 26 (January 1762), 32 and 41.
[25] *Monthly Review* 32 (February 1765), 138–9.

fiction. As in *Tristram Shandy*, Sterne created in these scenes many power-ful images of moved bodies moving, but here they are surrounded not with pseudo-scholarship but with commentary from Yorick which reflects upon and confirms their eloquence. Yorick, as protagonist and narrator of *A Sentimental Journey*, is forever drawn to record the minutiae of the somatic exchanges in which he becomes involved – postures, hand movements, looks, and blushes, together with the delicate but highly charged moments of physical contact experienced *en route* through a land of strangers and new acquaintances. Indeed, he delights in observing these minutiae. In a scene in a Paris bookshop, for example, Yorick donates a crown to a young *fille de chambre* whose display of gratitude enchants him: 'The young girl made me more a humble courtesy than a low one – 'twas one of those quiet, thankful sinkings where the spirit bows itself down – the body does no more than tell it. I never gave a girl a crown in my life which gave me half the pleasure' (p. 88). A language of gesture mediates Yorick's meetings with others, but it is also the very thing that Yorick, with his narrative eye fixated upon the eloquence of bodies, is shown most to appreciate in these encounters. So far as Yorick is concerned, '[t]here is not a secret so aiding to the progress of sociality, as to get master of this *short hand*, and be quick in rendering the several turns of looks and limbs, with all their inflections and delineations, into plain words' (p. 77). *A Sentimental Journey* is itself a rendering into words of a catalogue of eloquent gestures – whether these words are entirely 'plain', however, is another matter.

A Sentimental Journey was undoubtedly successful in delivering a good deal of 'polite' reading pleasure to many early readers. Ralph Griffiths was certainly satisfied to find that Sterne had put aside *Tristram Shandy* to pursue 'a new plan', and in the *Monthly Review* he applauded the senti-mental virtues that were apparent to him in the new work. Of a scene in which Yorick aids a group of beggars, Griffiths averred that 'the heart of the humane reader will revel in all the luxury of benevolence',[26] and he was even more effusive over Yorick's encounter in the bookshop with the *fille de chambre*: 'What delicacy of feeling, what tenderness of sentiment, yet what simplicity of expression are here! Is it *possible* that a man of *gross ideas* could ever *write* in a strain so pure, so refined from the dross of sensuality!'[27] For Griffiths, *A Sentimental Journey* shows Sterne at last approaching the zenith of his potential as a polite, sentimental author, and he has achieved these

[26] *Monthly Review* 38 (March 1768), 183.
[27] *Monthly Review* 38 (April 1768), 311.

literary heights by significantly relinquishing 'sensuality' – by accepting and
reproducing an elevated idea of the body which transcends 'low' carnality
and shows no 'addiction to brutal and corporal pleasures', as Johnson
wrote of 'sensuality' in his *Dictionary*.[28] Arguably, though, Griffiths has
read as 'pure' here a scene which can alternatively be taken to be charged
with carnal tension and innuendo, albeit that these competing energies are
conveyed indirectly through a subtly suggestive narrative which does not
foreclose the possibility of 'pure' interpretation. There are several aspects of
the narration which can be taken to eroticise the scene in the bookshop – to
render it very much concerned with 'corporal pleasures'. Yorick's fiscal
benevolence to the *fille de chambre*, for example, is related with an extravagant attention to the physical details of the transaction, so that in its
telling the gesture is not merely an exchange of money, but a careful
insertion of Yorick's 'crown' into the girl's 'purse'– a 'very small one' to
which Yorick returns repeatedly and to which he devotes lingering descriptive detail as he relates what he calls his 'virtuous convention' with the girl
(pp. 87–8). The suggestiveness surrounding the details of the transaction
here may seem difficult to overlook, and when faced with this scene, even
the most prudish modern editor of *A Sentimental Journey*, Gardner
D. Stout, finds himself drawn to wonder 'Is there, perhaps, a sexual
innuendo here based on the meaning of "purse"?'[29] Readers who read it
as an innuendo are certainly following a lead that Sterne makes available
here, and there are other suggestive aspects of the scene which can corrob-
orate and further bring into relief an erotic subtext – the fact that the *fille de
chambre* is in the bookshop to buy *Les Egarments du cœur & de l' esprit*
(1736–8), a novel that was known for licentiousness, may have signalled to
some early readers that they were on the brink of something other than a
simple lesson in sentimental virtue.[30] But as Ralph Griffiths's account of
the scene suggests, sexual innuendo does not absolutely *have* to be noticed
here, and when it is not, the scene can still provide gratification for readers
– it can still 'work' without innuendo having been triggered, and it then
does so without straying from the realms of polite literature.

---

[28] Johnson, *Dictionary*, vol. II, 'Sensuality'.

[29] Laurence Sterne, *A Sentimental Journey through France and Italy*, ed. Gardner D. Stout, Jr
    (Berkeley and Los Angeles: University of California Press, 1967), p. 188.

[30] Regarding Sterne's reference to this novel by Claude-Prosper Jolyot de Crébillon, Brissenden
    suggests that 'Sterne probably derived a certain pleasure from mentioning Crébillon's witty
    romance in *A Sentimental Journey*. The book has a pious title . . . [b]ut there is no more piety in it
    than in that "most tawdry [story] . . . of a nun who fancied herself a shell-fish, and of a monk
    damn'd for eating a muscle"' (*Virtue in Distress*, p. III).

In *A Sentimental Journey*, Sterne has not surrendered to a circumscribed ideal of the polite body; he has not produced a work which is complicit with any idea that 'sensuality' is 'dross', as Ralph Griffiths would have it. Sterne has rather produced a narrative which purportedly participates within a discourse of polite literature, but which at the same time suggests the limitations of that discourse by subtly narrating aspects of embodiment which politeness typically fails to accommodate. In different ways, *A Sentimental Journey* repeatedly introduces 'sensuality' into a narrative which declares itself sentimental; by doing so, it does not necessarily satirise and undermine sentimental values, as has sometimes been argued, but it does suggest that those values are typically founded upon an incomplete notion of embodiment.[31] Where other fictional men of feeling, such as Mackenzie's Harley, are largely desexualised creatures, Yorick is lustful and flirtatious. His interest in the many women he encounters in France often emerges obliquely from his telling – indeed, the first-person narrative of *A Sentimental Journey* is remarkable for its suggestion of motives and desires within Yorick which he does not divulge explicitly, or which run counter to those he claims underlie his actions. There are other moments, though, where Yorick is more open with regard to his roving passions and indeed presents them as integral to his benevolence. He has 'been in love with one princess or another almost all my life', he states at one point, adding 'I hope I shall go on so, till I die, being firmly persuaded, that if I ever do a mean action, it must be in some interval betwixt one passion and another' (p. 44). And later he defends his passions, asking: 'If nature has so wove her web of kindness, that some threads of love and desire are entangled with the piece – must the whole web be rent in drawing them out?' (p. 124).

Through Yorick, Sterne makes an argument for the inseparability of sentiment and erotic desire, in which, Yorick assures us, 'there is no sin' (p. 44) since he conquers his desires rather than acts upon them. Elsewhere in the work 'sensuality' is brought into the text through 'low' body humour, conveyed through various forms of innuendo with varying levels of subtlety. The scene in which Yorick gives the *fille de chambre* his crown provides just one of many passages in *A Sentimental Journey* where Sterne has moulded his Rabelaisianism into forms more indirect than those of *Tristram Shandy*, so that demonstrably Rabelaisian passages gain the possibility of being

[31] For two influential readings of the work as a satire of sentimentalism, see: Rufus Putney, 'The Evolution of *A Sentimental Journey*', *Philological Quarterly* 19 (1940), 349–69, and Ernest Nevin Dilworth, *The Unsentimental Journey of Laurence Sterne* (New York: King's Crown Press, 1948).

assimilated as polite. When Yorick arrives in Paris, for example, he looks
through his hotel window and sees 'all the world in yellow, blue, and green,
running at the ring of pleasure. – The old with broken lances, and in helmets
which had lost their vizards – the young in armour bright which shone like
gold, beplumed with each gay feather of the east – all – all tilting at it like
fascinated knights' (p. 65). The passage can be taken simply as a depiction of
Parisian street life couched in vivid chivalric imagery, but an alternative mode
of reading can unleash a string of sexual innuendoes here.[32] 'Running at the
ring' is a sport in which horsemen attempt to catch a suspended metal hoop
with a lance, and the easy capacity of this exercise to function as a sexual
metaphor had been exploited by Rabelais in *Gargantua and Pantagruel* (trans.
1653–94). Sterne had earlier borrowed the image from Rabelais in *Tristram
Shandy* (p. 649), and in its reuse here its suggestiveness is discreet but, if
detected, can readily multiply the *entendres* of the 'broken lances', the 'helmets', the 'armour' (a contemporary euphemism for a contraceptive), and the
general 'tilting' (a slang term for copulation). Indeed, the *clustering* of terms
which *might* be read bawdily arguably renders such reading quite compelling,
but bawdry need not necessarily spill forth from this superficially polite
passage.

   In places in *A Sentimental Journey* a bawdy interpretation is more
difficult to avoid, as at the work's conclusion when Yorick, recumbent in
a darkened bedchamber which he has been obliged to share with a lady and
her maid, reports:

when I stretch'd out my hand, I caught hold of the Fille de Chambre's
                      END OF VOL. II.   (p. 165)

Sterne's literary career concludes with probably his most famous aposiopesis –
one which 'politely' circumvents direct naming of the lower body, but
which none the less nudges the lower body into the minds of readers.
A lewd interpretation of this ambiguous passage evidently occurred to
Ralph Griffiths, who was consequently disappointed by the ending: 'so it
is, and so it ever was with poor Yorick; who could never take leave of his
readers without some pleasantry of the *lower species*. Thus the volume
before us concludes ... bordering rather on sensuality than sentiment.'[33]
Sterne's transgression of Griffiths's standards for proper literature
depends paradoxically upon *A Sentimental Journey* having caused

[32] For a discussion of this passage and of Virginia Woolf's reading of it as 'pure poetry', see my
   introduction to *A Sentimental Journey* (London: Penguin, 2001), p. xxix.
[33] *Monthly Review* 38 (April 1768), 318.

Griffiths himself to fill a textual silence with something 'of the *lower species*' which then offends him. It has made him think of aspects of the body which polite discourse typically represses or contains by means of silence – but not the type of *suggestive* silence which Sterne creates.

Where the body is concerned, polite discourse is, in a sense, itself aposiopetic. As I have aimed to show, eighteenth-century polite culture makes a huge investment in the body as a signifier, but it *stops short* of narrating or performing particular aspects of somatic experience – it produces a truncated version of the natural body, and it is partly in this cropping of nature that politeness is symbolised. Sterne's fiction articulates – with an indirectness and apparent politeness which increased as his *oeuvre* grew – those aspects of embodiment which eighteenth-century polite discourse left unmentioned. It shows how in the face of an attempt to systematise or control the eloquence of bodies, bodies themselves will overflow and disturb the symbolic roles allotted them.

Bibliography

Alcock, Mary, *Poems* (London, 1799).

Anthony, Sister Rose, *The Jeremy Collier Stage Controversy, 1698–1726* (New York: Blom, 1937).

Aston, Antony, *A Brief Supplement to Colley Cibber, Esq; his Lives of the late Famous Actors and Actresses*, in Colley Cibber, *An Apology for the Life of Mr Colley Cibber*, ed. R. W. Lowe, 2 vols. (London, 1889).

Bacon, Francis, *The Advancement of Learning*, ed. Michael Kiernan (Oxford: Clarendon Press, 2000).

Bacon, Wallace A., 'The Elocutionary Career of Thomas Sheridan (1718–1788)', *Speech Monographs* 31 (1964), 1–53.

Bakhtin, Mikhail, *Rabelais and his World*, trans. Helene Iswolsky (Cambridge, MA: Massachusetts Institute of Technology Press, 1968).

Ballaster, Ros, *Seductive Forms: Women's Amatory Fiction from 1684 to 1740* (Oxford: Clarendon Press, 1992).

Barker-Benfield, G. J., *The Culture of Sensibility: Sex and Society in Eighteenth-Century Britain* (Chicago and London: University of Chicago Press, 1992).

Barrell, John, *English Literature in History, 1730–80: An Equal, Wide Survey* (London: Hutchinson, 1983).

Bell, Ian, *Henry Fielding: Authorship and Authority* (London: Longman, 1994).

Benzie, W., *The Dublin Orator: Thomas Sheridan's Influence on Eighteenth-Century Rhetoric and Belles Lettres* (Leeds: Scolar Press, 1972).

Blair, Hugh, *Lectures on Rhetoric and Belles Lettres*, ed. Harold F. Harding, 2 vols. (Carbondale and Edwardsville: Southern Illinois University Press, 1965).

Bordo, Susan, 'Bringing Body to Theory', in Donn Welton (ed.), *Body and Flesh: A Philosophical Reader* (Oxford: Blackwell, 1998), pp. 84–97.

Boswell, James, *Life of Johnson*, ed. R. W. Chapman (Oxford: Oxford University Press, 1980).

Bradford, Richard, *Silence and Sound: Theories of Poetics from the Eighteenth Century* (London: Associated University Presses, 1992).

Brewer, John, *The Pleasures of the Imagination: English Culture in the Eighteenth Century* (New York: Farrar, Straus and Giroux, 1997).

Brewster, Dorothy, *Aaron Hill: Poet, Dramatist, Projector* (New York: Columbia University Press, 1913; repr. New York: AMS Press, 1966).

Brissenden, R. F., 'Sterne and Painting', in John Butt (ed.), *Of Books and Humankind: Essays and Poems Presented to Bonamy Dobrée* (London: Routledge and Kegan Paul, 1964), pp. 93–108.

Virtue in Distress: Studies in the Novel of Sentiment from Richardson to Sade (London and Basingstoke: Macmillan, 1974).

Brooke, Henry, *The Fool of Quality; or, The History of Henry Earl of Moreland,* 5 vols. (London, 1792).

Brooks, Peter, *Body Work: Objects of Desire in Modern Narrative* (Cambridge, MA and London: Harvard University Press, 1993).

Bulwer, John, *Chirologia; or, The Naturall Language of the Hand* (London, 1644).

Burgh, James, *The Art of Speaking* (London, 1761).

Butler, Judith, *Bodies that Matter: On the Discursive Limits of 'Sex'* (London and New York: Routledge, 1993).

Cash, Arthur H., 'Voices Sonorous and Cracked: Sterne's Pulpit Oratory', in Larry S. Champion (ed.), *Quick Springs of Sense: Studies in the Eighteenth Century* (Athens: University of Georgia Press, 1974), pp. 197–209.

Laurence Sterne: The Early and Middle Years (London: Methuen, 1975; repr. London and New York: Routledge, 1992).

Laurence Sterne: The Later Years (London: Methuen, 1986; repr. London and New York: Routledge, 1992).

Cheyne, George, *The English Malady*, 3rd edn (London, 1734).

Chouillet, Jacques, 'Une source anglaise du *Paradoxe sur le comédien*', *Dix-huitième siècle* 2 (1970), 209–26.

Cibber, Colley, *An Apology for the Life of Mr Colley Cibber*, ed. B. R. S. Fone (Ann Arbor: University of Michigan Press, 1968).

Cibber, Theophilus, *The Lives and Characters of the Most Eminent Actors and Actresses of Great Britain and Ireland* (London, 1753).

Cicero, Marcus Tullius, *De Oratore*, Loeb Classical Library, vols. 348–9 (Cambridge, MA: Harvard University Press; London: Heinemann, 1942).

Clark, Peter, *Sociability and Urbanity: Clubs and Societies in the Eighteenth-Century City* (Leicester: Victorian Studies Centre, University of Leicester, 1986).

Cohen, Murray, *Sensible Words: Linguistic Practice in England 1640–1785* (Baltimore: Johns Hopkins University Press, 1977).

Colley, Linda, *Britons: Forging the Nation 1707–1837* (New Haven: Yale University Press, 1992).

Collier, Jeremy, *A Short View of the Immorality and Profaneness of the English Stage* (London, 1698).

Copley, Stephen, 'Commerce, Conversation and Politeness in the Early Eighteenth-Century Periodical', *British Journal for Eighteenth-Century Studies* 18:1 (1995), 63–77.

Corbett, Edward P. J. and James L. Golden (eds.), *The Rhetoric of Blair, Campbell, and Whately* (New York: Holt, Rinehart and Winston, 1968).

Cumberland, Richard, *Memoirs of Richard Cumberland* (London, 1806).

Cunningham, Valentine, 'Vile Bodies', *Times Higher Education Supplement*, 8 March 1996, 15 and 18.

Curll, Edmund, *The History of the English Stage, from the Restauration to the Present Time. Including the Lives, Characters and Amours, of the most Eminent Actors and Actresses. With Instructions for Public Speaking; Wherein The Action and Utterance of the Bar, Stage and Pulpit are Distinctly considered. By Thomas Betterton* (London, 1741).

Davies, Richard A., 'Tristram Shandy: Eccentric Public Orator', *English Studies in Canada* 5:2 (1979), 154–66.

Day, R. A., *Told in Letters: Epistolary Fiction before Richardson* (Ann Arbor: University of Michigan Press, 1966).

Descartes, René, *The Philosophical Writings of Descartes*, trans. Joseph Cottingham, Robert Stoothoff, and Dugald Murdoch, 2 vols. (Cambridge: Cambridge University Press, 1985).

Diderot, Denis, *Selected Writings on Art and Literature*, trans. Geoffrey Bremner (Harmondsworth: Penguin, 1994).

Dilworth, Ernest Nevin, *The Unsentimental Journey of Laurence Sterne* (New York: King's Crown Press, 1948).

Donoghue, Frank, *The Fame Machine: Book Reviewing and Eighteenth-Century Literary Careers* (Stanford: Stanford University Press, 1996).

Doody, Margaret Anne, *A Natural Passion: A Study of the Novels of Samuel Richardson* (Oxford: Clarendon Press, 1974).

Douglas, Aileen, *Uneasy Sensations: Smollett and the Body* (Chicago: University of Chicago Press, 1995).

Douglas, Mary, *Natural Symbols: Explorations in Cosmology*, 2nd edn (London: Barrie and Jenkins, 1973).

Downer, Alan S., 'Nature to Advantage Dressed: Eighteenth-Century Acting', *PMLA* 58 (1943), 1002–37.

Downey, James, *The Eighteenth-Century Pulpit: A Study of the Sermons of Butler, Berkeley, Secker, Sterne, Whitefield and Wesley* (Oxford: Clarendon Press, 1969).

Dryden, John, *Plays*, The Works of John Dryden, vol. 13, ed. Maximillian E. Novak (Berkeley: University of California Press, 1984).

Dwyer, John, *The Age of the Passions: An Interpretation of Adam Smith and Scottish Enlightenment Culture* (East Lothian: Tuckwell Press, 1998).

Eaves, T. C. Duncan and Ben D. Kimpel, *Samuel Richardson: A Biography* (Oxford: Clarendon Press, 1971).

Elias, Norbert, *The Civilizing Process*, trans. Edmund Jephcott, vol. I, *The History of Manners* (New York: Pantheon, 1978); vol. II, *Power and Civility* (New York: Pantheon, 1982).

Engstrom, Alfred G., 'The Single Tear: A Stereotype of Literary Sensibility', *Philological Quarterly* 42 (1963), 106–9.

Evans, Theophilus, *The History of Modern Enthusiasm, from the Reformation to the Present Times*, enlarged 2nd edn (London, 1757).

Fagan, Patrick, *The Second City: Portrait of Dublin 1700–1760* (Dublin: Branar, 1986).

Field, Clive D., 'Anti-Methodist Publications of the Eighteenth Century: A Revised Bibliography', *Bulletin of the John Rylands University Library of Manchester* 73 (1991), 159–280.

Fielding, Henry, *The History of Tom Jones*, ed. R. P. C. Mutter (London: Penguin, 1966).

    Joseph Andrews with Shamela and Related Writings, ed. Homer Goldberg (New York and London: W. W. Norton, 1987).

Fielding, Sarah, *The History of the Countess of Dellwyn*, 2 vols. (London, 1759).

    Remarks on Clarissa, Augustan Reprint Society Nos. 231–2, ed. Peter Sabor (Los Angeles: William Andrews Clark Memorial Library, 1985).

    The Adventures of David Simple, ed. Linda Bree (London: Penguin, 2002).

Finke, Laurie, 'Mystical Bodies and the Dialogics of Vision', *Philological Quarterly* 73 (1988), 439–49.

Fish, Stanley, *Is There a Text in This Class?: The Authority of Interpretive Communities* (Cambridge, MA: Harvard University Press, 1980).

Fisher-Lichte, Erika, 'Theatre and the Civilizing Process: An Approach to the History of Acting', in Thomas Postlewait and Bruce A. McConachie (eds.), *Interpreting the Theatrical Past: Essays in the Historiography of Performance* (Iowa City: University of Iowa Press, 1989), pp. 19–36.

Fordyce, James, *An Essay on the Action Proper for the Pulpit* (London, 1753).

Forell, Madeleine and Janet Todd, *English Congregational Hymns in the Eighteenth Century* (Kentucky: University of Kentucky Press, 1982).

Foucault, Michel, *Discipline and Punish: The Birth of the Prison*, trans. Alan Sheridan (London: Allen Lane, 1977; repr. 1991).

Gallagher, Catherine and Stephen Greenblatt, *Practicing New Historicism* (Chicago and London: University of Chicago Press, 2000).

Garrick, David, *An Essay on Acting: In which will be consider'd the Mimical Behaviour of a certain Fashionable Faulty Actor* (London, 1744).

    The Letters of David Garrick, ed. David M. Little and George M. Kahrl, 3 vols. (London: Oxford University Press, 1963).

Gentleman's Magazine, the (London, 1731–1868).

Gerrard, Christine, *Aaron Hill: The Muses' Projector 1685–1750* (Oxford: Oxford University Press, 2003).

Gildon, Charles, *The Life of Mr. Thomas Betterton, The late Eminent Tragedian. Wherein The Action and Utterance of the Stage, Bar, and Pulpit, are distinctly consider'd* (London, 1710).

Goldsmith, Oliver, *Collected Works of Oliver Goldsmith*, ed. A. Friedman, 5 vols. (Oxford: Clarendon Press, 1966).

Goring, Paul, 'B for Broomstick? A Consideration of Aaron Hill's "Revolutionary" Acting Theory', *Leading Notes: Journal of the National Early Music Association* 13 (Spring 1997), 19–23.

    'Thomas Weales's *The Christian Orator Delineated* (1778) and the Early Reception of Sterne's Sermons', *The Shandean* 13 (2002), 87–97.

Graves, Richard, *The Spiritual Quixote; or, The Summer's Ramble of Mr Geoffry Wildgoose*, ed. Clarence Tracy (London: Oxford University Press, 1967).

Green, Thomas, *A Dissertation on Enthusiasm* (London, 1755).

Grub Street Journal, the (London, 1730–7)

H. W., *A Letter to David Garrick Esq; On Opening the Theatre* (London: 1769).

Haberman, Frederick William, 'The Elocutionary Movement in England, 1750–1850',
unpublished Ph.D. thesis, Cornell University (1947).

Habermas, Jürgen, *The Structural Transformation of the Public Sphere: An Inquiry
into a Category of Bourgeois Society*, trans. Thomas Burger (Cambridge: Polity
Press, 1989).

Hammond, Brean, *Professional Imaginative Writing in England, 1670–1740: Hackney
for Bread* (Oxford: Clarendon Press, 1997).

'Mid-Century English Quixotism and the Defence of the Novel', *Eighteenth-
Century Fiction* 10 (1997–8), 247–68.

Harris, Bob, *Politics and the Rise of the Press: Britain and France, 1620–1800*
(London and New York: Routledge, 1996).

Hempton, David, *Methodism and Politics in British Society 1750–1850* (London:
Hutchinson, 1983).

The Religion of the People: Methodism and Popular Religion c. 1750–1900 (London
and New York: Routledge, 1996).

Henley, John, *The Appeal of the Oratory to the First Ages of Christianity* (London,
1727).

Oratory Transactions. No II. To be occasionally publish'd (London, 1729).

Highfill, Philip H., Jr, Kalman A. Burnim, and Edward A. Langhans, *A Biographical
Dictionary of Actors, Actresses, Musicians, Dancers, Managers, and Other Stage
Personnel in London, 1660–1800*, 16 vols. (Carbondale: Southern Illinois University
Press, 1973–93).

Hill, Aaron, *The Art of Acting* (London, 1746).

*The Works of the Late Aaron Hill, Esq; in Four Volumes. Consisting of Letters on
Various Subjects, and of Original Poems, Moral and Facetious. With an Essay on
the Art of Acting*, 4 vols. (London, 1753).

Hill, Aaron and William Popple, *The Prompter* (London, 1734–6).

The Prompter: A Theatrical Paper (1734–1736), ed. William W. Appleton and
Kalman A. Burnim (New York: Blom, 1966).

Hill, John, *The Actor; Or, A Treatise on the Art of Playing*, revised edn (London,
1755).

To David Garrick, Esq; The Petition of I. In Behalf of Herself and her Sisters
(London, 1759).

Holtz, William V., *Image and Immortality: A Study of* Tristram Shandy (Providence:
Brown University Press, 1970).

Howell, Wilbur Samuel, 'Sources of the Elocutionary Movement in England:
1700–1748', in Raymond F. Howes (ed.), *Historical Studies of Rhetoric and
Rhetoricians* (Ithaca, NY: Cornell University Press, 1961), pp. 139–58.

Eighteenth-Century British Logic and Rhetoric (Princeton: Princeton University
Press, 1971).

Howes, Alan B. (ed.), *Sterne: The Critical Heritage* (London and Boston: Routledge
and Kegan Paul, 1974).

Hughes, Leo, 'The Actor's Epitome', *Notes and Queries* 20 (1944), 306–7.

'Theatrical Convention in Richardson: Some Observations on a Novelist's Technique', in C. Camden (ed.), *Restoration and Eighteenth-Century Literature: Essays in Honor of Alan Dugald McKillop* (Chicago: University of Chicago Press, 1963), pp. 239–50.

Hume, Robert D., *The Development of English Drama in the Late Seventeenth Century* (Oxford: Clarendon Press, 1976).

Hunter, J. Paul, 'The Novel and Social/Cultural History', in John Richetti (ed.), *The Cambridge Companion to the Eighteenth-Century Novel* (Cambridge: Cambridge University Press, 1996), pp. 9–40.

Jay, Martin, *Downcast Eyes: The Denigration of Vision in Twentieth-Century French Thought* (Berkeley: University of California Press, 1993).

Johnson, Samuel, *A Dictionary of the English Language*, 2 vols. (London, 1755).

Jones, Robert, *Gender and the Formation of Taste in Eighteenth-Century Britain: The Analysis of Beauty* (Cambridge: Cambridge University Press, 1998).

Kelly, Veronica and Dorothea von Mücke (eds.), *Body and Text in the Eighteenth Century* (Stanford: Stanford University Press, 1994).

Keymer, Thomas, *Sterne, the Moderns, and the Novel* (Oxford: Oxford University Press, 2002).

Keymer, Thomas and Peter Sabor (eds.), *The* Pamela *Controversy: Criticism and Adaptations of Samuel Richardson's* Pamela, *1740–1750*, 6 vols. (London: Pickering & Chatto, 2001).

Kinkead-Weekes, Mark, *Samuel Richardson: Dramatic Novelist* (Ithaca, NY: Cornell University Press, 1973).

Klein, Lawrence E., *Shaftesbury and the Culture of Politeness: Moral Discourse and Cultural Politics in Early Eighteenth-Century England* (Cambridge: Cambridge University Press, 1994).

Knowlson, James, *Universal Language Schemes in England and France 1600–1800* (Toronto: University of Toronto Press, 1975).

Knox, R. A., *Enthusiasm: A Chapter in the History of Religion* (Oxford: Clarendon Press, 1950).

Konigsberg, Ira, *Samuel Richardson & the Dramatic Novel* (Lexington: University of Kentucky Press, 1968).

Korte, Barbara, *Body Language in Literature* (Toronto: University of Toronto Press, 1997).

Langford, Paul, *A Polite and Commercial People: England 1727–1783* (Oxford: Oxford University Press, 1989).

Le Brun, Charles, *The Conference of Monsieur Le Brun, Chief Painter to the French King, Chancellor and Director of the Academy of Painting and Sculpture; Upon Expression, General and Particular. Translated from the French* (London, 1701).

Le Faucheur, Michel, *An Essay upon the Action of an Orator; As to his Pronunciation & Gesture. Useful both for Divines and Lawyers, and necessary for all Young Gentlemen, that study how to Speak well in Publick. Done out of French* (London, 1702?).

The Art of Speaking in Publick; or, An Essay on the Action of an Orator; As to his Pronunciation and Gesture. Useful in the Senate or Theatre, the Court, the Camp, as well as the Bar and Pulpit. The Second Edition Corrected. With an Introduction relating to the Famous Mr. Henly's present Oratory (London, 1727).

An Essay upon Pronunciation and Gesture, Founded Upon the Best Rules and Authorities of the Ancients, Ecclesiastical and Civil, and Adorned with the Finest Rules of Elocution (London, 1750).

Leder, Drew, *The Absent Body* (Chicago and London: University of Chicago Press, 1990).

Lentricchia, Frank and Thomas McLaughlin (eds.), *Critical Terms for Literary Study* (Chicago: Chicago University Press, 1990).

Lessinich, Rolf P., *Elements of Pulpit Oratory in Eighteenth-Century England (1660–1800)* (Cologne: Böhlau, 1972).

Locke, John, *The Educational Writings of John Locke*, ed. James L. Axtell (Cambridge: Cambridge University Press, 1968).

London Magazine; Or Gentleman's Monthly Intelligencer, the (London, 1732–83).

Lyles, Albert M., *Methodism Mocked: The Satiric Reaction to Methodism in the Eighteenth Century* (London: Epworth Press, 1960).

Lyons, Nicholas, 'Satiric Technique in *The Spiritual Quixote*: Some Comments', *Durham University Journal* 35 (1974), 266–77.

McKendrick, Neil, John Brewer, and J. H. Plumb, *The Birth of a Consumer Society: The Commercialization of Eighteenth-Century England* (London: Europa, 1982).

McKenzie, Alan T., *Certain Lively Episodes: The Articulation of Passion in Eighteenth-Century Prose* (Athens: University of Georgia Press, 1990).

Mackenzie, Henry, *The Man of Feeling*, ed. Brian Vickers (Oxford: Oxford University Press, 1987).

McKillop, Alan Dugald, *Samuel Richardson: Printer and Novelist* (Chapel Hill: University of North Carolina Press, 1936).

Malcolm, J. P., *Anecdotes of the Manners and Customs of London during the Eighteenth Century* (London, 1808)

Markley, Robert, 'Sentimentality as Performance: Shaftesbury, Sterne, and the Theatrics of Virtue', in Felicity Nussbaum and Laura Brown (eds.), *The New 18th Century: Theory, Politics, English Literature* (New York: Routledge, 1987), pp. 210–30.

Maslen, Keith, *Samuel Richardson of London, Printer: A Study of his Printing based on Ornament Use and Business Accounts* (Dunedin: University of Otago, 2001).

Mason, John, *An Essay on Elocution; or, Pronunciation. Intended chiefly for the Assistance of those who instruct others in the Art of Reading. And of those who are often called to speak in Publick* (London, 1748).

Mauss, Marcel, 'Les Techniques du corps', *Journal de la Psychologie normale et pathologique* 32:3–4 (1936), 271–93.

Mayoux, Jean-Jacques, 'Laurence Sterne', in John Traugott (ed.), *Laurence Sterne: A Collection of Critical Essays* (Englewood Cliffs, NJ: Prentice-Hall, 1968), pp. 108–25.

Midgley, Graham, *The Life of Orator Henley* (Oxford: Clarendon Press, 1973).

Mohrmann, G. P., 'The Language of Nature and Elocutionary Theory', *Quarterly Journal of Speech* 52 (1966), 116–24.

Monthly Review, the (London, 1749–)

Moran, Michael G. (ed.), *Eighteenth-Century British and American Rhetorics and Rhetoricians: Critical Studies and Sources* (Westport, CT: Greenwood Press, 1994).

More, Hannah, *Poems* (London, 1816).

Mullan, John, 'Hypochondria and Hysteria: Sensibility and the Physicians', *The Eighteenth Century: Theory and Interpretation* 25 (1984), 141–74.

  Sentiment and Sociability: The Language of Feeling in the Eighteenth Century (Oxford: Clarendon Press, 1988; repr. 1997).

New, Melvyn, 'Sterne's Rabelaisian Fragment: A Text from the Holograph Manuscript', *PMLA* 87 (1972), 1083–92.

  review of Mullan, *Sentiment and Sociability*, in *The Scriblerian* 23 (1991), 247–50.

  'Sterne as Preacher: A Visit to St. Michael's Church, Coxwold', *The Shandean* 5 (1993), 160–7.

New, Melvyn, with Richard A. Davies and W. G. Day, *The Life and Opinions of Tristram Shandy, Gentleman: The Notes*, The Florida Edition of the Works of Laurence Sterne, vol. 3 (Gainesville, FL.: University Presses of Florida, 1984).

Parsons, James, *Human Physiognomy Explain'd: In the Crounian Lectures on Muscular Motion* (London, 1747).

Petrakis, Byron, 'Jester in the Pulpit: Sterne and Pulpit Eloquence', *Philological Quarterly* 51 (1972), 430–7.

Pittard, Joseph, *Observations on Mr. Garrick's Acting; in a Letter to the Right Hon. the Earl of Chesterfield* (London, 1758).

Pope, Alexander, *The Poems of Alexander Pope, Volume V: The Dunciad*, ed. James Sutherland (London: Methuen; New Haven: Yale University Press, 1943; repr. 1965).

Porter, Roy, *English Society in the Eighteenth Century*, revised edition (Harmondsworth: Penguin, 1990).

Potkay, Adam, *The Fate of Eloquence in the Age of Hume* (Ithaca and London: Cornell University Press, 1994).

Punday, Daniel, 'Foucault's Body Tropes', *New Literary History* 31 (2000), 509–28.

Putney, Rufus, 'The Evolution of *A Sentimental Journey*', *Philological Quarterly* 19 (1940), 349–69.

Rack, Henry D., *Reasonable Enthusiast: John Wesley and the Rise of Methodism* (London: Epworth Press, 1989).

Redford, Bruce, *The Converse of the Pen: Acts of Intimacy in the Eighteenth-Century Familiar Letter* (Chicago and London: University of Chicago Press, 1986).

Regan, Shaun, 'Translating Rabelais: Sterne, Motteux, and the Culture of Politeness', *Translation and Literature* 10:2 (2001), 174–99.

Richardson, Samuel, *The Correspondence of Samuel Richardson*, ed. Anna Lætitia Barbauld, 6 vols. (London, 1804).

Clarissa: Preface, Hints of Prefaces, and Postscript, Augustan Reprint Society No. 103, ed. R. S. Brissenden (Los Angeles: William Andrews Clark Memorial Library, 1964).

Selected Letters of Samuel Richardson, ed. John Carroll (Oxford: Clarendon Press, 1964).

The History of Sir Charles Grandison, ed. Jocelyn Harris, 3 vols. (London: Oxford University Press, 1972).

Pamela; or, Virtue Rewarded, ed. Peter Sabor (Harmondsworth: Penguin, 1980; repr. 1988).

Clarissa; or, The History of a Young Lady, ed. Angus Ross (Harmondsworth: Penguin, 1985).

Pamela; or, Virtue Rewarded, ed. Thomas Keymer and Alice Wakely (Oxford: Oxford University Press, 2001).

Richetti, John, *The English Novel in History: 1700–1780* (London and New York: Routledge, 1999).

Rivers, Isabel, *Reason, Grace, and Sentiment: A Study of the Language of Religion and Ethics in England, 1660–1780, I: Whichcote to Wesley* (Cambridge: Cambridge University Press, 1991).

Roach, Joseph, *The Player's Passion: Studies in the Science of Acting* (Newark: University of Delaware Press; London: Associated University Presses, 1985).

Ross, Ian Campbell, *Laurence Sterne: A Life* (Oxford: Oxford University Press, 2001).

Rousseau, G. S., 'Nerves, Spirits and Fibres: Towards Defining the Origins of Sensibility', in R. F. Brissenden and J. C. Eade (eds.), *Studies in the Eighteenth Century 3* (Canberra: Australian National University Press; Toronto: Toronto University Press, 1976), pp. 137–57.

'John Hill, Universal Genius *Manqué*: Remarks on his Life and Times, with a Checklist of his Works', in J. A. Leo Lemay and G. S. Rousseau (eds.), *The Renaissance Man in the Eighteenth Century* (Los Angeles: University of California Press, 1978), pp. 45–129.

Rymer, Michael, 'Satiric Technique in *The Spiritual Quixote*', *Durham University Journal* 34 (1973), 54–64.

Sandford, William Phillips, 'English Theories of Public Address, 1530–1828', unpublished Ph.D. thesis, Ohio State University (1929).

Schwartz, Hillel, *The French Prophets: The History of a Millenarian Group in Eighteenth-Century England* (Berkeley: University of California Press, 1980).

Scott, Walter, *The Private Letter-Books of Sir Walter Scott*, ed. Wilfred Partington (London: Hodder and Stoughton, 1930).

Sheldon, Esther K., *Thomas Sheridan of Smock-Alley* (Princeton: Princeton University Press, 1967).

Shepherd, T. B., *Methodism and the Literature of the Eighteenth Century* (London: Epworth Press, 1940).

Sheridan, Frances, *The Memoirs of Miss Sidney Bidulph*, ed. Patricia Köster and Jean Coates Cleary (Oxford: Oxford University Press, 1995).

Sheridan, Thomas, *British Education; or, The Source of the Disorders of Great Britain* (London, 1756).

An Oration pronounced before a Numerous Body of the Nobility and Gentry (Dublin, 1757).

A Course of Lectures on Elocution: Together with Two Dissertations on Language; and Some other Tracts relative to those Subjects (London, 1762; repr. Menston: Scolar Press, 1968).

A General Dictionary of the English Language, 2 vols. (London, 1780; repr. Menston: Scolar Press, 1967).

Shortland, Michael, 'Skin Deep: Barthes, Lavater and the Legible Body', *Economy and Society* 14 (1985), 273–312.

'The Power of a Thousand Eyes: Johann Caspar Lavater's Science of Physiognomic Perception', *Criticism* 28 (1986), 379–408.

'Moving Speeches: Language and Elocution in Eighteenth-Century Britain', *History of European Ideas* 8 (1987), 639–53.

'Unnatural Acts: Art and Passion on the Mid-Eighteenth-Century Stage', *Theatre Research International* 12 (1987), 93–110.

Shuttleton, David E., ' "Pamela's Library": Samuel Richardson and Dr. Cheyne's "Universal Cure" ', *Eighteenth-Century Life* 23:1 (1999), 59–79.

Smallwood, Angela, 'A Study of the Representation of Character and Passion in the Novels of Fielding and Sterne, by Comparison with the Representation of these Subjects on the Stage and in Painting in the Period', unpublished D.Phil. thesis, University of Oxford, 1981.

Smith, Adam, *Lectures on Rhetoric and Belles Lettres*, ed. John M. Lothian (London: Nelson, 1963).

Smith, Raymond, *Charles Churchill* (Boston: Twayne, 1977).

Smollett, Tobias, *Travels through France and Italy*, ed. Frank Felsenstein (Oxford and New York: Oxford University Press, 1981; repr. 1992).

Some Rules for Speaking and Action; To be observed at the Bar, in the Pulpit, and the Senate, and by every one that Speaks in Publick. In a Letter to a Friend, 3rd edn (London, 1716).

The Spectator, ed. Donald F. Bond, 5 vols. (Oxford: Clarendon Press, 1965).

Sprat, Thomas, *History of the Royal Society for the Improving of Natural Knowledge*, ed. Jackson I. Cope and Harold Whitmore Jones (St Louis: Washington University Press; London: Routledge, 1959).

Stafford, Barbara Maria, *Body Criticism: Imaging the Unseen in Enlightenment Art and Medicine* (Cambridge, MA: Massachusetts Institute of Technology Press, 1991).

Stallybrass, Peter and Allon White, *The Politics and Poetics of Transgression* (Ithaca, NY: Cornell University Press, 1986).

Staves, Susan, 'Don Quixote in Eighteenth-Century England', *Comparative Literature* 24 (1972), 193–215.

Stephen, Leslie (ed.), *Dictionary of National Biography*, 66 vols. (London, 1885–1901).

Sterne, Laurence, *Letters of the Late Rev. Mr. Laurence Sterne, To his most intimate Friends . . . published by his Daughter, Mrs. Medalle*, 3 vols. (London, 1775).

Letters of Laurence Sterne, ed. Lewis Perry Curtis (Oxford: Clarendon Press, 1935).

A Sentimental Journey through France and Italy, ed. Gardner D. Stout, Jr (Berkeley and Los Angeles: University of California Press, 1967).

The Life and Opinions of Tristram Shandy, Gentleman, The Florida Edition of the Works of Laurence Sterne, vols. 1–2, ed. Melvyn New and Joan New (Gainesville, FL: University Presses of Florida, 1978).

A Sentimental Journey through France and Italy, ed. Paul Goring (London: Penguin, 2001).

A Sentimental Journey through France and Italy and Continuation of the Bramine's Journal: The Text and Notes, The Florida Edition of the Works of Laurence Sterne, vol. 6, ed. Melvyn New and W. G. Day (Gainesville: University Press of Florida, 2002).

Stevens, George Alexander, *Distress upon distress* (Dublin, 1752).

The Birth-Day of Folly: An Heroi-Comical Poem (London, 1755).

Stone, George Winchester, Jr and George M. Kahrl, *David Garrick: A Critical Biography* (Carbondale: Southern Illinois University Press, 1979).

Styan, J. L., *The English Stage: A History of Drama and Performance* (Cambridge: Cambridge University Press, 1996).

Swift, Jonathan, *A Proposal for Correcting, Improving and Ascertaining the English Tongue* (London, 1712).

The Tatler, ed. Donald F. Bond, 3 vols. (Oxford: Clarendon Press, 1987).

Thomas, David (ed.), *Restoration and Georgian England, 1660–1788*, Theatre in Europe: A Documentary History (Cambridge: Cambridge University Press, 1989).

Todd, Janet, *Sensibility: An Introduction* (London and New York: Methuen, 1986).

The Sign of Angellica: Women, Writing, and Fiction 1660–1800 (London: Virago, 1989).

Tracy, Clarence, *A Portrait of Richard Graves* (Cambridge: James Clark, 1987).

A True History of the Scheme for erecting a new Seminary for Education (Dublin, 1769).

Trusler, John, *Memoirs of the Life of the Rev. Dr. Trusler* (London, 1806).

Turner, Cheryl, *Living by the Pen: Women Writers in the Eighteenth Century* (London: Routledge, 1992; repr. 1994).

Turner, James Grantham, 'Novel Panic: Picture and Performance in the Reception of Richardson's *Pamela*', *Representations* 48 (Fall 1994), 70–96.

Van Sant, Ann Jessie, *Eighteenth-Century Sensibility and the Novel: The Senses in Social Context* (Cambridge: Cambridge University Press, 1993).

Walker, John, *Elements of Elocution*, 2 vols. (London, 1781).

Waller, Edmund, *The Poems of Edmund Waller*, ed. G. Thorn Drury, 2 vols. (London: Routledge, 1905).

Walsh, John, 'Methodism and the Mob in the Eighteenth Century', in G. J. Cuming and D. Baker (eds.), *Popular Belief and Practice*, Studies in Church History 8 (Cambridge: Cambridge University Press, 1972), pp. 213–27.

Ward, John, *A System of Oratory, Delivered in a Course of Lectures Publicly read at Gresham College, London*, 2 vols. (Hildesheim: Olms, 1969).

Warner, William B., *Licensing Entertainment: The Elevation of Novel Reading in Britain, 1684–1750* (Berkeley and Los Angeles: University of California Press, 1998).

Watkins, John, *Memoirs of R. B. Sheridan* (London, 1817).

Weales, Thomas, *The Christian Orator Delineated* (London, 1778).

Wesley, John, *Directions concerning Pronunciation and Gesture* (Bristol, 1749).

West, Shearer, 'Polemic and the Passions: Dr James Parsons' *Human Physiognomy Explained* and Hogarth's Aspirations for British History Painting', *British Journal for Eighteenth-Century Studies* 13:1 (Spring 1990), 73–89.

Whyte, Samuel, *Miscellanea Nova* (Dublin, 1800; repr. New York and London: Garland, 1974).

Wilkins, John, *Ecclesiastes, Or, A Discourse concerning the Gift of Preaching: As it falls under the Rules of Art*, 4th edn (London, 1753).

Williams, Raymond, *Marxism and Literature* (Oxford: Oxford University Press, 1977).

Wollstonecraft, Mary, *A Vindication of the Rights of Woman*, ed. Miriam Brody (Harmondsworth: Penguin, 1992).

Woods, Leigh, *Garrick Claims the Stage: Acting as Social Emblem in Eighteenth-Century England* (Westport, CT and London: Greenwood Press, 1984).

Index

acting, 5, 52, 114, 116
and bodily eloquence, 7
classical, 119, 122–7, 129–30
discourse, 118
and 'elocutionary discourse', 13
facial, 117, 123
and imagination, 130–2
and imitation, 130–3
manneristic, 125, 126
manuals, 7–9,
'natural', 118, 120–2, 134, 136
non-classical style, 119
and oratory, 129
and the passions, 1, 3–4, 130, 158
and politeness, 25
rules for, 130–1
science of, 135, 137
and sensibility, 137–40
styles of, 118, 119–22
techniques, 1
theory, 2, 140–1,
actresses, 120
Advice to a Parson; or, the true art of preaching
(anon.), 11
affectation, 110
Alcock, Mary
'A Receipt for Writing a Novel', 149,
165, 180
Althusser, Louis, 24, 25
Anglican preachers, 36–9, 79, 81, 85
Anglicisation of language, 100, 100–1,
aposiopesis, 189–90, 200
Aristotle
Poetics, 2
Aston, Antony, 122–3
Aubin, Penelope, 167
audiences, 25
oratory, 60, 64, 70, 72–4, 78
paying, 65–6, 99, 101
theatre, 114–16, 115, 129
see also readers; reading
Austin, Gilbert
*Chironomia; or, a Treatise on Rhetorical
delivery*, 10

Bacon, Francis
The Advancement of Learning, 102
Bacon, Wallace A., 96
Bailey, Nathaniel
*Dictionarium Domesticum, being a new and
compleat houshold dictionary for the use
of city and country*, 104
*An Orthographical Dictionary, shewing both
the orthography and the orthoepia of the
English Tongue*, 106
Universal Etymological Dictionary, 104, 106
Barker-Benfield, G. J., 20, 49, 180
Barrell, John, 28
Barry, Elizabeth, 122
Beck, Cave
The Universal Character, 103
Bee, The, 77, 78, 79
Behn, Aphra, 167, 168
benevolence, 109, 113
Benzie, W., 96, 98, 100
Betterton, Thomas, 121, 122–7, 192
see also Gildon, Charles
Blair, Hugh
Lectures on Rhetoric and Belles Lettres, 100
blushing, 151
bodies
eloquent, 107, 153
heroic, 75
national, 91
sentimental, 6, 13, 74
unruly, 26, 60–3, 90
bodily actions, 68, 185
bodily conduct, 64
bodily discharges, 160
bodily eloquence, 5, 13–16, 107, 111, 153
and acting, 7
and oratory, 11, 34
and reading, 14
bodily responses, 145
body, the
and 'appearances', 24–5
baser aspects of, 187, 193
and cultural history, 16–20
and femininity, 150–1

language of, 43, 47, 108, 110, 125
  see also gestures, language of
and the language of sentiment, 143
performance, 2, 146–7
physiological origins of, 193
and politeness, 201
and reading, 143–4
representation of, 146
and sentiment, 44, 96, 118, 143, 174
  see also sentimental bodies
and the theatre, 116
and virtue, 56
body image, 13, 82
  'classical', 13, 43, 118
  'non-classical', 118
  'sentimental', 13, 43
  sentimentalisation of, 118
'body studies', 16–20
book reviewing, 179
Booth, Barton, 125
Boswell, James, 23–4, 54, 99, 107
bourgeois class, 20–1, 44
Brewer, John, 20, 24
Brissenden, R. S., 192–3
Britishness, 92, 93, 99
Brooke, Henry, 14, 146
  The Fool of Quality, 157–9
Brooks, Peter, 146
Bulwer, John
  *Chirologia; or, The Naturall Language of the
    Hand*, 10, 31, 43
Burgh, James
  The Art of Speaking, 31, 38, 43
Burke, Edmund, 116
Butler, Judith, 17

Cash, Arthur, 184
Cave, Edward, 69
Cervantes (Saavedra), Miguel de
  Don Quixote, 83, 85
charity, 109
Chesterfield, Philip Dormer Stanhope, 4th Earl
  of, 105
Chetwood, William Rufus
  *A General History of the Stage, from its Origin
    in Greece down to the present Time*, 8
Cheyne, Dr George, 14, 160
  The English Malady, 5
church services, 32, 33
Churchill, Charles
  The Rosciad, 8
Cibber, Colley, 122–3, 126
Cibber, Jane, 126
Cibber, Susannah Maria, 120–1
Cibber, Theophilus, 125

Cicero, Marcus Tullius
  De Oratore, 45
class
  bourgeois, 20–1
  élite, 104
  lower, 64, 70, 98
  poor, the, 81
  upper-class women, 151
'classical decorum', 43, 52, 61, 112
  competing attitudes to, 52
  rules of, 54–5
classical rhetoric, 23–4, 52
Cleese, John, 153
Cocker's English Dictionary, 104
Coles, Elisha
  An English Dictionary, 104
Colley, Linda
  Britons: Forging the Nation 1707–1837, 91
Collier, Jeremy
  *A Short View of the Immorality and
    Profaneness of the English Stage*, 114
commercialism, 65–6, 101, 102
conduct, 7, 10, 54, 64, 116–17
consumption, 26
Cox, Nicholas, 46
Critical Review, the, 77, 179
cultural history, 5, 16–20
culture
  and nature, 6, 16–20
  see also nature
Cumberland, Richard, 118, 139
  Memoirs, 119–22
Cunningham, Valentine, 17
Curll, Edmund
  *The History of the English
    Stage*, 127, 192

Dalgarno, George
  Ars signorum, 103
declamation, 119–21, 125, 126, 129, 131, 135
Defoe, Daniel, 167
delivery of speech, 11, 37–9, 56, 63
'Demoniacs', 188
Descartes, René
  Les Passions de l'âme, 39, 131
Diderot, Denis, 117
  The Paradox of the Actor, 138
'docility', 16
Douglas, Aileen, 18
Douglas, Mary, 49, 139
  Natural Symbols, 19
Downer, Alan S., 9
Downey, James, 44
Dryden, John, 103
  Cleomenes, 115

eccentricity, 61–2, 63
Eliot, T. S., 163
élite class, 104
ellipses, suggestive, 189
elocution, 11, 35, 39, 91
'elocutionary discourse', 6, 7–16, 183
  and acting, 13
  and bodily eloquence, 13–16
  and medicine and anatomy, 15–16
  and the Methodist movement, 70
  and oratory, 13
  and sentimental fiction, 141, 142–7
  and the visual arts, 15
'elocutionary movement', the, 11–12, 35–45
eloquence, 6, 78, 111
  'classical' and 'non-classical', 43
  and femininity, 150–1
  and Henley, 64, 66, 67
  natural, 91
  and the passions, 39, 158
  and public performance, 34–5
  reform of, 92
  and society, 107, 153
  see also bodily eloquence; polite eloquence
emotion, 2, 145, 151–3
  communal, 109,
  language of, 109, 112
  and oratory, 39, 47
  and performance, 38
  and politeness, 39, 139
  and public speakers, 109
Engstrom, Alfred G.
  'The Single Tear: A Stereotype of Literary
    Sensibility', 138
entertainment, 66, 98
enthusiasm, 62, 63, 70–1, 72–4, 139
  anti-enthusiasm, 70–4
  as an anti-social force, 88
  and Evans, 75–7
  and Goldsmith, 77–81
  and Graves, 86–90
  and Green, 74–5
  and Sheridan, 112
*Essay on the Stage, or the Art of Acting: A Poem,
  An* (anon.), 7
Evans, Theophilus, 60
  The History of Modern Enthusiasm, 75–7

femininity, 150–1
feminist literary history, 53
Fielding, Henry, 8, 83
  Joseph Andrews, 69, 84
  Shamela, 169–70
    preface to, 173
Fielding, Sarah, 146

The Adventures of David Simple, 152, 157–8,
  176–7
  The History of the Countess of Dellwyn
    preface to, 176–7
  Remarks on Clarissa, 177–9
Fish, Stanley
  'interpretive community', 15, 145–6
  'rhetorical man', 23
Foote, Samuel
  *A Treatise on the Passions, So far as they
    regard the Stage*, 7
Fordyce, Revd James, 52, 187
  conduct literature, 53
  An Essay on the Action Proper for the Pulpit,
    27, 44, 52–9, 67
  and Le Faucheur, 55
  Sermons to Young Women, 53
Foucault, Michel, 16–17, 19, 25
  Discipline and Punish, 16
France
  compared to England, 38, 78, 93–4
French Prophets, 71

Gallagher, Catherine and Stephen Greenblatt
  Practicing New Historicism, 18
gallophobia, 93
Garrick, David, 13, 25, 34, 54, 117–18, 195
  acting style, 119–20, 121–2, 134–5
  and declamation, 126–7
  and emotional vacuity, 138
  An Essay on Acting, 134
  and *Macbeth*, 134
  and theatre audiences, 115
Gentleman's Magazine, the, 36, 69, 84
gestures, 47, 48, 125, 131, 132
  arm and hand, 50–1, 54, 110, 123, 129
  facial, 48
    'disagreeable', 49–50
    eyes, 48, 58, 110, 112
    see also acting, facial
  and feeling, 57
  language of, 110–11, 124, 149, 180, 197
  see also tears
Gildon, Charles, 131, 139
  language of the body, 125
  *The Life of Mr. Thomas Betterton, The late
    Eminent Tragedian*, 7, 9, 52, 123–7, 192
    and Le Faucheur, 124
Goldsmith, Oliver, 27, 77–81
  critique of society, 80–1
  and eloquence, 78
  endorsement of Methodism, 79–81
  French preachers, 38
  as 'H. D.', 80
  and politeness, 78, 80–1

'Some Remarks on the Modern Manner of
    Preaching', 36
'A sublime Passage in a French Sermon', 78
'good breeding', 128
Graves, Richard, 27, 63
    and body image, 82
    cultural critique, 81
    and enthusiasm, 86–90
    The Spiritual Quixote, 11, 71, 81–90, 112
    and sentimental writing, 84
    Wildgoose, 82, 84–90
Green, Thomas
    A Dissertation on Enthusiasm, 74–5
Greenblatt, Stephen
    see Gallagher, Catherine and Stephen
        Greenblatt
Greenwood, James
    *An Essay towards a Practical English
        Grammar*, 103
Greenwood, Richard, 184
Griffiths, Ralph
    review of *A Sentimental Journey*,
        197–8, 200
    review of *Tristram Shandy*, 196–7
Grub Street Journal, the, 68

H. W., 4, 117–18
Haberman, Frederick, 11
Habermas, Jürgen, 20
Hammond, Brean, 20, 22, 83
Hare, Arnold, 126
Harris, Bob, 21
Haywood, Eliza, 167, 168
Hempton, David, 70, 74
Henley, John 'Orator', 11, 26, 27, 46, 61–2, 63–70,
        90, 139
    bodily actions, 68
    commercialism, 65–6
    The Compleat Linguist, 65
    criticised, 68–70
    and eloquence, 64, 66, 67
    Guide to the Oratory, 65
    *The History and Advantages of divine
        Revelation*, 67
    An Introduction to English Grammar, 65
    and Le Faucheur, 67
    lectures on delivery, 63
    and the lower classes, 70
    Miscellanies, 65
    non-verbal expression, 67
    obituary, 69
    publications of, 65
    Transactions, 65
    writing about, 69–70
heroic bodies, 75

'Hibernian Society', 98
Hiffernan, Paul
    Dramatic genius, 127
Highfill, Philip H., Kalman A. Burnim, and
        Edward A. Langhans
    *A Biographical Dictionary of Actors, Actresses,
        Musicians, Dancers, Managers, and
        other Stage Personnel in London,
        1660–1800*, 9
Hill, Aaron, 1–5, 29, 114, 137, 139, 148, 168
    and acting, 114
    acting theory, 127–35
        revised, 131–5
    The Art of Acting, 1–5, 3, 7, 8, 141
        1746 version, 3
    'dramatic passions', 131, 132, 133
        astonishment, 133
        joy, 132
    'Essay on the Art of Acting', 3, 131–3, 140
    and gestures, 131, 132
    and Le Faucheur, 133
    letters to Richardson, 170–5
        misinterpreted, 174
    in the preface to *Pamela*, 173–5
    prologue to *The Tuscan Treaty*, 3
    The Prompter, 7, 127–31
    on Quin, 120
    rules for acting, 130–1
    'The Actor's Epitome', 4
    as a writer, 4
Hill, Sir John, 135
    The Actor: A Treatise on the Art of Playing, 7,
        42, 136–40
    and 'good taste', 135
    as the Honourable Juliana-Susannah
        Seymour, 136
    scientific writing, 136
    and stage practice, 35
Hitch, Charles, 46
Hogarth, William
    The Analysis of Beauty, 191, 192
Holtz, William V., 192–3
Home, John
    Douglas, 175
Howell, Wilbur Samuel, 11, 12, 52, 55
    *Eighteenth-Century British Logic and
        Rhetoric*, 53
Hughes, Leo
    'Theatrical Convention in Richardson', 148
Hume, David, 14, 94

illness
    see sentimental novels, and illness
individual, the, 17, 94
inspiration, 72, 75

'interpretive community', 15, 145–6, 179
    'polite', 174
    sentimental, 177, 179

Jay, Martin, 13
Johnson, Samuel, 54, 72, 198
    A Dictionary of the English Language, 104
    and Sheridan, 95, 106, 107, 113
journals, 7
    and book reviewing, 179
    the *Critical Review*, 77
    the *Public Advertiser*, 98
    the *Royal Magazine*, 80
    The Spectator, 36
    the *Theatrical Monitor*, 7
    the *Weekly Journal*, 68
    the *Weekly Magazine*, 77
    Gub Street Journal, the; *see also Bee*, the;
        Gentleman's Magazine, the; *Monthly
        Magazine*, the; *Lady's Magazine*, the;
        Prompter, the *Monthly Review* , the;
        Tatler, the

Kelly, Veronica, and Dorothea von Mücke
    Body and Text in the Eighteenth Century, 18
Klein, Lawrence, 20, 22
Korte, Barbara
    Body Language in Literature, 147

lachrymosity
    see tears
Lady's Magazine, the, 36, 77, 79
Lane, A.
    A Key to the Art of Letters, 106
Langford, Paul, 20, 80
language
    Anglicisation of, 100–1,
    court, 106
    English, 105–8, 107–108
        standardisation of, 92, 102–7
    Latin, 36, 103
    see also speech
language academy, 103
latitudinarianism, 37, 185
Le Brun, Charles, 192
    *Conférence de M. Le Brun sur l'expression
        générale et particulière*, 40
Le Faucheur, Michel, 122–3, 192
    Essay Upon the Action of an Orator, 9
    and Fordyce, 55
    and Gildon, 124
    and Henley, 67
    and Hill, 133
    Traitté de l'action de l'orateur, 27, 44, 45–52, 58
        editions, 46

    and Wesley, 73
Le Sage, Alain René
    Gil Blas, 83
Leder, Drew, 18
leisure, 25, 166
Leonardo da Vinci
    A Treatise of Painting, 192
Lessinich, Rolf P.
    *Elements of Pulpit Oratory in Eighteenth-
        Century England*, 11, 12, 44
Letter to David Garrick, A (H. W.), 4, 117–18
literacy, 31, 33
Locke, John
    Some Thoughts Concerning Education, 104
    on teaching English, 36
Love, James, 35
lower classes, 64, 70, 98

McKenzie, Alan T., 39
Mackenzie, Henry, 14, 146
    The Man of Feeling, 142, 144–6, 152, 157
    tour of Bedlam, 163–5
Macklin, Charles, 35, 121, 136
madness, 76, 85, 87, 162–4
    eloquent, 163
    polite, 164
Manley, Delarivière, 167, 168
masculinity, 9, 58
Mason, John, 187
    An Essay on Elocution, or, Pronunciation,
        10, 52
Mauss, Marcel, 17
Mayoux, Jean-Jacques, 153
medical theory, 15–16, 144, 159, 164
'method actors', 3
Methodist movement, 27, 61–3, 72, 90
    anti-Methodism, 70–4, 82
    and 'elocutionary discourse', 70
    and Goldsmith, 79–81
    and Graves, 81–90
    and polite eloquence, 85, 88
    preachers, 26, 70–1
    and sensibility, 75
    and Sheridan, 112
    theological objections to, 73
    see also enthusiasm
Midgley, Graham, 64, 68
Monthly Magazine, the, 180
Monthly Review, the, 179, 196, 197
morality, 126, 148, 155
More, Hannah
    Sensibility: A Poetic Epistle, 180
Mücke, Dorothea von
    see Kelly, Veronica and Dorothea
        von Mücke

Mullan, John, 15, 143, 150, 152, 160
  Sentiment and Sociability, 14

nation, the
  and the individual, 94
  and oratory, 91–6, 113
nature
  and acting, 120–2
  and art, 111–12, 133
  and culture, 6, 16–20
  language of, 47–9
  rhetoric of, 19
nervousness
  and virtue, 24
New, Melvyn, 75, 186, 188
'non-classical' decorum, 43
nonconformists, 71, 72–4, 75

oratory, 5, 9–12, 13, 44, 92, 193–4
  and acting, 9, 129
  and Anglican clergymen, 36–9
  and bodily action, 185
  and bodily eloquence, 11, 34
  and the British nation, 91–6, 113
  and church services, 33–4
  claims for, 94–5
  and conduct, 10
  delivery of, 11
  discourse on, 33
  and emotion, 39, 47
  and fiction, 11, 144, 147, 194
  lectures on, 11
  and men, 9
  non-verbal techniques, 45
  and politeness, 25, 34
  pulpit, 54, 56
  reform of, 37–45
  sentimental, 193
  and social order, 47
  standards of, 35–9, 91
  and women, 10
  writing on, 52
  see also public speaking; speech
'Oratory', the, 11–12, 63–6
  first venue, 66
  and lower classes, 64
  second venue, 66

Parsons, James
  *Human Physiognomy explain'd: In the Crounian
    Lectures on Muscular Motion*, 41
passions, the, 107–8
  and acting, 1, 3–4, 158
  bodily language of, 43, 47
  contagion of, 158–9

and eloquence, 39–42, 158
and faltering speech, 139
literary language of, 149
'natural', 133
and oratory, 47
and painters, 40, 2
and performance, 40
see also emotion
pathognomy, 41–2
  auditory, 42
performance, 2, 9, 23, 34–5, 40, 142–7, 163
periodicals
  see journals
persuasion, 46, 51
phrenology, 41
physiognomy, 41–2
physiology, 137, 164, 187, 193
Pickering, Roger
  *Reflections upon Theatrical Expression in
    Tragedy*, 7, 127
Pittard, Joseph
  Observations on Mr. Garrick's Acting, 25, 117
polite discourse, 20, 26, 60
polite eloquence, 61–3
  challenges to, 26
  deflation of, 187
  and the Methodist movement, 85, 88
polite society, 6, 9, 80–1
politeness, 6, 20–6, 78
  and actors, 25
  and the body, 201
  and emotional expression, 39, 139
  language of, 21–3
  and oratory, 25, 34
  and performance, 9, 23
  physiological origins of, 187
  and the sentimental, 43
  and sentimental novels, 146, 165, 166
  and the theatre, 114–18
  see also reading, polite
Polwhele, Richard
  The Art of Eloquence. A Didactic Poem, 11
poor, the, 81
Pope, Alexander
  The Dunciad, 62, 69
Popple, William, 127
Porée, Charles
  *An Oration, In Which an Enquiry is Made
    whether the Stage Is, or Can be Made
    a School for Forming the Mind to
    Virtue*, 128
Porter, Roy, 15
preachers, 44, 57, 89
  Anglican, 36–9, 78, 79, 81, 85
  in France, 38, 78

preachers (cont.)
    Methodist, 26, 70, 71
    see also enthusiasm; Henley, John 'Orator';
        Methodist movement
prefaces, 175–7
    see also Richardson, Samuel, *Pamela*
Presbyterianism, 54
print culture, 21, 31, 32, 65
    see also journals
Pritchard, Hannah, 120–1
Prompter, The, 7, 127–31
pronunciation, 47, 106
    standardisation of, 33, 34
Public Advertiser, the, 98
public speaking, 10–12, 31–3, 54
    and emotions, 109, 112
    guides to, 10–11
    training in, 57
    see also oratory
Punday, Daniel, 19

Quin, James, 119–20, 121–2, 123, 125
Quintilian (Marcus Fabius Quintilianus), 129
    Institutio Oratoria, 45
quixotic narrative, 81, 83

Rabelais, François, 186
    Gargantua and Pantagruel, 200
Rack, Henry D., 73
Raphael (Raffaello Sanzio)
    St Paul Preaching in Athens, 56
readers, 167–8, 170, 171–3, 179
reading
    and the body, 143–4
    communal, 171–3, 175
    modes of, 176–7
    as performance, 142–7
    polite, 144, 146, 168, 170, 172, 174, 176
        instruction in, 175–9
        and sentimental fiction, 146
    reform of, 166
    sentimental, 180
    of sentimental novels, 5, 14–16, 143, 146, 165
religion, 56, 81, 112, 126, 168, 172
    see also church services; nonconformists;
        preachers; Presbyterianism; sermons
Richardson, Samuel, 14, 83, 146, 195
    and *The Art of Acting*, 1–2, 4–5, 140–1, 167
    and body language, 147
    Clarissa, 1, 83, 150, 152, 168
        'Author's Preface', 175
        and illness, 161
    and eloquence, 6
    and generic developments, 168
    and heroic bodies, 75

    and morality, 148
    Pamela, 141, 146, 150, 151, 168–70
        letters from Hill, 170–5
        misreadings of, 169–70, 174
        preface, 173–5
        role of the body, 149
        witnesses to eloquence, 153–7
    and politeness, 24
    and *The Prompter*, 127
    and sensibility, 150
    Sir Charles Grandison, 41, 83, 147, 152, 168
        and illness, 161
    and theatricality, 148, 157
    and Thomas Sheridan, 98
    and virtue, 147, 167
Roach, Joseph, 130, 137
Ross, Ian Campbell, 188
Rousseau, G. S., 15
    'Nerves, Spirits and Fibres', 160
Rowe, Nicholas
    The Fair Penitent, 119
Royal Magazine, the, 80
Royal Society, 102

Sainte Albine, Pierre Rémond de
    Le Comédien, 136
Sandford, William Phillips, 11, 37
school of elocution, 11
schoolmasters, 103
Schwartz, Hillel, 71
scientific knowledge, 102
    see also medical theory
Scott, Sir Walter, 144
Scottish accent
    Anglicisation of, 100
Select Society, 99
sensibility, 49, 137–40, 145, 150
    and acting, 137–40
    deranged, 162
    and the feminine body, 150–1
    and the Methodist movement, 75
    opposition to, 138, 180–1
sentiment, 143
    and the body, 44, 96, 118
    language of, 143, 174
    and sexuality, 174, 199
sentimental bodies, 6, 13, 74, 181
sentimental novels, 29, 141, 143, 147, 165, 166, 179,
    194
    and acting, 144, 147
    and bawdry, 189, 194, 195, 200
    and death, 161, 164
    and 'elocutionary discourse', 141, 142–7
    and eloquent bodies, 153
    and the heroic body, 75

and illness, 144, 159–65
and literary instruction, 175–9
and madness, 162–4
male heroes, 151–3
'men of feeling', 157–9, 199–201
and morality, 148
and oratory, 144, 147, 194
and politeness, 146, 165, 166
and pornography, 173
reading of, 5, 14–16, 146, 180
and sexuality, 150, 174, 198, 199–201
and *The Spiritual Quixote*, 84
theatricality of, 144, 146–7, 148
and witnessing, 153–7, 161, 162, 164,
sermons, 32, 44, 187
sexual innuendo, 174, 198, 200
Sheldon, Esther K., 96
Sheridan, Frances, 99, 102, 146
    The Memoirs of Miss Sidney Bidulph
    'The Editor's Introduction', 175–6
Sheridan, Richard Brinsley, 95
Sheridan, Thomas, 28, 31, 33–4, 53, 78, 187, 194
    as an actor, 97
    British Education, 91–6, 101, 104–5, 112
        review of, 36
    commercialism, 99, 101, 102
    and delivery, 38
    education of the élite, 104
    and eloquence, 92, 111
    and emotion, language of, 109
    A General Dictionary of the English Language,
        99, 101, 106
    and Johnson, 95, 106, 107, 113
    lectures, 94, 95
        in Cambridge, 98
        in Dublin, 97–8
        in Edinburgh, 99–101
        in London, 98–9
        in Oxford, 98
    Lectures on Elocution, 11, 12, 93, 97, 107,
        108–112
    and Lord Chesterfield, 105
    and making 'Gentlemen', 98
    and Methodism, 112
    *An Oration pronounced before a Numerous Body
        of the Nobility and Gentry*, 97
    and oratory, 113
    and pronunciation, 33, 34
    public life of, 96–102
    'Rhetorical Grammar', 100
    and sentimentalisation of the body, 96
    and the spoken word, 105–8
    and tone, 42
    and Wales, 101–2
Shortland, Michael, 12

Smith, Adam, 14, 38
Smollett, Tobias, 22
society
    critique of, 80–1
    disruption of, 74
    and eloquence, 107, 153
    interaction within, 23, 64
    and order, 47
    polite, 6, 9
    reform of, 128
Some Rules for Speaking and Action (anon.), 10,
    35, 52
sophistication, 94
Spectator, The, 36
speech, 108–12, 139
spelling, 107
Sprat, Thomas
    History of the Royal Society, 102
Stafford, Barbara Maria, 15, 41
Stallybrass, Peter, and Allon White, 61, 67, 115
Stanislavsky, Konstantin, 3
Staves, Susan, 85
Steele, Richard, 36
Sterne, Laurence, 11, 14, 29, 153
    and acting, 8
    and aposiopesis, 189–90, 200
    and the body, 183, 187, 188–90, 193
    and comedy, 185, 187
    and elocutionary writing, 194
    and eloquence, 183
    *The Life and Opinions of Tristram Shandy,
        Gentleman*, 182–3, 186, 189–90
        and the art of oratory, 193–4
        and bawdry, 189, 194, 195
        morality and lewdness, 194
        satire on 'elocutionary discourse', 190–2
        sentimental scenes, 195–6
    as Mr Yorick, 186
    as a preacher, 184–6
    'Rabelaisian Fragment', 183, 186–9
    A Sentimental Journey through France and Italy,
        157, 183
        and bawdry, 200
        eroticism, 150, 198
        and Rabelaisianism, 199
        scene in a Paris bookshop, 197–8
        'sensuality', 199–201
        sentimental scenes, 196–201
        sexual innuendo, 198, 200
    sermons, 32, 183, 185–6
    'The Abuses of Conscience', 193
    theories of acting, 195
    theories of oratory, 195
    theories of painting, 192–3, 195
    and wit, 185

Stevens, George Alexander
  The Birth-Day of Folly, 69
  Distress upon distress, 69
Stout, Gardner D., 198
Stuart, Lady Louisa, 144–6
  and *The Man of Feeling*, 142, 179–81
superstition, 80
Swift, Jonathan, 96
  Gulliver's Travels, 103
  *A Proposal for Correcting, Improving and
    Ascertaining the English Tongue*, 103
sympathy, 40, 108

Tatler, The, 36, 37, 59
tears, 48, 58, 113, 138
theatre, the, 8–9, 114–18, 116–17, 126
  audiences, 114–16, 129
  civilisation of, 115–18
  and Le Faucheur, 124
  and morality, 115, 126, 128
  and social reform, 114, 128
  see also acting
Theatrical Monitor, the, 7
theatricality
  of sentimental novels, 144, 146–7, 148
Thomas, David, 125
Tillotson, Archbishop John, 37
Todd, Janet, 143
tone, 42
Trusler, Revd Dr John, 11
Turner, Cheryl, 166
Turner, James Grantham, 174
Tyers, Jonathan, 66

'universal language' schemes, 103
unruly bodies, 26, 60–3, 90

virtue, 24, 34, 56, 58, 149, 163, 164
  promotion of by writers, 167, 168
  visibility of, 158

Waller, Edmund
  Of English Verse, 102
Walpole, Horace, 194
Ward, John
  A System of Oratory, 10, 11, 12, 40–1, 42, 79, 187

Warner, William B., 174
  *Licensing Entertainment: The Elevation
    of Novel Reading in Britain, 1684–1750*,
    166
  'The *Pamela* Media Event', 169–70
  on *The Whole Duty of Woman, Or an infallible
    Guide to the Fair Sex*, 167
Watkins, John, 99
Watt, Ian, 146
Wedderburne, Alexander, 100
Weekly Journal, the, 68
Weekly Magazine, the, 77
Welsh pronunciation, 101
Wesley, Charles, 82
Wesley, John, 73, 82
  *Directions concerning Pronunciation and
    Gesture*, 35, 192
  and Le Faucheur, 73
White, Allon
  see Stallybrass, Peter and Allon White
Whitefield, George, 70, 73, 76, 79
*Whole Duty of Woman, Or an infallible Guide to
  the Fair Sex, The*, 167
Wilkes, John, 184–185
Wilkes, Thomas
  A General View of the Stage, 8
Wilkins, Bishop John, 37
  *Ecclesiastes, Or, A Discourse concerning the Gift
    of Preaching*, 37
  *An Essay Towards a Real Character and a
    Philosophical Language*, 103
Wilks, Robert, 125
Williams, Raymond, 13
witchcraft, 80
Wollstonecraft, Mary, 53
women
  and acting, 120
  behaviour of, 150
  and education, 98
  lectures for, 100
  and oratory, 10
  upper-class, 151
  and wit, 151
  see also femininity

xenophobia, 81